MARK ARCHER
WITH ANDREW WOODS

the man behind
the mask

Published 2016 by Music Mondays, Unit A4, Broomsleigh Business
Park, London, SE26 5BN

Copyright © **Mark Archer 2016**
First Published in hardback in 2016
Cover design: Marc French
Foreword: Billy Daniel Bunter
Photographer credits: Peter Walsh, Ming De Nasty, Matthew R
Lewis, Stafford Newsletter & Network Records

Contributors: Moby / Darren Partington (808 State) /
Tommie Sunshine / Gez Varley (LFO) / Danny Taurus (Slo Moshun) /
Neil Rushton (Network) / Andy Meecham (Bizarre Inc), Tim Garbutt
(Utah Saints) / Ian Bland (Dream Frequency) / Andrew Harrison /
Mark Goodier / Richard Benson (RAC) / Martyn Cresswell /
Neil Macey / DJ Kiddo / Lee Fredericks / Mark Mortimer /
John McCready / Jon McDonald / Pete Bromley / Josh Doherty /
Scotto / Michelle Kidd

A catalogue record for this book is available from the
British Library
ISBN: 978-0-9934732-1-0
Printed in 2016 by Dolman Scott Ltd.
www.dolmanscott.co.uk

DEDICATED TO FREDRICK JAMES ARCHER

"Altern 8 occupy a unique position in dance music history..." **Moby, Los Angeles 2016**

"Dancing in a field in the middle of England... what could have been better than that? It seems such a majorly substantial thing and yet no one has really told the story. The greatest youth movement of the past 30 years and it's hardly been documented beyond 1988/'89. What happened in 1991? 1992?" **Tommie Sunshine, New York City 2016**

Acknowledgements

My Mum and Dad for letting me follow my own path. Nikki for being the most amazing person I've ever met and Paul and Amanda for being the best brother and sister-in-law. Emma, Liam and Harry are the three best kids a dad could wish for and love to Ellie and Bobby (my extended little family). My aunties and uncles: Ann, Keith, Peter and Helen. The 'In-Laws': Bob, Lyn, Fleur, Kev and Val for all your help over the past seven years. Matt (Pickle Pants) Zalepa for giving me a chance when I needed it most and Fat Scuba Jay 'Don't kiss no Rastas'. Shaun Crist for listening to me when no one else would. Robert Bobzilla Page for the vector image. Wayne Bayles for being a true mate and Josh Doherty and James Bangface for keeping my career going – without you two I'd have probably given up. Crez and Rory the A8 dancers, Benson and Neil Macey for being musical inspirations and Neil Rushton for inventing reggae on a Tuesday. Ben and Rach, Josh and Kelly and all the crew at Bangface. Ben 'Skimmy' Stott, Lee Whitney, Mike Bell, Danny and Jen, Shaun, Lou, Paul and Barry. Eamon Downes, (CISTMAP) Graham Podmore, Geoff Hibbert, Daz 808 State, Derrick May, Kevin Saunderson and Juan Atkins. Baby Ford, Jay Denham for the 909, Bunter and Sonya for believing in me more than I do. Jack SDC, Chris and Gemma, Edzy and Sam, Neal Howard and Nathan Gregory Wilkins. Andy Roberts and the Ideal Trax crew. Kiddo, Gez Varley, Mark Gamble, Winston Hazel, Cass Roc and Andy Meecham. Slipmatt and Rach, Shades Of Rhythm, Ratpack, Ian Bland and Charlotte. Baby D and Phil Fearon, Frank Fieber, Conor and Gavin Feeney. Sam Greenwood, Ele, Henry Leon and all the FM crew, Andy Daisy and Gout. Alain, Davi and Kleber, Bert and Ruben at Detuned.

Kristoff and Kurt at ROS. Rennie Foster, Keith Tenniswood, DJ Marky, Andy Ceephax, Ed DMX, KiNK, Neil Landstrumm and Shadow Dancer. Mark Breeze RocketPimp, King Yoof, The Hacker, DJ Phantasy, Dan and all the crew at Rubadub. Jackmaster, 2 Bad Mice, Nightwave, Jerome Hill and David Sumner. All at Infrastructure NYC, Michelle, Sonia and Lisa. Andy 808 State and Charlie B. Maximum boost to Deano, Marts and Bugzy. The Malta ILA crew, Mark and Gary Broom and Andy 'DJ Stan The Devil Tune Man' Stanley. Dave Barker, Omar and Guille at Moog. James at Arcadia, Tommie Sunshine and Daniela, Cardopusher. Nehuen, Mudfoot Blapps, TAC and all the Toon Crew. Move D, Placid, Chevron and Datasette. MC Man Parris and Mark Butler. To all the Southport wedding crew for making it such an amazing day. And of course, Andrew Woods for the perfectly-timed phone calls.

Andrew Woods would like to thank Jennie, Tillie and Ivy, as well as Mum, Dad and Lesley. Thanks to Wendy Matthews, Imogen Lees and Georgia Almkvist for their help with the book and props to Kieron Bain 'The Hook-up'.

All interviews conducted by Andrew Woods

A message from the publisher...

"Mark appeared in my book The Love Dove Generation (2015) and one particular line in his interview blew me away. In fact, I thought his contribution was the best thing in the book. The line was: 'Our support act for that gig was none other than Take That...' I saw that line and thought 'this guy needs a book of his own'. Take That were his support! You see, this fella's story is not that well known and the more I found out about what he's done and been through, the more fascinating it became. So, here is The Man Behind The Mask and what better way to cement Mark Archer's place in the history of dance music. It's an amazing story." **Billy 'Daniel' Bunter, London 2016**

Let The Music Use You

There are so many tunes I wish I'd made. The Night Writers' Let The Music (Use You) – a Frankie Knuckles production from 1988 – is one of them. It's such uplifting music. This song gets you every time. It has a cowbell (a Roland TR-727 a-go-go Latino preset) all the way through it, which is odd, because usually in house, bits come in and out, but this cowbell continues all the way through. There was a Roland TR-707 that featured in early Chicago and acid and then came the TR-727. The 707 had rocky, 'real drum' sounds while the 727 was purely percussion with no kicks or snares. The 727 had bongos, vibra-slaps, wind chimes, whistles and timbales. I bought a 727 from a guy in the car park of Shelley's nightclub (in Stoke), one time. The Night Writers track has this consistent pattern all the way through it. Risqué III's Essence of a Dream also features the same sound.

The vocal to Let the Music (Use You) is so uplifting yet this is not a song about peace and love, it's about losing yourself in music. The chord pattern is sublime and was later sampled by Slipmatt on SL2's DJs Take Control, which used the entire keyboard break. Let The Music (Use You) is actually quite tinny as there's no heavy-duty bass; it just pootles along on the highs.

Another track I would have loved to have done is Voodoo Ray by A Guy Called Gerald. Voodoo Ray is that good you wouldn't want to remix it. I was offered the chance to remix Rhythim Is Rhythim's Strings of Life once and turned it down because I couldn't make it any better than the original. I guess that's a sign of a true classic. The first time I heard *Voodoo Ray* was at Frenzy in Stoke, and we were totally stunned when that klonky bit came in. Wow! 1988 was Year Zero I guess, and every time someone did something different, it changed things. It was a great time.

When I stopped going to the 'copping-off clubs' like Top Of The World in Stafford and turned up to warehouses instead, it was a revelation. These were no chintzy clubs and everybody there was into the same music as you. There was no pulling or fighting. You heard the music you liked all night long. It was properly done.

I remember New Year's Eve (1990) at the Aston Villa Leisure Centre and Eddie Richards played a bootleg he'd done of an old house track by Ralphi Rosario called *You Used To Hold Me* (1986), which he mixed with *Salsa House* by Richie Rich. On the vinyl, there's a deliberate needle skip and everybody simply stopped dancing thinking he'd fucked it up, but then right on the beat *Salsa House* came in and the place erupted. That was an amazing night, hearing all the big tunes from that year. I still had hair then and the porting on the speakers actually blew it about, as there was so much sub bass. I stood there, eyes closed tight, head pointing to the ceiling, as the smoke, lasers and pounding music sailed around me. Sometimes I'd catch the eyes of another raver pulling the same face as me and we'd both know. This tune was the shit! **Mark Archer, Redditch 2016**

Contents

The Men In Masks

Like two pharaohs, The Men In Masks floated across the sea of heads on an enormous bed. Thousands of people screamed as the music shot down from the heavens through a man in the sky. The masked men looked all around, surveying the scene, jaws dropped. 'It's the moment they've all been waiting for!' The bed travelled upon the arms of the worshippers to every corner of their vast kingdom, as The Men In Masks nodded their heads and pointed people out. 'It's the moment they've all been waiting for!' The Men In Masks finally took to the stage. Arms behind their backs, heads bowed, they waited for the signal. When it came, delirium filled the air. 'It's the moment they've all been waiting for!'

The Archers, The Muggos And Zombie Nuns

The umbilical cord had wrapped itself around the baby's neck. The midwife checked the heart rate, stethoscope shaking, and wanted to call an ambulance. The midwife was young and inexperienced and Fredrick had little confidence in her. 'There isn't time!' said the expectant father. 'I'll take it from here!' Easing the midwife to one side, Fred rolled up his sleeves despite the protests against. However, Fred was the coolest man on the planet and certainly the most together person in that suburban home. It was clear that the baby was almost out and although the pinky, fleshy coil was in danger of strangling it, Fred could see what needed to be done. Fred dealt with life as if he had an instruction manual in the glovebox for any situation. If the baby needed to come out, then let's bloody well see it! Fred bent down and gently eased the baby out into the world, whilst calming Beryl and keeping the cord away from the tiny throat. Fredrick Archer was the coolest man on Earth and if it hadn't been for him... Well... **July 7th 1968, Bishopswood, Staffordshire**

Dad slapped his guns on. Whenever someone, or some*thing*, needed sorting, he would always announce that – just like John Wayne – he was reaching for his holster. Dad had a right face on him. 'I'm not having this!' he said, marching out of the house. My older brother Paul and I followed behind our angry father; my six-year-old body suddenly empowered as our posse made its way to the village playground.

Thirteen miles from the town of Stafford (Staffordshire, West Midlands), the tiny hamlet of Bishopswood was not known for drama, although King Charles II once hid in an oak tree at nearby Boscobel House to evade Oliver Cromwell. If a child let slip a word as shocking as 'ruddy' for example, it was panic stations in Bishopswood. 'Woah! Someone has sworn! They said the word *ruddy*!' But usually when the jungle drums started beating in Bishopswood, it was because of one particular family: The Muggos.

I don't want unfairly to demonise in print what were then mere children, so let's just say that the Muggos were *characters*. If we went down to the playground and the Muggos were there, they'd be up to no good. Or at least it felt that way. I'm sure they weren't up to mischief every minute of every single day; it just felt like that. If a child was on the roundabout, the Muggos would speed him up until he was sick and crying for mum. If you had an ice cream, they might take it off you and drop it to the ants in the sand pit, which was pretty traumatic for a kid.

Dad was a total hero though and if the Muggos were taunting the kids and pushing people about we would run off home to get him. Dad always knew something was up if we came home early. 'Why the hell are you back?!' he'd ask, as if we'd lost our tiny minds.

-   'The Muggos are there! They're picking on us!'
-   'Right, that's it! I'm slapping me guns on!'

Slapping his guns on was a reference to the Western movies that seemed to be on TV throughout the entire seventies and once the mythical holster was slapped on, Dad would appear on the scene, ready for a shoot-out.

The Muggos were picking on Andrew Bugey, who had a slight speech impediment and Mr Bugey was already there. 'You can't take the law into your own hands, Fred!' Mr Bugey told my fuming father.

-   'You just fucking watch me!'

Without having to touch anyone, Dad just gave the Muggos 'the look'. Dad was never violent, but 'the look' threatened some terrible brand of awfulness if you didn't heed it. The Muggos could see which way the wind was blowing; their faces dropped to the floor and they started whimpering, although stopping short of an apology. 'OK, I want you two running around that field until you're ready to say sorry!' Dad boomed. The Muggos duly started to canter around the cow field. These were the bullies of the village and they were properly bleating as we watched their laps of dishonour. Looking back, I feel a little differently about the Muggos now. As an adult I can see that these bullies were clearly not that happy within themselves and so they simply harassed others to get the upper hand. One of the Muggos – and not the sharpest knife in the drawer – had a shock of white curly hair, which presumably got him some serious stick and so I guess he was just getting his retaliation in first. A few laps in and the Muggos stopped in front of Dad. 'We're sorry,' they mumbled, well out of puff.

The Muggos were at the heart of the biggest scandal to hit Bishopswood. At the end of class every Friday afternoon, Mrs Povey would treat each child at St John's Primary School to a sweet from her enormous jar. This jar held such significance in our tiny world that it proved too much of a temptation to the Muggos who broke into the school one weekend and filled that giant container of sweets with milk, thus ruining all its contents. It was the biggest scandal in the village for quite some time and tells you a lot about Bishopswood that a jar of sweets getting damp was still getting talked about for years afterwards. Still, Dad had no respect for the reputation the Muggos were building for themselves and I can still picture the two brothers now, running around that cow field, crying their little eyes out.

It was comforting to me that Dad was happy to play sheriff, as I was quite a soft touch. I was, and still am, very trusting of people. I am scared of the cops. Not exclusively fearful of the police, but I always try to avoid confrontation and danger. If a policeman comes up to me in the street, I start to worry that I've done something wrong. I've had that kind of respect for authority throughout my life and I try to avoid things that could get me into hot water. I guess there was more of a pressure to respect authority figures when I was a kid. Our parents had been brought up in much stricter circumstances and the war didn't seem that distant, as most parents and all grandparents had experienced it in some way.

Although we were out and about on bikes and playing in fields, we were constantly reminded of the dangers of mischief thanks to those harrowing Public Information Films about electricity pylons, child snatchers and rabies. 'Charley says...' Those films terrified me. I remember one about a couple returning home from hospital with a child and Dad slipping on a rug, babe in arms. 'Placing a rug on to a newly polished floor is like setting a DEATH TRAP!' The world was full of adventure, sure, but it was also full of death. *Apaches* featured these kids playing on a farm, and so we were very conscious of that particular film, living as we did in a rural area. The film started with five friends in a classroom and then cut to a barn where a massive metal gate or something falls on top of one of them; the next day their desk is empty. Then they're playing again, passing around a bottle like a peace pipe – playing cowboys and Indians – and one of them takes a sip from the bottle. Rat poison! So his desk was now empty too... So with all this potential peril out there, it was nice to have a dad who would look out for me and my brother.

Dad was tall and thin. He was always lean. I, my dad and Paul all have a hiatal hernia. Dad had very bad indigestion as a child and they pretty much sliced him open to try and sort it and the resultant scar was a proper Frankenstein job, right across his chest and all the way around his back. It looked like he had been sliced in half with these really wide stitches marking out the biggest scar I have ever seen. Because Dad had a tube fitted into his stomach he would often feel sick as a result and would never eat an awful lot. He would always say, 'I feel a bit flat.' If you asked him if he wanted anything to eat, he'd say, 'Nah, I'm alright. I've just had a grape.' A big plate of food really fazed him. 'I can't eat all that!'

Although most kids idolise their parents, Paul and I knew that Dad was cool. I mean, Dad was a *dude*. A painter/decorator who worked for Birmingham Co-op doing shop fittings, Dad designed exactly how the shops would look, which was an amazingly ambitious profession given that he was colour blind. Dad had this mad thing where he could look at a colour and know exactly what it was – and not what he was actually seeing – by making an adjustment in his head. Dad was a proper old-school painter as well who could turn his hand to signwriting and marbling effects, all the stuff done by computers these days. Dad was also in a band.

Dad was lead singer in The Bob Gough Sound, who regularly played their rock/soul/croony covers around the local towns and villages at weddings and dinner functions. Harry Pardoe, who lived opposite us on Whiteoaks Drive, was the band's drummer. Dad would also take up percussion at times by playing bongos and congas. Uncle Harry, as he was known to us, had a big Ford Granada and was a generous soul; he once gave me and Paul some bongos, hi-hat cymbals (with stand) and two snare drums, which was proper cool. The Bob Gough Sound would play at comedy nights, social functions and working men's clubs all over the Midlands. Dad was always 'on trend' too. I found some old photos of Dad recently and on the back of one was a 'note to self':

'This jacket and waistcoat is a bad choice.' Dad was the coolest man on the planet.

Auntie Ann would come over and babysit us, when my parents went off to a function. Dad really looked the business, all done up in his red velvet jacket. Looking back, it must have been quite an inspiration to me, that somebody in my house was an actual member of an actual band. That world wasn't as distant to me as it might have been for others, I guess. My dad was a lead singer!

Dad belted out these big powerful ballads and we would be treated to sneak previews on a Sunday when he cranked up the record player, having opened every door and window in the house. Dad would sing along at the top of his voice, often accompanying his vocals with some serious 'air drumming'. The stereo was an old sideboard record player; a cabinet on legs with sliding doors. One side of the cabinet housed knick-knacks, the other contained Dad's vinyl. That cabinet had a really distinctive smell. In there were 16s, 78s, 45s and 33s.

Paul and I didn't really have records of our own when we were primary school age. The playgroup ditty *The Big Red Bus and The Thirsty Little Mini* was my first record. We were given an eight-track cartridge machine at some point, probably out of somebody's car and we had a couple of those clunky cartridges by easy-listening artists. Still, Paul and I were more than happy to sift our way through our parents' collection. There was always music on in the house and I would love to say that I was exposed to the latest avant-garde sounds from Düsseldorf, in a home that sailed close to the cutting edge, but we weren't. We had Beatles records, but I never heard them played. The music at home wasn't very edgy. I imagine my parents probably preferred The Beatles before they went weird.

Mum and Dad would often host dinner parties and I would listen to the muffled sounds from my bedroom late at night. There'd be a strip of light underneath the door of my darkened room and I would lay in bed, falling to asleep to the faint strains of Detroit Spinners, The Stylistics and Johnny Mathis. Mum always swore that she could *turn* Johnny Mathis, she fancied him that much. I remember wishing that I was old enough to attend a dinner party. I would have loved to have got my hands on that turntable.

Dad always had the radio on in the car and I would like just about everything on there. Radio back then represented such a broad church of music, as did *Top of the Pops* on a Thursday night, which was a rare opportunity to *see* the bands that occupied the all-important charts. Although punk was exploding across the UK in 1976, it had little effect on life in Bishopswood. Johnny Mathis bossed Johnny Rotten in most suburban homes back then.

Then one day Paul and I were given one of those record players that sat inside a case with the speaker across the front. You had the on/off button and a tone dial for more treble and bass. It was either very tinny or completely muffled, but you could place a whole load of 7" singles on there and it would play them all in turn, dropping each new disc from the stack. A family friend had given us a load of Bakelite 78s and these were heavy-duty slabs of vinyl. The Bakelite that had the biggest effect on me was *Let There Be Drums*, which was an old sixties thing. I used to play that record all the time, jumping up and down on the bed to it. Bakelites were well thick and so it would only have to tap a standard vinyl record next to it and CRACK! The disc was absolutely shattered. *Let There Be Drums* was instrumental with a guitar-driven, percussion-heavy vibe, which I really don't like at all now, but it got me suitably excited back then.

I've never been one to question things too much. It was only when I reached 16 that I discovered that Auntie Ann and Uncle Keith were brother and sister. Keith was a big musical influence on me, in that he loved some pretty heavyweight bands of the time, like King Crimson, Yes, Camel and Nice. Keith had these futuristic white headphones with a black curly cord and a volume control on each can. Keith was a cool uncle and seriously into his music. I remember he had that King Crimson album with the painting of a man's screaming face on the front, mouth wide open. Keith's records showed the wild directions music could take and his collection was nothing like my parents'.

Life was pretty sweet back then. Mum was a dinner lady at my primary school for a while, which was cool. Mum had worked in Richard Shops when she was younger. Dad spotted her working in the women's clothes store one morning and told her colleague that he was going to take her out; a confident man. But like many women of the time, Mum eventually stayed home after their subsequent marriage and kids. As conventional as our home life seemed back then, both my parents were quite quirky really and were always off doing exciting things like water-skiing and diving, when Dad wasn't playing gigs. My folks wouldn't dream of wasting a day watching TV.

Some weekends we would go and visit my relatives in Wolverhampton and we would sing songs in the car all the way there.

I'd ask Dad where we were going and he'd always reply: 'Off our heads!' I never really knew what that meant.

I was not the cleverest of kids, but I was pretty happy at St John's Primary School, five doors down from our house. Mrs Ellis was a teacher from school and also a family friend. Mrs Ellis – or Doreen as we were allowed to call her out of work – was very strict at school. She got right into your face when she told you off and didn't quite know which of your eyeballs to look at, so her eyes switched left to right and back again. But out of school, she was ace.

I would go home for lunch back then to watch TV. I loved going home for lunch. I will never forget Paul scaring the living daylights out of me one lunchtime, a few years later, by putting *Armchair Thriller* on the telly. I had nightmares for years after watching the episode that featured a terrifying nun with a skull for a face. That programme really shocked me and I just couldn't erase this zombie nun's face from my mind. It scared me so much it put me off watching any horror film or even spoof, right up until today. Cheers Paul!

Bishopswood was really tiny and we could walk around the whole village until quite late without any fear of getting lost or falling into too much trouble, although there was always the ever-present danger of electricity pylons and rabid dogs. The little village had fields all around it with walkways out of the centre that led you down the country lanes to little brooks where we would play, catching sticklebacks with nets and jam jars. The soil was made of clay and Paul would make these little pots out of it. We would go to the brook, scoop up the clay and make all these bowls and old-fashioned pipes. We'd make all sorts of weird things out of that clay, which would eventually go brittle once dried.

There was this particular pond in Bishopswood that was obscured by high hedges and people would dump their rubbish in it. This was a notorious fly-tipping area, known affectionately by the locals as 'the dump'. We would always be down the dump on our bikes. There'd be all sorts of stuff in that pond. We once found a Honda C90 in there. The bike was minus the engine, but it had the wheels and so we pushed it all the way back to the village and took it in turns to sit on it and push it down the drive.

We would spend the weekends, summer holidays and nights after school playing 'army' in the fields that surrounded the village. When the farmers had finished the harvesting, they'd leave the hay bales and we would make castles from them, or simply take the stack apart and jump into it from a tree. It was proper country living. Grazed knees and rosy cheeks.

Paul and I were brothers, and very close friends. Many people thought we were twins although Paul was two years older than me. We spent summer days walking around Bishopswood for hours, kicking up dust whilst looking for 'treasure'. If we found 2p, we'd walk straight to the sweet counter of the little village shop, where you could come away with four halfpenny sweets, which represented a nice little haul. Paul and I hung around a lot together and he was my best friend, I guess.

***

Every year we went to Wales on holiday as my mum's eldest brother moved somewhere near Cardigan where he ran a garage. We were in Wales all the time. Even at Christmas we'd load up the car with presents and drive to Cardigan. Then in 1976, Uncle Harry sorted us some free accommodation in Ibiza. Harry's daughter Sue was engaged to a chef called Vicenti who worked at the Nautilus Hotel, which is how we ended up staying at their villa. Thanks to Freddie Laker's cheap flights, we were off abroad during the sizzling summer of 1976, which was possibly the worst time to leave Britain. Still, this was my first time on a plane to that strange continent known as 'abroad'.

This villa was in the middle of nowhere and it was well exciting. Everything was different. I remember having breakfast on the villa terrace and trying apricot jam for the first time. There were no red bricks or grey office buildings in Ibiza. Everything seemed so white and bright.

We went to the hotel Nautilus for lunch as guests of Vicenti. The Nautilus was where Happy Mondays shot the video for *Step On*, Shaun Ryder hanging off the 'E' in the HOTEL sign. I can remember Javier, the head waiter, asking us what we wanted for lunch. 'Anything from the menu,' he said. Paul and I asked for spaghetti on toast. Vicenti was quite disgruntled as we could have had lobsters and all this lovely fresh seafood, but we were the fish out of water. We didn't really cotton on. I guess he was insulted. It was mad hot out there and I can remember the pain of Mum combing my hair as she hit against the tops of my sunburnt ears with the brush.

Mum and Dad were really into diving and water-skiing and so Ibiza was all about getting in the water. Back in the UK my parents were often diving at weekends. I got told off by a teacher once for a 'what I did at the weekend' piece of writing. We had been to Stoney Cove (Leicestershire), so Mum and Dad could go diving down into this deep lake to explore an aeroplane fuselage that had been placed there. Dad had the diver's watch, wetsuit and, like Action Man, the dagger strapped to the side of his leg. Honest. So I wrote: 'Mum and Dad went diving in a lake inside a big aeroplane...' The teacher wrote back to my parents saying I had a 'wild imagination... and told terrible fibs'. So Dad slapped his guns on and went straight to school to put them right.

So Ibiza featured lots of swimming and diving. Paul and I were into catching these black sea urchins, covered in spines. We'd take these creatures back to the villa at the end of the day where we'd place them on top of the entrance to this massive ants' nest. By the next morning the ants had cleaned away all the insides and the skin, leaving these brightly coloured blobs: all greens, purples and mad patterns. I loved diving. You got to wear a mask.

***

Although I was a bit of a soft touch, I got into quite a few scrapes at home. We had one of those old-fashioned storage heaters in mine and Paul's bedroom, which was a metal rectangular box filled with bricks that warmed up and glowed. I don't know if I had just learned to do a forward roll or not, but I had this fantastic idea to roll across the top of this heater. I was only small so I could stand along the top, but I went off the end, post-roll and smacked my head on a protruding plug socket. I've still got the scar on the back of my head. A year later, I decided to try and walk along the side of the bath while it was wet and covered in soap. My legs went from underneath me and my arm went right back, causing a fracture. So twice I was rushed to RAF Cosford hospital, not far from Bishopswood. Another game we played was 'death darts'. We'd throw these darts right up in the air and time how long you could stay still before you legged it. I ended up with a dart in the leg after one such hollow victory.

Paul was a proper 'tatter'; someone who was constantly fiddling with inventions and gadgets. Instead of simply assembling model aeroplanes before painting and hanging them from the ceiling, Paul would have to modify them by making the undercarriage go up and down. He'd tinker with things all the time. He once built a LEGO bus from the normal bricks, but made the double-decker hollow and melted a hole into one of the thin parts of the roof. Just in front of one of the rear wheels, Paul left a brick missing and filled it with talcum powder. So as you moved the bus, you could blow through the hole in the roof and this talc would poof out of the side, just like the fumes from an exhaust. Paul had kitted out model helicopters with drones before you could even buy cameras for them. He joined the RAF when he was 17. Paul loved building rockets, making them bigger and bigger. Rather than just a firework that went up and down, he'd get rockets to fly in stages like the Apollo missions. As a young man, Paul once lined up all these rockets up in a cornfield in Cambridge and set all the stubble alight. The fire service had to put out the ensuing blaze.

As well as listening to bizarre old-fashioned records and making clay pipes, Paul and I were both into *Star Wars*. We had heard on the grapevine that this film was going to be incredible and to whet our English appetites comic strips started to appear in UK newsagents between the US release in August 1977 and the eventual UK release that Christmas. The film came out just as Dad was starting to think about moving us out of Bishopswood. Dad didn't like living on an estate with neighbours overlooking your garden and everyone knowing your business and he wanted to get away. Dad wasn't a grumpy bloke, but he didn't like being 'on show' and so he often expressed a desire to move out to the middle of nowhere.

1977 was a classic year. Owing to the Queen's Silver Jubilee, Raleigh brought out a silver-edition Chopper that had big, thick aluminium-spoked wheels like a BMX. The handlebars were closer together and it had drum brakes on the back. The bike was not great for long distances, but it made my summer. I spent hours on that bike and kept it until I was 16. It's quite rare now. Chopper peaked in '77 before BMX took over. I was very lucky to get that bike, especially as we never had a lot of money. In fact, Paul and I never asked for things off our parents as we knew things were tight.

I loved watching TV and was a massive fan of *Tomorrow's World* on Thursday nights (BBC1), just before *Top of the Pops*. It would be called a gadget show now, but *Tomorrow's World* was far more informative. There was no buggering about on hover boards; this was proper science and very nerdy and dry. Sometimes I didn't quite get it. I remember the episode with the microwave oven – years before they came out – and I couldn't accept that this would end up in every kitchen. 'No way is that an oven! You can't just stick food in that! There's no heating element!' I loved gadgets and really lusted after this tag gun which shot buttons back on to clothes. 'Mum! Why can't you see the genius of this thing?'

Dad loved these factual programmes too and watched every nature documentary going. Religion never got a look-in, though. As soon as *Songs of Praise* came on, Dad would bristle. 'You can get that shit off, right away!' We'd be having Sunday dinner listening to this particular DJ on Radio 2 and after his show was always *Sing Something Simple* and Dad would get the proper hump. 'Get that crap off, now!' Dad also had a strange hatred for the singer/actress Anita Harris. I'm not really sure why.

Star Wars was becoming huge, though and it was the talk of the playground at Brewood Middle School. We were looking for houses around the time we started collecting the *Star Wars* comics. I remember this one particular afternoon distinctly. 'Get your best clothes on, we're going to look at houses,' announced Dad. My brother and I hated looking at houses. How could we have an opinion on such a thing? So, with proper faces on, we found ourselves standing in front of the Odeon in Wolverhampton. I guess we thought we must be waiting to go into an estate agents or something. We also visited Gran in Wolverhampton at the weekends so we were often in the town centre. We still hadn't clicked, even when we turned around and saw the poster. 'What are we doing here?'

-   'What do you think we're doing here?' Dad gruffed. 'We're here to see *Star Wars*!'

We didn't know it at the time, but the magazines we were collecting were serialising the whole of the film by following the movie script. When we finally got to see the film, we were like, 'No way! Dad, Dad, we know what's going to happen!' Serialising the script was a bit of an ill-conceived idea, really, but the movie still had us reeling for weeks after. Well, for years.

Headbangers, Lapwings And Kraftwerk

If you didn't like heavy metal, you got your head kicked in. The West Midlands refused to let go of heavy rock, no matter how explosive punk had been, and if you were asked to put forward an opinion on Whitesnake or Black Sabbath, your answer had better be positive. So important was a love for metal I would study the sleeves of rock compilations for the names of bands and songs in case such a conversation should arise. You would always bang your head at school discos even if you detested songs about motorbikes, wizards and loose women. I didn't mind it, but when we eventually moved to the new house in the sleepy village of Gnosall in 1979, you had to like heavy metal or you'd get a boot up the arse.

Things were very tribal back in the late seventies. People knew what music you liked by what you wore and Gnosall was a real rockers' domain, as was much of the West Midlands, home to Led Zeppelin, Black Sabbath, Judas Priest and their ilk. Later on, Ozzy Osbourne moved near to where we lived as if to ensure that no one in his heartland ever stopped listening to the heavy-duty power rock that some say evoked the steel and car-making industries of the area.

I was a square kid, really, with the bowl haircut and crap clothes; nothing 'on trend' whatsoever. I wasn't 'cool' as such. There's a Polaroid of me (just before we left Bishopswood) looking well dapper in a tank top and flares. I had a Wembley football tucked under my arm. It was odd that I was posing with a football as I was crap at sport. Dad was a very good goalkeeper and so he was forever persuading me to take it up, so I guess I thought I'd impress my dad in this particular snap. Although I was getting into electronica and the New Romantic scene, I hadn't cottoned on to the fashions or hairstyles of the time. There was a big stigma attached to flares in the late seventies, but it hadn't reached me yet. Mum still chose all my clothes.

There was a regular kids' disco in Gnosall and I thought it might be a good way of making friends as I was so excruciatingly shy and had moved away from all my mates in Bishopswood. So I went to the disco on my own to see what was going on. There was this lad Colin Gallagher there who was two years above me at school and he had the Doc Marten boots and a pair of punky tartan trousers which he proceeded to drop to his ankles in the middle of the dance floor. I remember looking at Colin Gallagher's buttocks thinking, 'Why on earth have we moved here?' That just about summed up punk for me. Only a punk or a headbanger would show their bum off at a kids' disco. That said, if Rainbow, Whitesnake or Status Quo came on, I banged my head with the best of them. The year below mine at Heron Brook Middle School liked anything by The Police and The Jam and they were doing that funny skipping-about dance, wearing these little jackets with targets on the back and that seemed somewhat preferable to the denim-and-leather brigade.

My first new friend in Gnosall was Graham 'Poddy' Podmore and we would listen to Thin Lizzy, Whitesnake and Rainbow together. I didn't detest metal and I really liked Motörhead, who seemed to be the one metal band even punks liked. I told Poddy that we were going to appear on *Top of the Pops* one day in a band of our own. We were air-guitaring to Deep Purple's live album *Made in Japan* at the time and I made sure we knew exactly what our roles would be once we were booked on to the show to perform our ear-bleeding brand of hard rock.

Music had become very important to me, particularly after leaving Bishopswood to relocate in Gnosall. Our new home was a 300-year-old cottage slap bang in the middle of nowhere, on the very fringes of Gnosall. In Bishopswood you knew everyone in the village and all the local kids were your friends, but in Gnosall we were isolated and I found it tough settling in. Listening to music was an escape for me, and with the advent of affordable ghettoblasters and the mind-blowing revolution that was the personal stereo, music was fast becoming an obsession.

I loved electronic music even though I couldn't really shout about it. The music that got the 11-year-old me excited back in 1979 was about as far removed from the macho world of Scorpions and Saxon as you could get. My heroes were moody, immaculate automatons standing impassively behind keyboards rather than scruff bags in tights assaulting guitars whilst unrolling their tongues. The electronic musician looked like a C&A mannequin and couldn't/wouldn't dance for toffee. I guess the first proponents of this were the generation who got into Nice, Tangerine Dream and Bowie. Many from the macho side of rock were very dismissive of electronic music. 'All you have to do is push a button to make a record,' but the prog rockers seemed to 'get it'.

The first record I ever bought was *Cars* by Gary Numan in 1979. I really liked *Are 'Friends' Electric?* that came before it by Numan's Tubeway Army, but was too scared to enter the record shop. I totally bottled it. Punks, skinheads and headbangers were in record shops, and as a kid, I found walking inside a store very intimidating. You wouldn't even look at 'them' in case they spat at you. So when *Cars* came out I thought, 'If I don't buy this, I'll miss this one as well.' So I plucked up the courage to get a copy of *Cars* and snagged *Are 'Friends' Electric*? while I was there. Bonus! I don't think the excitement of carrying records home has ever been bettered. Just a sneaky peek at the sleeve on the bus home or in the car was heavenly. What a rush. Streaming a track comes nowhere near.

I had started to spend less time with Paul in Gnosall as he was growing up with a load of new friends. Paul used to talk on my behalf when we were younger and always looked out for me, although he did once take a bite out of every piece of fruit in the fruit bowl – including bananas – before blaming it on me. We also covered the sofa in Sudocrem and talc-ed the entire house, but I was always the scapegoat. But we were very cool with each other. The age difference became more apparent in Gnosall, though. The distance between us was first made apparent one afternoon when we collected sticklebacks from the brook, back in Bishopswood. I was carrying this heavy glass jar of fish back on my own, as Paul scootered off in front of me. In a rush to catch up with Paul, I tripped over the poles of the fishing nets and fell onto the glass jar, which smashed to pieces. Dad then spent ages picking all the glass shards out of my belly with tweezers, all because I was trying to catch up with my big brother.

One thing Paul and I did have in common though, was music. As the seventies gave way to a new decade I was bewitched by the rap music coming over from the US, such as Sugarhill Gang's *Rapper's*

Delight, which was such a momentous tune. I remember my brother buying Kraftwerk's *Numbers* single from the *Computer Love* album in 1981, the title track of which was to serve as the basis for Soul Sonic Force's *Planet Rock*. With electro, I saw the future. My future. Kraftwerk predated the whole electro thing by years, though and those German pioneers represented the most drum-based music Paul was into; his record collection was full of Jean Michel Jarre and stuff like that. It was all terribly grown-up music with no real beats. Paul seemed to lap up anything that linked him to the technology he loved so much; he even built an AM radio from components once, which really impressed me.

Paul was a real stickler for sound reproduction and was the first person I knew to have a personal stereo (a really cheap one from Woolworths). Paul played a tape on his new machine – a big red plastic brick with a couple of black buttons on the side and the orange foam on the headphones. He was instantly angry. He ended up taking it back. He said to the assistant, 'Can't you hear the hiss?'

- 'Sorry, I don't know what you're talking about.'
- 'The hiss!'

It was just a cheap personal stereo playing a hissy tape, but eventually he put some money towards a better one. Although he wasn't into breakdancing, Paul had a brilliant ghettoblaster. We loved flicking through Mum's catalogues looking at the latest Sanyos, Philips and JVCs. I would spend hours with a catalogue looking at the wattage, noise reduction and graphic equalisers. 'If you had to pick any stereo off this page, which would it be?' I'd say to Paul. 'But you can only pick one!'

We ended up giving the old sideboard record player to Granddad when we upgraded to a Philips stereo system with tape deck and VU meters on the front, complete with moving needles. Sundays, Dad would still put his music on, only now he could really crank it up so it was blaring. There were no neighbours to upset either.

I used to judge music on face value back then. Now I explore it more and think about the production and meaning, but back then I thought: 'It's just a new Roxy Music album.' I didn't realise that Roxy would have used all the latest studio techniques and equipment. Popular music covered so many genres back then it was hard to know where to head. The Top 10 might have ABBA, Whitesnake, Chic, Bowie, Kraftwerk and Val Doonican all vying to be number one. It was a real mixed bag and many people had no issues with liking the entire lot. In fact, seeing your favourite band on *Top of the Pops* sandwiched between fogey bands, singing puppets and cabaret singers gave them even more edge.

I was forever taping stuff off the radio with one of those little Binatone cassette recorders with a speaker at the back and a row of buttons along the front. You'd pull a handle out to get the mic and then sit it next to the stereo, which was playing the Top 40. The Binatone had a condenser mic in it, so if anyone walked into the room talking, it would feature on the recordings. They were the worst recordings ever really, but that was what you were used to, I guess. You had to press 'stop' on the tape machine before the DJ butted in.

As I was always watching nature programmes with Dad, my head was full of useless information. If a bird flies overhead I can tell what it is – even now – purely by its silhouette. I got a pair of binoculars for my birthday one year and would spend afternoons staring at the lapwings for hours on end, listening to the birdcall. You could hardly see the lapwings because they were camouflaged by the mud, but it was lovely being out in the countryside. Dad was always good at spotting and nurturing an initial interest kids had and always encouraged from the side-lines. Dad was never pushy.

Although Dad was happy living in the middle of nowhere, I hated it. It was pitch dark where we lived on the edge of town, with no street lights. The cottage was warmed up by coal fires and the house was lined with asbestos. The walls were covered in fibrous chipboard with glossy yellow polystyrene tiles placed over the top; the colour thanks to the previous owners being heavy smokers. When we first moved in, Dad, Paul, Uncle Keith and I ripped all the asbestos out with no real health and safety concerns. Asbestosis hadn't become identified at that time and so we just tore into the potentially fatal material with not so much as a dust mask for protection.

Nights at the cottage were pitch black. Real country dark. I was shit scared to go to bed; I could hear the floorboards creaking all around me as night descended. Creaeeaaaakkkk! It was like someone walking right across the room. You can see why TV shows visit these old houses looking for spirits. Ten minutes of lying in bed listening to the house talking is enough to put the willies up the toughest of souls. It got to the point where I would pray for a car to come zipping past just so the lights would beam up into the room and assure me that a headless ghost wasn't about to cleave my bonce off. Then it would return to pitch black again. The combination of the dark, the floorboards creaking and the screams of the owls and foxes outside – like women being murdered – had me dreading bedtime. It was like something from *Armchair Thriller.* I ended up sleeping with my Timex wind-up watch in one ear and my finger planted firmly in the other. All I could hear was the comforting ticking that would eventually lead to morning.

***

Just as video games and home computers were becoming popular with our friends, Paul and I were hard at work helping Dad restore the cottage. Dad never saw the point of computer games as you didn't learn anything. Instead, we helped the old man rip a wall down and assisted him with the metalwork, woodwork and painting. I remember removing sections from underneath the brick wall so we could lay some foundations for the cottage. We used wood for a mould to pour the concrete in and then removed the planks, dug along a bit more and started again, one metre at a time.

It was fun exploring this old house, especially when we found an old coin from the time of Oliver Cromwell. The 'bit' was made from proper silver and had been clipped down the edge, a practice of people fallen upon hard times; the clipped portion of silver would be melted down to sell. Some old papers stuffed around the door frames turned out to be coal bills from 1822, back when coal was brought from Lichfield by horse and cart all the way to Gnosall. It was always fun helping Dad whilst honing our skills and furthering our knowledge of local history.

I also collected Whimsies; those little porcelain animals. I'm not sure why. You could get Whimsie trout or otter and I had quite a few of them. I was never a real collector as such, but people just kept buying them for me.

Often the only company I had in Gnosall was our tortoiseshell cat, Tispa. We never got to name any of the pets, as that was Dad's job. Then we got a black cat called Merlin. Then when my brother was followed home by a black and white cat that looked like it had been kicked in the face, he asked if we could keep it. The cat's nose was all mushed up and it was eating worms; its ears full of mites. 'If it's still here when your dad gets home we can keep it,' said Mum. It was still there when he got home and so Dad called it Mono because of its colouring. Tispa eventually disappeared the same week we saw a local news story saying that cats were being stolen. Apparently tortoiseshells were being used to make ladies' mittens. Then Merlin got knocked down dead. But scruffy old Mono lived for years and years, although it always looked as if it was on its last legs.

School was OK. I changed from Brewood Middle School to Heron Brook when we moved and I was still a very shy kid, although eager to please. I wasn't setting the academic world alight as such, but I was well-behaved. Mr Bates was a strict teacher, but funny with it. He was deaf in one ear and people would talk to him on his wrong side. He would launch blackboard rubbers at people with pinpoint accuracy. I think that was why I remained so quiet.

I really enjoyed art, but was crap at maths. I loved drawing cartoons, but that was never encouraged. Now, they will get behind you if they spot a talent, but back then you had to draw from real life, like a Mars wrapper or an old shoe. I was a real daydreamer and just loved making things. Mr Roy was a cool teacher as he didn't believe in giving kids homework. 'You work at school, play at home,' he'd say. I loved English until one of my assignments was used by a higher class one afternoon to point out just how rubbish it was. I can remember the kids coming out and laughing at me because my essay was no good. I'm not sure you could get away with that sort of bullying now, but it shattered my confidence.

My mate Poddy lived further out than us and we were really into playing outside. We would often hang out on an old train line after school that went from Stafford through a lot of the villages before eventually hitting Gnosall. The line was disused so there was no live track or anything, but it was ace riding your bike down it. Someone had left a burnt-out Mini down there and we would sit in the front pretending to drive it. Poddy produced a packet of Woodbines one afternoon and sparked one up. Woodbines must be the worst cigarette to start smoking with and I felt proper sick after a few lungful's.

Outdoor play to one side, I secretly lusted for a computer, but because money was in short supply at home I would always make do with playing on a mate's. I remember those old text-based adventure games that threw up various exciting options. 'You're in the forest – do you want to run or fight? Press F or R.' I actually found them really exciting although it was less sophisticated than sending a text. 'Do you want to fight the goblin?' Yes I did.

Oddly, for someone so into electronic music, I was pretty hopeless around computers when it came to programming. Much of computing back then was focused on actual programming. My high school, King Edward VI in Stafford, had a computer club, but only four kids ever went there. They had those beige BBC microcomputers and only the real spofs knew how to use them. So much so, that if you actually went in, there was a major chance you'd make a total dick of yourself. So everyone steered clear of computer club. The dawn of the computer age was sold to us in the dullest manner imaginable, looking back. It seemed that the peak of a computer's abilities was to revolutionise supermarket tills and increase data storage, things that were hardly going to excite the young.

Computers back then could do very little and it was all up to you to make it exciting. It's mental to think how things have changed. My brother's mate had a ZX Spectrum and we would sit there for ages waiting for a tape to load, reading magazines as it screeched away. Then, if someone touched the computer too much, the whole excruciating process had to start again. Screeeeeeech!!! Life seemed to be pretty sweet back then though, all things considered, until a mate really let me down.

Dark Times, World Wars And The Hell Diver

It was whilst at high school in 1982, that the rest of my life would be influenced by a single moment of stupidity, when my best friend at the time, Dave Robinson, decided as a joke, to convince everyone at school that I was gay. It wasn't a one-off jape that was forgotten about the following day; instead it was to trigger an ongoing campaign of bullying that lasted the best part of four or five years, shattering my confidence and destroying any chance I had of forming friendships.

Every day at King Edward VI (in Stafford) was awful. I was mocked continually and often beaten up. 'Backs against the wall, Archer's here!' they'd shout as I entered the classroom; I was always last to show, to limit the damage. I didn't want to go to school of course, but I wasn't the sort of person to skive off either – because I was scared of the cops – and so off I went every morning knowing what was waiting for me. I couldn't relax for a second. People would just walk up to me and slap me in the face because they felt like it. I was so miserable and the really sad thing was that I got used to it. I would spend lunch times sitting on my own in the classrooms to bypass any potential trouble in the playground. I couldn't see why anybody, male or female, would have any interest in me. It makes me sad now to look back at myself then. I used to engage eye contact with my form teacher in order to get some help, but she would just shrug her shoulders as if to say, 'What can *I* do about it?'

Dave Robinson left King Eddie's to go to a private school not long after, but sadly became one of the ringleaders outside of school. Dave and his mates would ring our house and shout down the phone at me. On the old phones, if you put the receiver down it only ended the conversation if the caller hung up; so of course they were still there when I checked. You couldn't phone anyone either while they were connected. Every time you picked the phone up they'd still be there, laughing on the other end.

We would often go cross-country at school, running down to the main road in Stafford. We then snaked our way around the rugby fields before circling all the way back up by Stafford Castle. Then it was back to the main road and school. When it came to my 14th birthday I heard a rumour that I was to be thrown into the biology pond during cross-country. That was the only time I skipped school. I went down to the old railway line in Gnosall and sat on my own until it was too late to go to school. At school the following day I froze when I heard that we were having PE; my day's skiving had been in vain. True to their word, these lads threw me straight into the murky pond, which was thick with stagnant water and weeds. It proper stunk. I had gotten a right mouthful of this mush and was very sick after. It was just one thing after another.

I remember this guy grabbing me by the neck one lunchtime and everyone gathered around to see the fun. This kid strangled me a little too hard, though, and I blacked out. When I came to, everyone was shitting themselves, but no one would see if I was OK as it would have marked them out as a target to the bullies. I was always in awe of my mate Poddy and considered him well cool. Poddy could handle himself. However, he contacted me on Facebook not long back and said he was getting bullied himself back then; being associated with me possibly didn't help.

I was sometimes relieved when there was inter-school rivalry between King Ed's and Blessed William Howard at the other end of the playing fields, because focus shifted from me for a bit. There were some ridiculous urban myths at the time regarding legendary battles between the two schools. One such myth was that King Eddie's saw off the entire Blessed Bills, with just one kid. I never saw any clashes though and as soon as the hype died down, all eyes were back on me.

I would go home and tell Paul about the bullying, but he wasn't interested; nor was my dad. I'd lost Paul as my mate I guess. I got punched on the school bus one afternoon and Paul just got off and walked home on his own. He didn't want to get involved.

Dad could get quite irritated by the bullying stories. 'People don't take the mick out of you unless you give them reason to,' he'd say, clearly not believing me. It was a really shitty time, but I just grinned through gritted teeth and got on with it. I was shy to begin with and so the bullying made me even more sensitive. I still don't like situations where people gang up on you. I can deal with one person taking the piss, but when three or four get on at me it reminds me of school and I have to remove myself from the situation completely. I would come home, watch TV, have my dinner and then sit with Dad and Mum in the living room. Failing that I'd be in my room listening to music.

There was one plus-side to being a recluse: 'pause button mixing'. With time on my hands and a few tape recorders and radios at my disposal, I made those first tentative steps into mixing. I would record something off the radio, wait until it got to a snare or something, then wind the tape back to that particular bit where it would line up with the tape head and then press pause and record. I would then wait until another tune came on. The tape would then kick off at the first kick drum or snare, which was cued into another on-beat. I used to do a lot of tapes like that. I was also learning with a record deck. I would play a track off a tape whilst using my finger to speed up or slow down a 7". You couldn't record it, but you could match them up and learn the principles of mixing. I was well into rap by now and loved Grandmaster Flash and Melle Mel, but it was *The Hurting* by Tears For Fears that I kept coming back to, over and over. So much so that a mate of Paul's went out and bought it the day after I first played it to him. I guess I listened to a whole mixture of music until a brand new scene opened up to me.

I knew Sean Lester back from when I lived in Bishopswood. Sean used to go around telling people he was my cousin just because he looked a bit like me. Sean Lester was quite cool though and was the one person I could relax with at high school. Sean had this sweet Adidas sports bag with all these mysterious names written on the side in marker pen: Shannon, B-Boys and 2 Sisters and all that. I was like, 'What's all this?'

-    'My mum's boyfriend is a DJ and he plays these people at the club,' he explained. 'It's called electro and it's what I'm into.'

There were literally three people at school who were into electro and we were all looked upon as freaks – so no change there! I loved it. It was such a futuristic sound. Andrew Hume, Sean Lester and I were the electro crew back in 1983. I never got into things really early on as a kid. I remember someone asking me, 'What kind of music do you like?' at school and I rather naively mentioned a new Cliff Richard record I liked. That was one of the worst things I could have said, of course. But once I heard electro, I was hooked and Cliff Richard this was not. I loved the clothes that went with electro too. Puma and Adidas tracksuits and white basketball hi-tops, the 'electro' look was well sharp. No bovver boots, leathers or parkas. It was a look that overlapped with the 'soccer casual' scene and it was hard to tell a football lad from a breaker until you saw the Dire Straits T-shirt beneath the Fila track top. The casuals also had the Lois cords and split-fades, but it was always the Dire Straits or UB40 T-shirt that gave them away. 'You're not into breakdancing!'

The year after I left school, King Eddie's was really down with breakdancing. It was majorly cool all of a sudden and the breakdance crew from Risingbrooke actually came to challenge the local lads. Why couldn't I have been a year younger?

Although electro was going to earn me some credibility, my first gig was a trifle naff. In 1983, a lad asked me if I wanted to see the then popular Nik Kershaw play in Hanley (Stoke-on-Trent). Stuart Harrison was a ginger-haired kid with a pronounced Adam's apple and I guess he considered me a kindred spirit. I'd like to say that my first concert was George Clinton and Funkadelic, but it wasn't. It was Nik Kershaw. That said, I wasn't really bothered by live music to be honest and it was to be many years before I attended my next gig. I am a stickler for how music sounds on record and for me that's perfection. So Nik Kershaw couldn't have bowled me over more if lasers had shot from his eyes and burned the venue down. My heart belonged to vinyl.

Another passion of mine was modelling. As I couldn't hang out with kids my own age for fear of bullying, a lot of my time was spent indoors. I had loads of World War II figures and vehicles in my bedroom and I would spend hours assembling and painting them. I had a whole town laid out on my bedroom floor. Paul's best mate Michael had a massive war diorama in his loft. The intricate set-up was Michael's dad's and we would often go up there to play 'wargaming' with a dice. Roll a six and you could kill however many people or move your tanks thus far. My dad wasn't that keen on games or films that glamorised war however and was always keen to point out that people actually died during wars. I always respected my dad for that.

My father was also a stickler for 'scale'. Let's say you had a Matchbox set with a helicopter and a car; Dad could get quite irate if it wasn't to scale. 'That's not to scale!' he'd say. 'That person driving the Mini is as tall as the helicopter! They're not to scale.' There was 1/32 scale with 5cm tall figures and 1/72 scale with figures that were just 1cm tall and so painting them was a painstaking job. The soldiers' flesh, socks and shoes were all different colours and you didn't want to cross-contaminate the paint. I was quite fascinated by war – being part of a generation that avoided the actual horror of it – and loved all the military uniforms and apparel. At first school, the kids would shout, 'All join on if you want to play army!' They'd put their arm around your shoulder, and then you'd hook the next person to join up. We would hunt for sticks and make machine gun noises whilst pointing them at people. I really wanted a gas mask when I was younger. I'd say to my parents, 'Please get me a gas mask! They're so cool!'
- 'What would you do with it?'
- 'I'd wear it.'
- 'Then what?'

I guess war was an escape from the constant bullying and harassment and was a world where bigger concerns were kicking off.

***

The scooters would circle around our cottage, beeping their horns as the riders laughed and shouted insults. Standing inside the cottage, peering through the living-room curtains, I felt trapped and humiliated. It was awful hearing all this at home; the one place that up until that point had offered some comfort after the constant bullying at school. But the telephone pranks and now the mopeds had taken away my only escape route. I was fast becoming isolated and depressed.

I had no way of meeting any friends due to the bullying and even if I rode my bike round Gnosall, I'd end up being chased. Even if a single member of the gang spotted you, they'd be off to get the others. It was awful. Within minutes you'd have four or five mopeds after you. As the bullying centred around some lies, there wasn't anything I could do to change things. If I had been overweight, I guess I could have lost some timber or something, but I wasn't. There wasn't anything I could do other than suck it up. I found it increasingly hard to think about anything else. You bully a shy kid and the results can be devastating

– as they can be for anyone, shy or not – and seemingly impossible to shake in later life.

CB radio (Citizens Band Radio) had been very popular in the late seventies and early eighties after the success of the trucker film *Convoy* and TV shows like *BJ and The Bear*, *Dukes of Hazzard*, *The CB Bears* and *CBTV Channel 14* and it was perfect for a recluse like myself. I sold one of those Pong video games with the block-graphic bats for £5 one weekend and decided to invest in a CB radio from Tandy. CB was essentially communicating to people through a two-way radio receiver usually used by truckers. There had been a massive boom in home ownership of CB, although it was illegal for many years, as it sometimes interfered with police radio. The weird thing was that you never really knew who you were talking to as you'd have a CB name or 'handle'. I named myself 'Hell Diver' after a model aeroplane that hung from my ceiling.

I was in a bit of a crappy area for CB reception as there was a bloody big hill between Gnosall and Stafford and so you would only get to communicate with people who owned these tall 'sky ariels' that were capable of achieving a really clear signal. The only person I could reach in Gnosall was someone I didn't want to talk to, which was typical I guess. This was like having email, but only one email address; of someone you didn't like. You'd often hear all this squelching noise only to realise after a while that you were listening in on someone else's conversation. Sometimes you would go to a channel and bark, '1.4. for a copy' and someone would reply. You would both then switch to an agreed channel. The conversations sometimes consisted of these mad three-way chats: 'Who is this I'm talking to?!' You also got these really anal truckers who would have a pop at you for using the wrong jargon. 'Eyeball eyeball, who's up for a 1.4.?' There was lots of jargon. The success of Hollywood movies like *Smokey and The Bandit* promised so much of these little gizmos and the reality of transmitting from a West Midlands bedroom was a little sad I guess; but I managed to pull on it, so who's complaining?

I persevered with CB as I had very little else to do and one day struck up a relationship with a girl called Black Lace. She seemed really nice and we would often chat about anything and everything. After a while, it became clear that meeting in person could work just fine and so we arranged to meet up at her house. Internet dating can be misleading when it comes to photographs and profiles, but I had no idea what Black Lace looked like. But I was very trusting. I hadn't actually considered this to be more than a friendly meet and so when she produced a boob within minutes of me arriving, I was more than a little shocked. I guess the red light bulb in her bedroom was a sign. 'Woah! I've seen a tit!' Initial relations with females to one side, CB really was a lifeline and for six months I had a girlfriend! My first one.

Not long after the meeting with Black Lace I met some lad on the CB from Newport, near Shropshire, and rode over on my bike to see him. Another time this same kid came back with me and we just spent the day listening to music and whatnot. I remember when it was time to go home, he produced a five-pound note from his pocket. 'This is yours,' he said. 'I could have nicked it, but I didn't.' With that he handed me back the crumpled fiver he'd clearly swiped. Yes, you met some characters on CB, but none one of them bullied me, so I didn't mind.

So I thank Tandy for providing me with that Realistic CB. I ditched it when it started stinking though; which was what happened to CBs when the batteries died. They stank.

CH. 4

Electro Friends, A Funky Moped And Tony Turner

8 Of The Best: Electro

1. Imperial Brothers – *We Dub To Scratch (Be Bop Scratch Mix)*
2. Aleem – *Release Yourself (Dub)*
3. Project Future – *Ray-Gun-Omics*
4. Davy DMX – *One For The Treble*
5. Key-Matic – *Breakin' In Space*
6. The Egyptian Lover – *Egypt Egypt*
7. Captain Rock – *Cosmic Blast*
8. Hashim – *Al-Naafiysh (The Soul)*

There was never any question of me staying on at school owing to the bullying and to be honest my grades were not good enough anyway. The end of school was a massive relief and after years of depression and abuse, and I slowly returned to a bully-free life.

During the eighties Margaret Thatcher's government introduced the Youth Training Scheme (or YTS) to train young job-seekers prior to work placements. Shortly before leaving school, Dad got a job working for the Stafford YTS as an instructor after losing his job at the Birmingham Co-op. He got so high up the chain at Co-op, they wanted him to start firing people. He refused to tell his friends that they wouldn't be having a Christmas that year and so he left and got a job as a YTS instructor in Stafford. Dad taught painting and decorating on the course, which also had teachers providing instruction on woodwork and brickwork. Trainees would go into each individual section while they were there.

I left school at 16 with virtually no qualifications, but no life of leisure was waiting for me. As soon as I left school, Dad was on at me. 'You need to get a job and earn some money for your board.' So I signed up to the YTS in Stafford where Dad worked. I got to do welding and learned how to paint windows while on the scheme. I also learned to lay bricks, did a bit of plumbing and tried my hand at carpentry and metalwork. I even built a rose arch for my parents' back garden.

My only previous experience of employment was working at a butcher's shop in Haughton during high school. That butcher really took the piss. I was 14 or 15 and he asked me to clean the big chopping table with a wire brush. I clearly wasn't cleaning the table properly as he grabbed the brush off me and said, 'No no, you have to do it like this! Like you're shagging your missus!' I was like, 'What?!' It was really embarrassing. At the end of the day the butcher called me over, after opening the till. With bated breath I waited for my first ever wage packet. The butcher smiled and pressed something into my open palm. I slowly unfurled my fingers. There in the centre of my palm was 5p. 'That's alright innit?' he said.

-    'Yeah, I guess.' What a tight sod.

Dad was someone you could talk to on the YTS scheme. There wasn't that division between 'them and us' with Dad – he was always one of the lads. If Dad thought a lad on his team's girlfriend was a bit rough he'd say so, basically making out that he could do better himself. He wasn't that PC to be honest and was never one to shy away from saying what he felt, but because of that, the trainees really liked him and felt relaxed in his company. The lads confided in Dad and when he heard that someone was selling a motorbike he asked me if I wanted to see it. I definitely wanted to see it. Dad always had his ear to the ground and had already taken a border collie pup off one of the trainees. Dad came home one night, unzipped his coat and produced this puppy, which he named Jimpy after a childhood pet.

One of my mates bought a moped the year before, when I still had a racing bike and I would desperately try and keep up with him. He would occasionally slow down, so I could put my hand on his shoulder. Then he'd taz off, dragging me with him on my bike. I can still recall being on a pushbike while going faster than I ever had before, with tears streaming down my face, scared to let go. The guy in question was Chris Sleight, from Ranton. He was an odd character who joined high school a week later than everyone else. He told all the girls that he'd be dead by the time he was 21 and this opened the floodgates. All the girls were like 'Poor Chris!' He never went short. Needless to say, this illness was a complete sham.

I fell off my pushbike the year before and smashed my two front teeth out and badly split both lips (with stitches in my lips and face). I eventually had my teeth replaced with porcelain ones. Anyway, I sold my racing bike to a lad on the scheme and bought this moped. The beast in question was a BSA Beaver. Everyone else had a Yamaha FS1E or a Honda DT50, but I had this little BSA. Whenever you crashed the Beaver it completely disintegrated. The seat would fly off, as would the side panels and tank. I came off it quite a few times. I was following a coach with Chris Slight one afternoon and a police car came the other way. Now because I'm scared of the cops, I looked around to see where it was going when this car turned and headed back. Chris had stopped because the bus had come to a halt and I went straight into him. I was lying on the floor star-shaped and winded. The Beaver's petrol tank had come off and was leaking petrol. There were only a couple of drops, but this geezer got out of his car and shouted, 'There's petrol! IT'S GONNA BLOW!' It was like a scene from *Die Hard*. What a drama. Needless to say, it didn't BLOW!

Some of the YTS lads were a little edgy, but they were OK and I was happy on that course until the bullying started up again. One of the trainees had a sister who had been to my school and she kindly opened the door to everything I was trying so hard to forget. The only positive of this act was that it opened Dad's eyes to what had been going on for the past four years.

It wasn't long before this gossip was brought to the attention of Matthew Kerr, who was one of the 'wilder' members of the team. Matthew stole a double-decker bus one afternoon and drove it around town picking up customers and charging them for the ride. This same lad also bullied and beat me up. Matthew wrote some graffiti about me in the toilets and it all kicked off. Matthew had massive ears and a really big nose and I think he was the type of lad who had to get his retaliation in first too – just like the Muggos.

The head of the scheme pulled all the lads together one morning in response to the bullying. 'Someone has written some graffiti about a fellow member of the scheme and I want to know who!' But no one would snitch or own up and they all just stood there, silent. Then the guilty party asked, 'Why, what does it say?' When the course leader refused to appease him, this lad blurted it out to everyone at which point they all laughed. My dad saw it all and finally the penny dropped. The bullying on the course came to a sudden halt after that.

***

Rap, electro and graffiti had been bubbling around for a few years, but these strands suddenly became enormous after the success of films *Breakdance* and *Beat Street* in 1984, which followed the influential *Wild Style* documentary released the previous year. The sound, style, graffiti and dance were now neatly packaged together for a mass audience. Only a year or two before we had been part of a select group of three in our year listening to this music, but now hip hop was a major cultural force. Breakdancing and rapping was now being featured on kids' TV programmes like *Blue Peter*, which was known more for its features on tortoises, postage stamps and Highland dancing than it was for street culture from South Bronx.

I went to see *Breakdance* and *Beat Street* on my own. All the idiots who were bullying me at home went to the same performance of *Beat Street*. These lads took the piss all the way through the movie until I stood up and shouted at them to 'Shut the fuck up!', which was very unlike me. *Breakdance* and *Beat Street* are, alongside *Star Wars*, my favourite films of all time and I soon started collecting the music featured in those inspirational movies. Music aside, the fashion really inspired me too and I started craving some white Puma trainers and a tracksuit. Ski-hats were popular too. The Bronx seemed a long way away from Stafford and Gnosall, which was one of its appeals I guess.

My childhood was quite sheltered in rural Staffordshire. Going into Wolverhampton I had seen people of West Indian and Asian origin, but not really known anyone as there were no ethnic minorities in Bishopswood. Noah Brown was the only black kid in school, and no one I knew ever had any close dealings with him other than, 'Dude your hair is different.' At break times he would just stand there while people touched his hair. But life on the YTS had me working alongside kids from all sorts of backgrounds, which was really cool *and* useful.

There were a few Rastas on the course and it was great working alongside people who liked the same music as me. Although I was too shy to make friends with them I would watch what was going on and listen to their music, which really broadened my tastes. My school friends were more likely to see *Footloose* at the cinema than *Breakdance* and even those who ventured to see *Beat Street* found it boring.

Although the breakdance films hit the UK in 1984, breakdancing had been bubbling away in the UK for at least a year before. Venues such as Rock City in Nottingham had been holding meets from 1983 following a performance by the US WFLA crew in the city's Old Market Square. B-boy became the catch-all term for someone who was a part of this scene. B-boys like Damian Darcy who walked around Stafford with his curly wet-gelled hair, all cut into a checkerboard at the back. He used to strut round town in the sun with his ghettoblaster on his shoulder, blasting out Kraftwerk's *Tour De France*. What a dude!

The YTS lads told me about a group of breakers who met up in Stafford of an evening and said I should go and meet them. I was mad into breakdancing, but you got beaten up if you didn't like heavy metal in Gnosall. As I didn't have any friends back home I would take my moped into Stafford, just for something to do. I had only ever seen breakdancing on TV until I was wandering around Stafford one night. I was pushing my moped along the pavement when I spotted these lads body-popping and breakdancing outside the supermarket Presto. I knew that these lads must have been the same crew the YTS boys had mentioned and so I parked my moped at a nearby car park and ran back to see them.

Watching breakdancing in Stafford was a headfuck. I couldn't believe it. Something from New York was actually happening in Stafford. I ended up staying there all evening, watching, and asked them if I could tag along the following night. 'Yeah yeah, and if we're not here we'll be over near Tesco.' I went straight back the next day and started hanging around with them all the time. They let me carry the lino and whatnot while I learned about body-popping and the music they were into. I even bought an album called *Breakdance You Can Do It*, which had a poster on how to do certain moves. Now, I'm no good with instructions on anything and I tried and tried and tried in vain to do the moonwalk from this poster; I eventually got there, but no thanks to that duff guide. So I learned some moves and tried to fit in, although I was more of a body-popper than a breaker. I could never throw myself down at the floor without causing an injury.

Meeting those Stafford breakdancers was pivotal in my life and a direct result of being pushed out of the village owing to the bullying. I could have stayed and got beaten up, but instead went to Stafford where no one knew me.

There was one lad who used to hang around with the breakdance lot called Steven Harrison and he said he knew somewhere I could put my bike when I came to hang out. Me being a trusting soul, I said, 'Cool!'

A little later someone said, 'Have you heard about Steven Harrison? He's been done racing away from the police on a motorbike.' It turned out that Steven was 14. Shit! I went to the police station and said that I believed my motorbike was there and they bunged me in a cell for a bit. I honestly didn't know he wasn't old enough, but as I've said, I'm a very trusting soul.

I slowly found out a few of the breakers' names; who were mostly a couple of years younger than me. Dean Meredith, John Parkes, Jon McDonald and Adrian 'Pez' Perry were wicked dancers and there was also Chilli, Mark Gray and Abdul. Dean Meredith and I seemed to have a lot in common when it came to music and we were always swapping tapes. Sometimes blokes would stagger out of pubs, totally pissed-up and would try and breakdance. 'I'll show you how it's done!' They'd fall onto the lino and attempt to spin, all the change coming out of their pockets. They were arseholed.

We were hanging around Stafford one evening when one of the crew announced that his sister had started dating some bloke who had given him some pirate radio tapes from Manchester or somewhere. These tapes were well cool: really good electro and hip hop. Because I lived out in Gnosall they wouldn't lend me the tapes for fear of not getting them back and so I started taping similar tunes off a local radio station from Stoke called Signal. Signal Radio used to have a network show that played across several stations around the country. Leaping Lee Finan's *ID 104* show would feature soul, funk, Brooklyn sounds and Bronx stuff as well as acts like SOS Band and Colonel Abrams. Each week, Finan would play a mix from one of the DMC albums and at a certain time of the night, ten of the tunes would all be mixed together. It was Leaping Lee and the electro albums that really got me into the mixing.

One of the tapes I did manage to get hold of from the Stafford crew featured tunes from *Beat Street* and *Breakdance*, and as I recall was essentially two records mixed together that just didn't work somehow. The mixer behind these tapes was a guy called Andy Meecham who knew Dean, and the mixes were really interesting even if they weren't that slick.

Next door to Tandy in Stafford was Lotus Records and I went in there one morning and bought two records with big red stickers on them that said: 'The real sound of hip hop.' They were *Hip Hop Bebop (Don't Stop)* by Man Parrish and *Planet Rock* by Afrikaa Bambaataa & The Soul Sonic Force, originally released back in 1982. I was obsessed with the music and wanted to hear more. The only breakdance club night near me was in Hanley, Stoke-on-Trent, on a Sunday. The Place was your average Ritzy venue, but down in the basement was Trevor M, and he played all the soul, funk and electro. Everyone would start body-popping to Maze and stuff. The Place was a real mix of white and black kids and I would travel there on the train for a weekly fix.

I got taxed by Andrew Gardener and his mates on my 17th birthday whilst on the train into Stoke to get to The Place. Gardener pulled me to one side and looked me straight in the eyes. 'Hand over your money!' He shook me down for what little money I had and moved on down the carriage. Penniless and shook up, I still had to get to The Place. All the breakdancing lads from the YTS were on the train too. Everyone had Puma, Fila and Adidas, but because my brother and I never asked for stuff, I had a no-name tracksuit and a pair of trainers from Tesco. I finally felt like I belonged somewhere however and had friends into the same things I was. There was this one guy called Chilli and he had all the newest clothes and I kept wondering where this dude was getting his money from.

I wasn't the only one getting taxed on that train however. Steven Moore was a basketball player and a friendly geezer and his younger brother Roger had also been taxed on the train to Stoke. The police were waiting for ticket dodgers at the other end and we all got bundled into a police cell because we had our train tickets stolen. Roger was asked his name, which caused a stir. 'Roger.'
-   'Roger what?'
-   'Roger Moore.'
-   'Pull the other one.'
-   'Seriously, it is!'

The police ended up phoning his parents to see if he was lying while we sat in the station for an hour or so. Eventually they let us out and we took the long walk across Hanley to get into The Place. It was a top night out, though.

Every major town had a breakdance crew and many of them turned up to The Place. Stafford had Electro Shock, Wolverhampton was home to the B Boys and there was Smack 19 from Sheffield. Broken Glass from Manchester ended up making a record and they turned up to The Place one week and took everyone on. Broken Glass totally wiped the floor with everybody. That 17th birthday was fun despite the mugging, although it was marred somewhat by the very long walk home back to Gnosall.

8 Of The Best: Eighties Soul/Funk

1. D Train – *You're The One For Me*
2. Maze – *Twilight*
3. Change – *You Are My Melody*
4. SOS Band – *Just Be Good To Me*
5. Prince – *Erotic City*
6. Mtume – *Prime Time*
7. Cheryl Lynn – *Encore*
8. Rose Royce – *Magic Touch*

The YTS found me a work placement in a small town outside Stafford called Stone, working for some sports trophy engravers. I would travel from Gnosall to Stafford on my Beaver and then on to Stone to etch names on to snooker trophies and golf club medals. I knew I would have to get a proper job at some point, but I didn't really enjoy the engraving game much, although it gave me enough money to buy another BSA Beaver for sorely needed parts.

I got into trouble at the trophy place one afternoon when I accidentally set fire to a load of stock I'd lumped on to the bonfire, mistaking it for rubbish. The work placement ended shortly after that fire.

I got my first proper full-time job at Fisher Decorations in 1986. Everyone there was about 25 upwards and seemed ancient to me. They were all talking about U2 and Simple Minds. My nickname at Fisher was Mega as all I banged on about were 'mega mixes', which were popular at the time. Being the youngest I got all the shit jobs. It was quite a demanding role and the managers always wanted you to work faster and better, but there was no one there with the time to show you how. So I was really slow at first and yet they were really getting on at me to speed up. They suggested I learn on my own time so I was more efficient at work. Yeah, right.

You'd be up on these rickety ladders, wobbling all over the place. You'd pay good money to experience a ride like that at a theme park. One foot brushing against the ladder at the bottom, and you'd be well nervy at the top, painting the chimneys. The bottom of the ladder would sometimes be on a tiny, busy pavement with cars whizzing along below. It was a health-and-safety nightmare.

There was a lad at Fisher called Melvin and he loved playing practical jokes. At break, everyone would sit down on a paint can to have their sandwiches, crisps and a cup of tea, whilst others would play cards. Melvin would often whip the tea bag out of his cup and place it on the paint tin just as you were about to sit down. As you had jeans on and a white overall you couldn't feel this tea bag, but when you stood up – in the white bib and bracing – it looked like you'd shat yourself. Sometimes you'd be walking around all day looking like you were covered in diarrhoea.

Not all of Melvin's jokes were opportunistic, however. Some of them were executed with a bewildering amount of preparation and precision. He once bought a box of chocolate éclairs, unwrapped them all when he got home, drilled a hole in one end of each and sucked all the chocolate out. He then stood them on one end and filled the middle with vinegar, before heating a knife and putting the toffee back on to the end to seal the éclair. He then wrapped them all back up and brought them to work the following day. You know what it's like when you have an éclair and you think, 'I'm not going to chew this one, I'm going to suck all the chocolate out...' Then, after a couple of seconds of sucking, your mouth was full of vinegar.

Melvin was constantly pulling pranks. I'd take a bottle of milk to work each day and place it next to me as I worked. All day I'm checking that the milk and sandwiches are still there, and then suddenly the milk was gone. Melvin had emptied it. That was it, you'd have no drink for the rest of the day, so it was well annoying. So instead of pressing my thumb into the foil top of my milk one morning I grabbed the outside really firmly and lifted the top off without pressing the dimple in the middle. I drank the milk, filled it up with water and white emulsion and placed the foil lid back on. I put it next to my sandwiches and I kept checking and checking, until 'Eurgh!' Melvin had taken a gobful.

There was no thought about safety at all back then. We never wore masks. We used spray paint to mark an area around a pothole or something, but instead of depressing a nozzle you just stuck two fingers in and sprayed it straight out of the can. The fumes were incredible! I didn't know what I was doing. Still, I earned enough to pay for my board although my Christmas bonus was a measly five quid that had to last me over the festive period while I wasn't working.

Luckily it only cost a pound to fill up the tank of the Beaver, which was good for 70 miles and that would last a week. Dad really helped me around this time. Working made me realise that this wasn't for me; my driving desire was to make music and Dad bought me a sampling keyboard on hire purchase to encourage me. I paid Dad off a bit each week. Dad was great at helping you get to where you needed to be. The keyboard was nothing flash, but De La Soul would go on to use it on *Three Feet High And Rising*. I always wanted to make music myself and I knew that investing in equipment was a good idea. Dad also got me my first decks not long after with a load of post-dated cheques. Coolest man on the planet!

It was around 1986 that I decided to sharpen my image. I perfected a caterpillar moustache and got my hair permed. I had deathly straight, dark brown hair and so I had some tight curls put into it. I had started going out to a nightclub in Stafford called Top Of The World and would get the first bus into town on a Friday or Saturday evening. I would be at Top Of The World for 8pm, although the club actually opened at 9pm.

Top Of The World was another 'townie' venue, but the music policy wasn't that bad. You got a bit of pop, indie and then some disco/dance. I'd sometimes pop into this pub called Dappers before Top Of The World. There was this DJ from the local RAF base at Dappers called Tony who would play soul, funk and electro. It could get quite rammed in there and it was a nightmare getting to the bar, so you ordered yourself two pints each time. It was only when you got out that you realised just how drunk you were, because you weren't being held up by all the people inside. I would then walk the full length of Stafford to Top Of The World. This was a time of Farah slacks, slip-on shoes, untucked shirts, thin gold chains and curly perms. Sounds horrendous, but it was as cool as fuck back then. You know what? That was possibly the coolest I have ever felt in my life. Especially as the following year, I started losing my hair.

I was hanging around with a bloke called Tony Turner at Top Of The World who was a bigger version of me. Tony had curly hair, 'tache and a paisley button-down shirt. He was a few years older and a lot more confident. Tony Turner would walk around the club and all the girls would come up and give him a kiss and a cuddle. 'I want to be Tony Turner,' I thought, watching him marching around like a giant hairy peacock. I was Tony Turner's little shadow, I guess. I didn't realise it at the time, but I was quite possibly pissing Tony Turner off by following him around as he always had business to attend to. Then one night we came across this drunken girl holding on to the cigarette machine at the top of the stairs, who was batting her eyelids at Tony. Just as Tony started to walk off he looked back at the girl and said, 'Stay here, mate! You're in there!'

- 'Really?'
- 'Yeah, yeah, yeah. Go and talk to her!'
- 'Shit!'

So I started talking to this girl. She was dead drunk. 'Let's go for a dance,' she suggested. We were dancing away when I saw this geezer I knew from school who couldn't dance in time with the music. If I'm ever dancing and I clock someone who can't, it completely throws me. So I started taking the piss out of him and this girl thought I was taking the mick out of her and cleared off. I waited for a half hour, but she didn't show. So I went downstairs and there she was. I went straight over and put my hands in her pockets. I don't know why I did that. I put my hands in her pockets! Weird. Anyway, Karen and I ended up seeing each other. I didn't see Tony Turner much after that, which might have had something to do with a shirt I got him from my mum's catalogue. A shirt I ended up paying for. Still, I lost a shirt, but gained a girlfriend, all thanks to Tony Turner.

After years of low self-esteem, I suddenly felt confident. I felt I looked as good as I ever had, was often out clubbing and now I had a girl on my arm. I was going out a lot more with Karen and her friends throughout 1987. It was a carefree time. Even when I lost my job at Fisher a year later – in a case of 'last in, first out', when the work dried up – Karen kept me in cider. I was also starting to tinker about with the keyboard more at home, just as an underground form of dance music was about to explode…

Jon McDonald *"Early to mid-eighties I was really into breakdancing and used to hang around in a small community of dancers based in*

Stafford. We'd have the ghettoblasters, lino and all that sort of thing. I was a massive electro fan, still am.

I met Mark through Dean Meredith and I can remember hearing the news a few years later, that they were working together at a studio in Stafford."

Acid, Tandy And The Blue Chip

8 Of The Best: Acid House

1. The Love Story – *Ecstasy*
2. 808 State – *Flow Coma*
3. SLF – *Show Me What You Got (Acid Mix Part 1)*
4. Fast Eddie – *Acid Thunder (Fast Eddie Mix)*
5. Fast Money – *One $*
6. R+R – *Acid Off A Way (Part 1)*
7. Mike Dunn – *Magic Feet*
8. Armando – *Downfall*

New clubs, new music, new fashion and a brand new drug. Did the late eighties produce the UK's last great youth movement?

I knew all about house music from being into electro and going to Top Of The World late '87 where you would hear the odd tune. When I first heard Steve "Silk" Hurley's *Jack Your Body* or the *House Music Anthem* by Marshall Jefferson, I wasn't mad keen as they weren't like the soul and funk I was used to. I look back now and see just how revolutionary those tunes were, but at the time it just seemed to follow on from electro and other electronically based music. Karen was really into the sound, though and so I would stand at the side of the dancefloor laughing at her and poking fun while she was dancing. But slowly I started to get into house. More and more we would go round people's houses to listen to tracks from Chicago and New York and it really started to excite me. House was a form of music that seemed to offer endless possibilities and was truly modern.

I was walking back into town one night to get a bus when I spotted Dean, the breakdancer I used to hang with back in '85. Dean was still at school and was on a work experience placement at Stafford Co-op. I went into the supermarket and we started chatting. It had been a few years since we'd hung out, but we were both still into music. 'You'll have to come round my house, I've got some decks,' he suggested. With that, off I went to Dean's one morning with my little keyboard under my arm. I had a Casio SK-1 sampling keyboard from Dixons, which had a small microphone that allowed you to record and sample. Once your recordings were stored, you could play that sample up and down the keyboard. I used to sample loads of bits and pieces from electro records. There was no firm idea that I was going to make a career out of this or anything; it was more of a hobby really.

Dean and I spent the day trying different techniques and it felt as if we could actually make a track if we put our minds to it. It was at the very least a great way of spending time. Dean's mate Gareth was there one day and the three of us had some fun messing around with the equipment. Dean had decks and a mixer and I was dead impressed that he could do the 'transformer scratch'; he even showed me how, which was handy as I had no decks of my own at home.

When I failed my first driving test, I cheered myself up after by going into Tandy to get a Realistic Mixer. I would stand there with the transformer switch pretending to do the scratch with one hand, although I couldn't do the other bit until I had some decks. That was the liberating thing with electronic music: you didn't have to learn guitar for years and years, you just had to have the passion and a little know-how.

When Dean moved to a village on the way to Cannock, I would often go to his house with my keyboard. We would put some sounds into the sampling keyboard, play it back and record it to tape. We would then put that recording back into his mixer and play other bits over the top, constantly overdubbing. I still have the original tape we recorded, over a white CBS cassette. I scratched the names of the tracks off and put RMD over the top, which stood for Rhythm Mode: D. At one point, Dean, Gareth and I were divvying up duties to be carried out on our inevitable appearances on *Top of the Pops,* as I had done with Poddy years before. 'I'll do the scratching and you do the keyboards…' You had to be organised.

I had seen in the local Stafford newsletter that a new 24-channel recording studio was opening up in town. It felt like a real opportunity. There weren't many towns as small as Stafford that had recording studios and so I thought I'd chance my arm. We had nothing to lose. So we took the tape we made and played it to this record producer Kevin Roberts who was the owner of Blue Chip Studios. Looking back, I'm amazed I had the nerve to approach them. Kevin was a Northern Soul DJ and a bit of a character. Kev didn't hang about either. 'Right lads, I want to sign you up!'

- 'You what?!'

I had gone from nothing – no job, no experience, nada – to a record deal. One demo tape produced at Dean's house and BOOM! We had a recording contract! We were just having a laugh really and maybe that helped in some way, in that we weren't too desperate or anything. But whatever way you looked at it, Blue Chip Recordings wanted us to do a record. Mind. Blown.

We told Kev Roberts that we wanted to do acid house, but he wanted a *Pump up the Volume*-style hit and we just agreed with whatever he said. Lots of people were sampling Michael Jackson at the time, and so when Kev booked a recording session for us they replayed *I Want You Back* by Jackson 5 and we simply scratched over the top to this terrible drum beat. That 'tune' became the first ever Rhythm Mode: D single.

The artwork for *So Damn Tough* was abysmal. Somebody wrote Rhythm Mode: D across the top in really bad graffiti, which was disappointing. Still, it felt incredible to have a record pressed. It wasn't that this music lark had even come about as a result of a prolonged campaign; it had happened before I'd even had a conscious thought to pursue it. Properly. I had initially wanted to be a DJ, a decision I made in Top Of The World one night. 'I want to be a DJ, not a painter/decorator.' I didn't know how I'd achieve this and I didn't even have the bottle to go into a club and say 'I want to DJ' so it was a weird one. But now we were going to have some vinyl out and that seemed to eclipse DJing completely.

I was in Stafford Our Price one afternoon, flicking through records with Dean when this tune came on and we both looked at each other and went bright red. 'It's ours!' We both walked straight out of the shop.

This thing we'd made was utter dog shit. We had no idea what we were doing and the bloke who owned the studio had no clue either although Kev was credited as Executive Producer. Kev was trying to lead this team of engineers who had their own way of doing things and he really wasn't into the music we were doing. So it was a bit of a shambles. Looking back though, it was a pretty amazing moment, even if the song did sound like something that had fallen off the back of a lorry.

Gareth left RMD pretty much straight after the single was pressed saying that these sessions at Blue Chip weren't really doing it for him. So it was suddenly just Dean and me. We would go in every morning, listen to piles of records and say, 'I like that bit… and this part.' Dean was better at scratching than me and so he took care of that. We both had loads of ideas which helped, and would tell the engineer exactly what we wanted to achieve. We learned loads as we went along.

Kev never registered us with MCPS (Mechanical Copyright Protection Society) and we knew nothing about writers' royalties. 'What's publishing, Kev?'
-   'You don't need to worry about that, lads.' It was a case of lambs to the slaughter.

It was all a bit of a whirlwind really and that's what hooks young talent into signing away their rights. It was amazing to get a copy of the record so quickly and that was enough. Wow! Unbelievable. Blue Chip was so shoddily run, though. We did a remix of the single and they went for a picture sleeve for this as the first release was in a basic black bag with a hole in the middle. 'You can draw!' Kev said to me. So, I got a piece of card the same size as a record sleeve and started doodling. Purely a doodle. Not even my best doodle. We were calling it the *On The Money Remix*, so I sketched a really shit hand holding a load of notes, and I even wrote 'money' on the notes, to show whoever it was that was supposed to be designing the sleeve that these motley-looking bits of paper were meant to be dollar bills. It was utter shit, but was more of a direction for the designer to take rather than the finished thing. Two weeks later, the covers turn up and my shit doodle of the hand is on the front of the sleeve. I was the designer! There were the dollar bills with 'money' written on them. Money being a concept we could never quite grab a hold of, ourselves, back then.

Although things were moving fast, they were never quite fast enough for Karen's mum. 'Why are you with him? He won't amount to anything. He's always skint!' This was 1988 and for the first two years we were at Blue Chip we didn't see a penny from anything. We were so obsessed with making music it didn't seem to bother us, though. It was other people who seemed to have a problem with our empty pockets. I guess it was handy having a dad who understood my love of music, but to others it was probably just a pipe dream that was never going to pay the bills. We got on to a government scheme, however, which paid us a certain amount of money each week for our placement at the studio and that helped. Although our income was small, we had no real responsibilities or decadent lifestyles and so it was a good time to experiment. I thank my parents so much that they allowed me this time to find my feet whilst living at the cottage. We were effectively working engineers at Blue Chip with a 24-channel studio at our beck and call and we were learning so much. I'm not sure we truly appreciated it at the time.

Dean rang the cottage one night and said, 'Do you want to go to an acid house night?' Acid house was like the naughty younger brother of Chicago house and appealed to me straight off the bat. Those squelchy basslines from the Roland TB-303 – first outed in Phuture's 1987 classic *Acid Tracks* – were amazing and the whole peace, love and unity vibe that went straight back to 1967 and the first 'Summer of Love' was both fun *and* subversive. Acid house was underground and overground, combining front-page tabloid headlines – concerning illegal raves and this new drug ecstasy – with considerable chart success. 'Yes, Dean. I'm up for it!'

Up until that point I had only been clubbing in Stafford in shoes, trousers and a Tony Turner-style shirt. Acid house nights were different, though. The dress code was more like that of a gig than a club; although straight-up house nights were more 'clubby'. People wore long-sleeved T-shirts to acid nights, usually featuring that smiley yellow face.

It was a Tuesday night in Stoke at a club called Excalibur, which was a gay bar. I drove to Excalibur after finally passing my driving test. I had so many driving lessons I ran out of money and ended up decorating the instructor's house as payment. I had never done wallpapering before and ended up covering the whole house and painted outside and in. I was there so long, every single day in fact, that the driving instructor's two-year-old daughter would ask me to wipe her bottom for her. Still, having passed my test, I spent my life's savings on a Mini which was taking me, Dean, Gareth, Pez (Adrian Perry) and Potty (Adrian Pottinger) to our first acid house 'rave'.

There was a bar upstairs at Excalibur with stairs leading down to a basement. I'm not sure if I really knew how this night would pan out. I had heard all about raves on TV and in the papers, but it was a definite step into the unknown. So there we all were, sat upstairs waiting for things to kick off. We thought you'd get there and it would just be *on*. Happening. But we were all just milling about, wondering when the night would start. There was a speaker at the top of the stairs and after a while it sparked into life. 'You can come down now!' Bearing in mind we had only been to smart clubs up to this point, we were quite shocked. This basement was a properly dark room with a UV light, smoke machine and strobe. There were huge black drapes along the walls and everything was black. I had been to HMV the day before and bought a smiley T-shirt – crap quality with shonky smiles on the face – but none of us were doing drugs. I'm not sure if many others were either. It was at Excalibur that I learned to do the acid dance and 'get right on one, matey!' This was it! The moment my life changed forever as pure acid and deep house pumped all night long. The night was called Frenzy and it turned everything on its head for us.

It was heaving in that smoky basement and you couldn't see your hand unless the strobe was on you. You'd often get bashed in the face by flailing arms and so you covered your face with your hand to stop yourself getting whacked. Northern Soul DJ Colin Curtis and a young lad called Daz Willot were manning the decks and the place was so dark I spent a while assuming that Daz was black. The mixing was non-existent really, just that 'herd of wildebeest' sound from *The Lion King*. But every tune was a banger and that night opened my mind to so much. This was real underground stuff from 10-2am.

I was naive and oblivious to drugs. I thought the face-scrunching and gurning was just an appreciation of the music. Even if I'd been offered E – which I wasn't at that time – I would have refused, convinced that I would be flinging myself off the roof of a car park or something. I guess those kids smoking a peace pipe in the public information film had really affected me. My mate Pez started acting weird one time and I thought he was on the funny fags. I was a complete novice when it came to drugs. I was purely there for the music, and far too scared of the cops to take a mind-bending pill that might give me nightmares. No point risking it. The thing is, I was enjoying the scene anyway. I believe that people tended to be on speed or acid early on in '88 as E hadn't really shown its little white face to our group as yet. Either way, I was high alright. High on acid house.

Frenzy had a massive effect on us. Dean and I wanted to make an acid house album as soon as we got back to Blue Chip. The great thing about being at Blue Chip was that we could just get on with stuff, inbetween mixing tracks for Kev Roberts, who clearly wanted to be the new Pete Waterman. Mid-1988, if something was in the charts, Kev would want a version of it. 'I want you to do something like this,' he'd say playing Yazz And The Plastic Population's *The Only Way Is Up*. So Kev got a girl down from Liverpool to come and sing and we sampled all the sounds off the Yazz record for this cover of a Northern Soul song; the track was under the name Dica And The Living Proof (Dica being acid backwards). We also worked on Kev Roberts' other projects, which included a Rick Astley-type singer called Jerry Pearce, and we would scratch over the top of his poppy dance music. I've got recordings of soul legend Edwin Starr coming into Blue Chip and re-recording vocals for this Jerry Pearce bloke. A bit like getting Salvador Dali in to paint your shed.

We were just two kids mucking about in a 24-track studio. We sometimes connected two mics to the pitch control on the FX units and made vocals sound high like Pinky and Perky and we recorded loads of stupid conversations. We could also alter the mic to sound very low like Frank Bruno and would talk loads of waffle in this strange deep voice. We had loads of catchphrases at the time like 'blip blop' and if we were scratching we'd shout, 'Dowit, kid. Dowit!' It was great fun.

Dean was definitely feeling the same sort of music as me. We both continued going to Frenzy and visited clubs in Stoke and Newcastle-under-Lyme. We loved the whole acid house scene. Neither of us could play keyboards and were rubbish with computers, but we were toying around with acid house while learning to engineer. We knew what sounded good, which was a start.

Kev loved the idea of an acid album – because they were selling well – and so he had the idea of putting out a 'compilation' album, although we were to do every single track. So we did six tracks and made up for names for each of the 'artists'. Side 1 of *Acid Trance* consisted of The Smiley People's *It Makes Me Haaappy, To The Acid House (Whistle Lampin)* by M.A.D.M (M.A.D.M. stood for Mark Archer and Dean Meredith) and Bubbleena's *Ah Ha Ha Haaa (Alright Matey Mix)*. Side 2 featured Blip Blop's *In A Trance (Doo It), Zoooommm* by

Jeuce and *Let Me Hear You Scream* by Thieves Of Bagdad. We thought the name M.A.D.M. was really cool, but not long after its release the studio got a solicitor's letter from a group in Leeds called MDMA saying we needed to change our name. We totally ignored it as they were our initials. MDMA ended up becoming Utah Saints.

Because we didn't have the set-up – the studio was for live rock bands really – we only had one keyboard and a rack of various things like samplers. There was no internet of course, so you didn't know how people made their tunes or what keyboards they were using, so we knew next to nothing, although we'd obviously heard of the Roland TR-808. I had never heard of the other drum machines being used and we didn't have the technology to make drum patterns so I would take a bunch of records to the studio each morning and we'd take a drum loop off of one, add a kick and a clap and build it up from there.

Acid Trance was us looking up to all the people from Chicago, Detroit and New York who were doing the acid stuff. You had the likes of Lenny D, Tommy Musto and Frankie Bones from New York and that M.A.D.M. track sampled a Frankie Bones loop. Frankie Bones did a tune a year or two later called *They Stole Our Break*, where he re-edited our record with a sample on top. 'Shit Frankie Bones is going to kill us!' We took that as a major compliment. We always sampled things we really liked. There are cases where it's a wholesale rip-off of course, and that's not good, but I find being sampled, really flattering. Dance music is all about recycling. Early house saw loads of examples of people putting out the same tunes such as *Love Can't Turn Around* by both Darryl Pandy and Farley "Jackmaster" Funk. The track by Jeuce was sampled too, by a label up north on a track by Panic called *Voices of Energy*. It was a big early hardcore record and they made a drum track over which they synced that Jeuce tune; it had the big countdown and everything. But all the tunes on *Acid Trance* were made of samples too with the acid coming from my Jen SX1000 and a SH-101 (owned by musician Andy Meecham), as the studio didn't have a 303 at the time.

We had a launch party in Stafford for *Acid Trance* and no one turned up. We'd had trouble with promotion as the flyers were deemed to be too risqué for some shops. EPMD had an album track called *Doing Damage* and as hip hop often went hand in hand with house, we put that phrase on the flyers. Our Price wasn't happy. 'You can't call it that; people will be expecting you to wreck the club!' The night itself

Me, Mom, Paul and Dad

Dad and Mom in Ibiza, 1976

Looking mighty flash in 1977

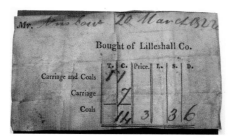

One of the coal bills from 1822 found at the cottage

Coal bill from 1822

The coin I found from 1651

The BSA Beaver

Aged 17 with my breakdancer's curly perm (1985)

My homemade smiley T-shirt from 1988

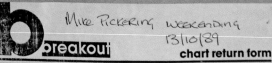

breakout — chart return form

Mike Pickering weekending 13/10/89

	artist	title	12"	lp	label
1	STATE 808	PACIFIC STATE	✓		CREED
2	LIASONS D	HEARTBEAT	✓		USA
3	SHALL WE ↔ FORGEMASTERS		✓		WARP
4	LA MIX	LOVE TOGETHER	✓		BREAKOUT
5	URIGINE 3	THE THEME	—		AVL
6	JAM MACHINE	EVERYDAY	✓		Deconstruction
7	CRY TALK	MIXDOWN HOUSE (A DUB)	✓		MIXDOWN
8	Mc BUZZ B	WHITE LABEL	✓		PLAY HARD
9	KITAH	U BROKE MY HEART	✓		Dance Mania Music
10	QUARTZ	MELTDOWN	—		WHITE LABEL
11	DE-LITE	WILD TIMES (MAMDAH)	—		CIRCA
12	DE LA SOUL	EYE KNOW	✓		BIG LIFE
13	MR LEE	GET BUSY	✓		JIVE
14	LIFE	FEEL SO GOOD	✓		PROPHET
15	NEXUS 21	STILL LIFE KEEPS MOVIN	✓		BLUE CHIP
16	TOT	WHAT U R	✓		DFM
17	SNOWBOY	SNOWBOYS HOUSE OF LATIN	✓		URBAN
18	CHUBB ROCK	YA BAD CHUBBS	—		CHAMPION
19	BLUE PEARL	NAKED IN RAIN (ACAPELLA)	✓		W.A.U
20	FIDELFATTI	JUST WANNA TOUCH ME	✓		MAGIC SERVICE
21	The SHAMEN	'62 PRE MIX	✓		DESIRE
22	TRP	THIS IS THE PLACE	✓		MG
23	GARY JACKMASTER WALLACE	PARTY TIME	—		House n effect
24	SHEILA	ACID KISS	✓		QUARK
25	NOUVEAU	ADIEU	✓		BARCLAY

this original copy to be sent to: James Hamilton, punch publications ltd, ludgate house,
245 blackfriars road, london se1 9uz. fax no: 01-928 5158
blue copy to be sent to: dmc ltd, p.o. box 89, slough sl1 8na.
yellow copy to be sent to: paul kindred, club promotions dept,
a&m records ltd, 136-144 new kings road, london sw6 4lz

Mike Pickering's Hacienda chart (13.10.89)

HOT ON PROMO — NOW AVAILABLE
NEXUS 21 —
(STILL) LIFE KEEPS MOVING
DETROIT TECHNO SOUL GROOVE. BLUE C34. CLUB + REMIX VERSIONS

DISTRIBUTED BY THE CARTEL

NEXUS 21	NEXUS 21
'(STILL) LIFE KEEPS MOVING'	'THE RYTHM OF LIFE'
THE REMIX	**THE ALBUM**

"DANCE MUSIC OF THE HIGHEST APPEAL, THE RYTHM OF LIFE!"
(KEV HILL, MIX MAG, NOV 1989.)
DISTRIBUTED BY BACKS / THE CARTEL

Nexus 21 magazine adverts 1989

First ever Nexus 21 photo shoot, 1990

Nexus 21 photo shoot at the Custard Factory, Birmingham, 1991

Another shot from the then disused Custard Factory

Stay calm Archer, stay calm. Me with Juan Atkins and Derrick May

Detroit Tigers vs Milwaukee Brewers baseball game with Kevin and Derrick - very surreal

Chris Andrews and Marc Kinchen in the KMS studios, Detroit

Marc Kinchen (19) and me (21). I've always been the shortest

Marc Kinchen adding the genuine Detoit techno flavour to our tracks.

Techno barbeque with Neil Rushton, Kevin Saunderson, Donna Black and Derrick May

Trying to act cool in the KMS studios with Kevin Saunderson and Anthony Shakir

featured just Dean and me. We agreed to hide the microphone from Kev Roberts. But failed. 'How you're doing y'all?!' he boomed into the venue, although there were only about ten people there. Embarrassed or what? I don't know if anyone ever bought *Acid Trance* as there were no sales figures, but apparently Luke Vibert loved it and still plays one of the tracks.

We enjoyed a prolific output at Blue Chip as we were in the recording studio every single day. We did a couple of breakbeat albums with loops from old funk tracks. The Rhythm Mode: D album *So Damn Tough* had a moody sleeve of me, Dean and Rob Bairstow on the cover. Rhythm was spelt 'Rythm' which was a little embarrassing. Dance music has been plagued by the word 'rhythm' with many examples of spelling errors making it on to the sleeve. Resident Hacienda DJ Graeme Park called *So Damn Tough* 'Gothic hip hop', due in part to the dark album sleeve I believe. It was a shit album. Half the ideas were put together as we were learning our craft.

While we were working at Blue Chip, Kev really wanted to get in with a big label (called Stone) so he asked us if we would remix *Donald Where's Your Troosers?* by Andy Stewart and we agreed, although we didn't get paid. We basically got a copy of the 7" single, scratched it over a hip-house beat, threw in some samples on top and it was pressed up as the 12" mix which Simon Mayo had the Radio One exclusive on. It was credited to The Party Posse; a name Dean and I made up so no one would know it was us. Until now! Oh well…

***

I had been buying a lot of Detroit techno from around late '87/early '88. Detroit techno seemed so futuristic and there was so much emotion within the tracks, especially Derrick May's. There were certain elements that reminded me of the early electro tracks and I'm a huge fan of 'tape and reverse edits', so they really stood out. The more techno I heard, the better it seemed to get. *Techno! The New Dance Sound of Detroit* (a Virgin/10 compilation compiled by Neil Rushton) was the Holy Bible of techno and every track blew me away. As acid house was starting to fade I really wanted to change direction slightly and get away from the sample-driven sound. I wanted to do a UK version of Detroit techno.

As Dean and I couldn't play keyboards and didn't have a computer, the studio put an advert in the local paper asking for keyboard players and computer programmers. The two lads who turned up had been to the same school as Dean, although a couple of years older. Andy Meecham and Chris Peat had also done some work on the *Acid Trance* album although I'd never actually met them. Andy had put together the *Breakdance/Beat Street* cassette I'd heard, back in the breakdance days. Small world and all that.

One of the Frenzy crew's catchphrases at the time was 'bizarre'. Everything was *bizarre*. If you saw someone with weird clothes on, you would turn to your mate and tap him on the shoulder. 'No way bizarre!' This led to the naming of this new venture: Bizarre Inc.

Early 1989, Bizarre Inc started on a track called *Technological.* Bizarre Inc was still essentially me and Dean, but we now had two more hands on deck. So it was a case of me and Dean bringing in tracks, sampling drums, playing bass lines and Chris or Andy doing the chords. Everything seemed to be moving along really nicely as we started to put an album together.

I guess there are always shifts in dynamics when you add new people to a team, and as Dean already knew Chris and Andy, I started to feel like the odd one out. It was just a feeling really, but working as four was very different to just the two of us.

In March I took a couple of days off for Karen's birthday and came back to the studio eager to get back on it. The rest of the lads seemed a little quiet, but I just put it down to paranoia, as I had been away for a day or two. After a while, I started to think that they might be sending me to Coventry. 'Maybe they're playing a prank,' I thought, but the silent treatment lasted the whole day. When it got to 4pm or whatever, I addressed the room. 'Look, I've been trying to talk to you all day, and each time I ask you something, you turn your back and start talking to one of the others. This has been going on all day. What the fuck is going on?'

- 'Ah, we don't like your attitude,' said Dean.
- 'So why didn't you say something?'
- 'No one wants to work with you,' Dean continued. I was absolutely shell-shocked.

I left for home that Friday evening feeling so depressed. What the hell had I done? My world had fallen apart. I knew that Bizarre Inc had the capacity to go somewhere and now here I was, on my own again. It brought back memories from the past, feelings of isolation and rejection. I had also lost an important part of my social life in Dean.

The following day was a Saturday and I awoke hoping it had all been a bad dream. I crawled out of bed and saw a note that had been posted through the door. It was dated from a few days before, so had been written and sent while I was off work with Karen. The letter was from Kev Roberts saying that I was to post the keys to the studio back through the letterbox. 'Don't use the keys. Don't come into the studio,' it said.

I sat at home not knowing what to think. How could this be happening? This was my job. Dad tried to shake me out of my stupor and slapped his guns on again and took me up to Blue Chip to see what was going on. We used my keys to get in and within seconds came face to face with studio manager Kev. 'What are you doing in here? I told you not to come in!'

- 'Woah there!'

We chatted a bit to Kev and his initial anger died down. It turned out that the other three had come to him with some concerns while I was away. One of them claimed that I had been stealing discs from the studio. Now, we used discs to compile sample libraries and so I had a disc and Dean had a disc, with all our sounds on. These took a while to put together and so you didn't leave them at the studio in case they got nicked. It wasn't that I had taken loads; I had two floppy discs. One disc had some house drums on and another was full of hip hop beats. I tried to explain this to Kev but he didn't want to know.

When I got home I phoned Dean up and said, 'What's going on?'
- 'I just want to work on my own.'
- 'Why didn't you just say that you wanted to go solo, rather than getting me the sack from my job?'

Dean didn't seem to understand my situation at all. 'You'll get yourself another job, won't you?' Dean seemed very matter-of-fact about it all. As quickly as this career had started, it was over. I couldn't quite work out what I could have done differently. I was shattered.

So I was back to signing on the dole for three or four months, whilst applying for jobs. I had got into the whole music thing by accident and we'd just started getting somewhere with Bizarre Inc and had done an album. I thought Dean and I worked well together, but looking back I guess there were signs. We were quite organised and sometimes we would go home to try and find samples to help certain tracks: 'You find the drums and I'll find the vocals, etc.' There was one day when I came in to find that Dean had decided to do the bit of the song I was doing, which meant that my entire plan for a mix went to Dean. So I had to do a completely different mix from scratch. It was shortly after this that I was sacked.

I later found out that any remixes that were done had my name removed. Kev kept putting his name down as producer and writer, although he wasn't even in the studio when we recorded the tunes. My crime? Maybe I was a bit too demanding. I guess I did try and gee people up when we were up against a deadline and I would always say what I thought of the work, even if people didn't want to hear it. Maybe that had upset them. I don't know. So Blue Chip stood by Dean and the boys and I was booted out. It left a really bad taste in my mouth although it's all cool with Andy now. Andy has always been sound and polite.

CH. 6

1989... Another Summer

There was fuck all to do in Gnosall. I had no job and no money, but music always seemed to fill the gaps. It wasn't like I was in London, New York or Chicago and part of a community that would link me up to other studios or musicians. I was skint and living at my parents' in the middle of nowhere and had been dumped by my band. I would stay upstairs in my bedroom and play on the Technics decks my dad got me, trying to work out what to do next. Music was so important to me I just couldn't turn it off. I was either listening to music, talking about music or making music. I was up in my room one day, thinking of ideas when I came across a birthday present from Karen.

For my 21st Karen bought me a Street Sounds box set called *Hits of House*: 14 albums of inspiration. I decided to go through that mass of music and make some notes: 'Sample that... loop this.' I was just identifying bits and bobs really. I sat for a while and thought, 'Why can't I do something similar? Something that's pure techno?' Inner City had just had a massive hit with *Big Fun* and if there was one thing Kev Roberts liked, it was a chart hit. So I plucked up the courage and phoned Kev. 'I've got an idea for a techno album.'

I got a frosty reception off Kev at first, but I could tell he was warming to the idea as I enthused about the possibilities of doing a UK version of this hip scene from Detroit. Eventually he relented. 'You can come in and get some studio time, but you'll have to work with Chris (Peat) as you can't play keyboards.' Wow! I couldn't believe it. I'd chanced my arm again and it had paid off.

I turned up to Blue Chip really motivated to make this new project work. It was a bit awkward with Chris because of what had happened with Bizarre Inc, but I hadn't known him before Blue Chip so it was a clean slate as such and Chris seemed genuinely excited about doing something different too. Chris was a massive fan of Depeche Mode and wasn't into clubbing at all and that actually added something original to our work together; we were coming into this from quite different perspectives.

Work was soon under way. I had a pile of ideas that kept us busy and we worked well together, with me directing the work whilst Chris got to grips with the more technical side of things. I really wanted to do a 'techno symphony' with a killer piano riff and so I played Rhythim Is Rhythim's (another misspelling of rhythm) *Strings of Life*. 'I want that kind of piano. Can you do something similar? Not the same, but similar.' We would jangle a way for bit until we got to a piece I liked and then we looped it to go up or down at the end. We'd build and build on the sound putting real graft into the layers. I'd do all the drums and ideas and Chris would play the keyboards and operate the computer.

Mark Hargreaves was the engineer at Blue Chip at the time and he knew all about the studio equipment. Mark wasn't into our music as such, but no matter what you played, it all sounded the same. Ha ha. When Mark had extra work on, he got a girl called Tina to help us out. Tina was well into heavy metal and Mark had taught her how to engineer. I was also taking notes. I would sit with Mark and scribble down bits and bobs. 'How to sample using the S-950. Press this button, scroll this way. Press that. Get an input…' I would put all these notes into a step-by-step book, so I could use them when I was on my own. I was learning how to engineer.

Tina got this toxic shock syndrome thing midway through the recording and so she wasn't about for a while and so my expertise in engineering came to the fore. The knowledge I had gathered was vital at this point with Mike and Tina doing other things. Not only did Tina leave us to engineer, but she also gifted me a verruca. Ha ha. I'm pretty sure it was from her as she used to walk around the studio barefoot.

Chris and I worked well together although I found him very difficult in one particular regard: his smoking. I used to get these terrible migraines owing to the constant cigarette fumes and I would get quite panicked as he reached for his ciggies. The migraines were excruciating and I would often be physically sick. Other than that we worked well together as our roles were quite defined.

We had a proper big studio, 48-channel desk, 24 tracks and a two-inch tape machine. Everything we did, we recorded down to tape which we striped with SMPTE code – a process that sounded like a fax machine or a computer game downloading. The code on one channel would start the computer running and then you'd go on to record extra channels, ensuring it all ran in time. You recorded so many things down in the first take and then you'd lay a bassline on a separate channel. As soon as you punched the code in, it was timed to come in with everything else on the tape so it all synced up.

We recorded a load of drum tracks. So track 1: kick drum. Track 2: sample. Track 3: hi hats. Track 4: snare. When we wanted to kick off a bassline you would start recording on the tape, press start on the computer in time with what was playing and use the 'plus/add and minus' arrow keys on the computer to keep it in time with the tape. You can hear certain tunes, on the acid album for example, where the bassline is slightly out of time and too slow for the drums because whoever was on the plus and minus keys was not listening properly. We hadn't learned all the engineering tricks as yet.

Our Jen SX1000 keyboard had no output, so there was no way of syncing it up with the rest of the music. It was like having an acoustic guitar. So when we were recording, someone had to play the riffs live, as you would with a piano, for seven minutes straight while someone else tweaked all the knobs. It was roughshod as we had no in-depth knowledge and the equipment was pretty basic. We bought the keyboard from Gareth who helped out on the first Rhythm Mode: D sessions. 'You can only get one noise from it,' he said. 'Give us a fiver!'

Kev Roberts would often drop by to stick his two-penneth in, pushing faders up and down. After he left, we'd put it all back to how it was, and then he'd come back in and nod. 'I told you it would sound better!' Kevin had the Reynolds Girls turn up to the studio once with a demo tape and he sent them packing. 'No way!' Six months later they were in the Top 10 with I'd Rather Jack.

That summer of 1989 was industrious and we were totally immersed in the recording of this album. I don't know if my desire was stronger because I'd been booted out of Bizarre Inc, but I really wanted to show what I was capable of. It was hard for me to gauge how Chris felt, however, as we never really got that close.

We would often be working late at Blue Chip and as a result were sometimes locked in. The car park at Blue Chip was inside a compound locked shut by these giant wooden gates and you couldn't climb over them. The studio was hidden away within these massive brick walls that were covered in broken glass and topped off with barbed wire, preventing anyone leaving or entering the compound during the night. Kev Roberts' girlfriend Sam was locked in one evening and like some armed robber on *The Sweeney* she simply drove Kev's Jag straight through this enormous gate, smashing it to matchwood. This wasn't your dream studio, but Blue Chip still played an important part in our lives.

So I'd come into Blue Chip each morning with a pile of tracks, samples, noises or whatever and Chris would vibe off it. We would loop things around until we got something that worked. I had recorded a load of instrumental tracks and sampled all the clean drum loops I could from my vast collection of techno records. I'd then take some bass lines too and Chris would do really nice pads and tinkles over the top. We had done *Technological* as Bizarre Inc and I really wanted to use that bassline again, but instead of it coming out of a keyboard we sampled the noise off the Bizarre Inc record and replayed the bassline slightly lower, so it was a deeper noise rather than sampled clean. We called the track *Logical Progression*.

Kev was still dropping by to stick his oar in. 'You need some vocal tracks,' he'd tell us, although we'd never written vocals or worked with a vocalist. Kev knew Edwin Starr and Junior Walker And The All Stars, and acts like that would often come in and we'd engineer for them. But we weren't brilliant at working with vocalists at all. So Kev got two singers in from Wolverhampton (Joanna Graham and Diane Grey) clutching some lyrics their manager Simon Greatbach had written (with his business partner Michael De Souza) and suddenly we had something akin to *Big Fun/Good Life* by Inner City. *(Still) Life Keeps Moving* was our take on Detroit techno with the same drums and stab and it was the first tune of ours to get some level of success that we actually knew about. We were getting some really positive DJ reaction reports back; the questionnaires popped inside white labels that were sent out to the big names. 'Another good Blue Chip record. Keep it up!!' (Mike Pickering, The Hacienda, DJ Reaction Report *(Still) Life Keeps Moving*). Mike Pickering was one of the three or four famous house DJs at The Hacienda and he loved *(Still) Life...* saying it was one of his top ten Hacienda tunes, along with *Voodoo Ray*. I had been to The Hacienda a few times and the atmosphere was amazing and knowing that something you made was being played there, was just... WOW! The next thing we knew there were adverts and reviews in music papers for our band: Nexus 21.

Most people thought the name Nexus 21 was from *Blade Runner* and the Nexus-6 replicants, but it wasn't. I was reading *Hip Hop Connection* at the time and there was some regular article with Dave Pearce where you could write in with a query. At the bottom of one letter it said: 'Nexus 14'. I thought it sounded quite techno-y and as Chris and I were both 21 at the time, we decided on Nexus 21. I checked to see if the name had been used for anything else and the only connection was a load of dating agencies who used the term 'nexus' because it meant 'together'.

I took *(Still) Life...* home and played it to Dad in the car. 'Listen to this!' I was so excited. Dad furrowed his brow and showed no emotion whatsoever, before he finally piped up. 'There are no crash cymbals!' I was proper gutted. But he was right. We had no drum machines or whatnot. Karen wasn't that enamoured either. I guess their reactions kept me grounded. I went to Central Park in Newcastle-under-Lyme with copies of *(Still) Life...* and gave them out to DJs. 'You probably haven't heard this, but see what you think.'

Around this time, I started keeping a scrapbook of adverts and reviews (good and bad) as I didn't know how long anything was going to last. One review said we were *"...as interesting as a used rail ticket..."* It could all end tomorrow though, I thought, carefully cutting them out and sticking them in. We weren't making any money out of music either, so I was looking at our careers through the eyes of a fan, to some extent.

'... heavy on melody and bang on today's pulse.' Kevin Hills' review of *(Still) Life Keeps Moving* from *Mixmag*, Nov, 1989

Blue Chip wanted help with the artwork for the album and as we'd seen what they were capable of (spelling mistakes on Rhythm Mode: D and Bizarre Inc covers as well as the crummy fist of money), we considered any control we could get over the direction of the artwork was well worth grasping. Leave it to them and you'd get any old crap. My brother Paul originally aspired to be a pilot in the RAF just so that he could join the astronaut programme, as that was the minimum requirement. His dreams were dashed, however, when he was sick on a passenger jet and so space travel was out of the window. He then went on to load missiles onto aircraft and repair ejector seats on Canberras. Paul's obsession with space travel meant that he had quite a collection of books on the subject and would regularly write to NASA, who sent back photos and brochures from various space explorations. Paul knew all about the Space Shuttle before it was even on the news over here. These books of Paul's often featured images of Earth from the Moon and so we got one of them blown up by a photographer in Stafford for *The Rhythm of Life* album cover. So, the album sleeve featured a picture from a book and I did the lettering using those Letraset transfer sets, carefully rubbing them onto the design with a pencil. Each letter was half a centimetre thick and all the Ss had been used, so we had to use a dollar sign. Some people claimed they liked the slightly disrupted effect of the logo, but that was an accident too, a result of blowing it up too much on the photocopier; there are dots all around the letters. Incidentally, you can't get that typeface anywhere now and we even used the same Letraset years later on another release. We were used to doing everything ourselves at Blue Chip. After all, if you left Kev alone with a record sleeve, he'd end up as writer, producer and composer. Whilst finishing off the album it became apparent that Blue Chip was struggling a little. I can only assume that Blue Chip wasn't making any actual money and they certainly never seemed to have any. We pressed Kev for some studio time, knowing that it was still very precious to us, especially as money was not forthcoming.

Blue Chip ran a weird operation, releasing records we never even knew were getting pressed. Chris and I did a Nexus 21 track with a techno remix on the B-side as C+M Connection (Chris and Mark), which I never even knew came out on Blue Chip until 2005. Kev's sister worked in a Nottingham record shop and he once asked Dean and I to mix a load of Depeche Mode tracks for her to play in the shop, which we did. A few weeks later this box turned up and it was all these 12"s called *Mode Mix*. He told us we were doing a tape for his sister and yet he had pressed it up for release.

So, Kev gave us the keys to the studio in exchange for our lack of royalties and warned us that we were not supposed to be in there. We recorded nine tracks in total before Blue Chip finally went bump. I was hoping that the studio would get saved at the last minute, but no such luck. We'd just started getting going and now the studio and the label were bust. Still, the album was out and getting some good reviews so it felt like we had some momentum bubbling, but where could we go now? Stafford wasn't New York or Chicago. There was no easy route back into the industry. So, armed with these nine tracks, we said goodbye to Blue Chip.

At this point Dad put it on the line: 'There's a job going in the village as a butcher. Butchery is a trade. You're always going to need butchers. Get good at being a butcher and you're always in demand. It's a guaranteed good wage. Or... you can carry on with this Nexus 21 thing. It's totally up to you.' I think Dad would have preferred me to take the butcher job, but he made it easy for me. 'Mind you, if you don't continue with the music thing,' he added, 'you might always look back and think *what if?*' Good old Dad.

"Stafford's Nexus 21 were probably among the first people, along with Baby Ford, to release a British techno track to get any real attention with the Inner City-influenced '(Still) Life'..." Record Mirror

***

Karen and I were still clubbing at the time and we would often go to a night in Longton, Stoke called Introspective at the Leisure Bowl. It had a sprung floor and was a big, fantastic place. Daz Willot from Frenzy and Pete Bromley from Central Park, DJed there. Central Park was Newcastle-under-Lyme's version of Top Of The World and DJs Danny and Kelvin played there too; they went on to become Candy Flip and Sure Is Pure who produced Robbie Williams and the rest. You knew you'd get quality on a Friday night at Introspective. I would also hang out at a little wine bar called No.7s in Burntwood near Stafford, which was gaining a reputation.

I went to No.7s one night with a copy of *(Still) Life* and offered the DJ a copy, but he simply rifled through his record box whilst I stood there. 'This is a bit rude!' I thought. Then he pulled out an identical sleeve. 'Already got it, mate!' He had a big smile on his face. 'Oh my God, someone actually bought my record!' That man was Neil Macey.

Neil Macey was a bit younger than me and a really nice chap and one of the biggest influences on my musical tastes. 'I'm thinking of giving all this up,' I told him one night. Neil was having none of it and told me to keep the faith. Neil really assured me that I had the chops to carry on with this music thing, which was really helpful. A week later, I was at No.7s again when Neil cornered me. 'I've been offered a job at Kool Kat,' he said. 'I think I can help you.' I knew Kool Kat very well as they had released a lot of acid house tracks as well as the proper big names of Chicago house and early Detroit techno. Kool Kat brought techno to the UK with the seminal compilation album *Techno! The New Dance Sound of Detroit.* Our Price had Kool Kat records. Kool Kat was a proper decent label.

Neil Macey (Kool Kat, Network and Ideal Trax) "*I was DJing in a local wine bar in Rugeley, just six miles away from Mark in Gnosall. I had been buying records in Burntwood and the guy who ran the record shop was a resident DJ at No.7s on a Thursday night. This was at the point where the rave scene was just kicking off and there were hardly any clubs in the whole of the Midlands where people played house all night long. There was Tressines in Birmingham and DJ Dick played there and then there was Scott at the Lord Raglan in Wolverhampton and Entropy in Stoke, but not much more.*

Mark had been buying records in Burntwood too and the guy who ran the shop, Pat Ward, was a Northern Soul guy and good friends with Neil Rushton who had already started releasing some Chicago records on Kool Kat. Pat had been a dancer who won competitions at Northern Soul gigs Neil had put on and so they were mates. Pat then invited me to DJ at No.7s in Burntwood as he was getting more and more interested in rave.

Pat invited me down on a Thursday night to play some records for an hour or two and so I took the 'Rugeley Crew' with me and we filled the 150-capacity club. Pat stood at the bar and let me DJ all night as a full-on rave broke out at this little provincial club until 2am. Before that, No.7s was known more for being an unofficial swingers club. There was a massive Jacuzzi upstairs for the lucky stragglers looking for a bit of 'afters'. But things changed that night. It was dark, all the lights off, strobes on full, with a finger on the smoke machine. This was so successful it soon became a regular night, such was the enthusiasm for Thursdays at No.7s. Shortly afterwards my mates starting losing their jobs as they weren't going to work on a Friday.

Mark appeared not long after we started up and approached me with a record he'd made. Mark was never into taking drugs and was certainly not your average raver; it was all about the music. 'I like the music you're playing,' he said, handing me a copy of Nexus 21's (Still) Life Keeps Moving. He was as pleased as punch when I pulled out my own copy from the record box. That surprised and delighted him. We started hanging out, chatting about this and that. Mark was dancing like crazy at these nights and it was there that he developed his moves, with all the pointing-finger action and proto shuffling.

It wasn't long before Pat Ward tipped Neil Rushton off about the Thursday nights. 'You won't believe what's going on over here! It's a full-on rave!' Neil would have been one of those in the Jacuzzi back in the day.

There weren't many DJs back then who owned enough records to work for hours on end, so it was rich pickings for the lucky few. An American import cost £6 a piece, so if you had the records, you got the gigs. Neil Rushton came down one night with some fantastic music. He started pulling out all this unreleased Inner City stuff and Derrick May's Rhythim Is Rhythim acetates. 'Play that one! And this one!' Suddenly this small-town provincial nightclub had become a seminal venue and a real focus in the development of techno.

I started chatting to Neil and he invited me down to the Kool Kat offices on the Monday, where he played me more stuff. He said he wanted to start a new, more contemporary label, called Network. By the end of the day he'd offered me a job. I was 19 at the time and had gone from working a local wine bar to being staff at a record label. My DJing took off too; right place, right time. I was made Head of Club Promotions at Network, which was essentially shoving records into mailers. Neil also asked me to A&R and wanted anything good that he could release. It was at that point that I thought of Mark and Nexus 21."

A couple of weeks later at No.7s, Neil (Macey) cornered me again. 'The boss is over there at the bar; he knows about Nexus 21 and wants a chat.' I froze. There was no way I could go over and talk to the boss of a record label. It must have taken me 20 minutes to walk 10 steps, really shitting myself, but eventually I sidled up next to this guy like a proper spare part. I said, 'Excuse me, I'm Mark from Nexus 21.' Straight away he turned around.

- 'No way! I've got your record in the office! Do you fancy a meeting?'
- 'Yeah!'

- 'I'm starting up a new label and I want you to be a part of it.' I wrote my number down to arrange a meeting and he carried on talking about his grand plans. What?!

So early one morning I popped round to Chris's to pick him up and off we went to Birmingham in my Mini. The record label occupied some floor space in a beautiful old timber building called Stratford House and we were blown away as soon as we walked through the door of this 15th century-listed mansion house. The Kool Kat office was full of trendy sofas and had this giant stereo system and DAT machine. Blue Chip this was not.

Neil Macey *"Mark was unhappy with the Blue Chip situation and was playing me the stuff he was doing with Chris, which I loved. Mark then came in and played Neil the first Nexus 21 LP, which sounded so right at the time. Neil Rushton wanted to sign them up, there and then. Neil was keen to get the rights of everything they had done thus far to prevent any dual releases and as chance should have it, he knew Kev Roberts from the Northern Soul scene. The negotiations for the back catalogue were done very quickly."*

I was 21, but I felt like a nervous five-year-old, completely out of my depth. As we sat in this grand office, the team were playing all these DATS which I later found out were the release schedule for the newly created Network. Tracks included Neal Howard's *Indulge*, *Mood* by Symbols and Instruments and *Take Me Back* by Rhythmatic from Nottingham, which actually blew the hi-fi speakers. Neil Rushton also had connections to Northern Soul, just like Blue Chip's Kev Roberts, but this guy was a player with direct links to the Detroit techno scene. Neil handed over a contract and advised us to go away and study it. We shook hands, walked back to the Mini and just stared at each other. Fucking hell!

As there were no music lawyers in Stafford, we were ill advised with regards to our contract by someone Chris knew. 'Yeah yeah. Looks decent, that.' And with that we signed away our music for life. Ha ha. Network owned the songs for life, but they undertook a sizeable risk in doing so. Looking back, it was pure naivety on our behalf, but that innocence was partly due to the £1250 advance, which was a lot of money to us even after it was split down the middle. All of a sudden I had enough money to buy a sampler. I remember thinking, 'This is proper! No messing about pretending to be on a record label. This *is* a record label!'

This advance was recuperable, which meant that the first thousand pounds we made would pay off the advance. What we didn't understand was that we would be racking up thousands and thousands in debt, which ultimately wouldn't get paid back for years. But we were young and desperate to make music and here we were getting paid to do it. That was an incredible thing. So I bought the sampler and Chris got an Atari computer so he could do demos from home. Now I could sample away back at my parents', building an extensive library for the studio work, which moved on the whole production process no end.

Network was amazing. We were now on the same label as the heavyweights of Detroit techno. One of the first things Neil did was to contact Kev Roberts in order to acquire all the master tapes to prevent him releasing anything that would disrupt their plans. Bizarre Inc's new label Vinyl Solution had already bought all of their previous work in a similar move. We didn't want records popping out of the Blue Chip vault just as we were making a name for ourselves.

Kev rang when he heard that we'd signed and said, 'Congratulations. But you do realise you can't sign for them? You signed with me.' The thing is, we hadn't. I gave it to him straight. 'You will never find a signature on any piece of paper Kev, as we didn't sign anything.'

-   'Oh.'

Network Records was a new direction for Neil and his business partner Dave Barker. Whereas Kool Kat was concentrating on Chicago and Detroit, Network was to be a lot broader in scope. Neil knew all the people in Detroit and not long after signing to Network they got the Nexus 21 single *(Still) Life Keeps Moving* from Blue Chip and sent the master tapes over to Detroit to be remixed. As ours was a respectful rip-off of *Good Life* and *Big Fun*, they sent it to Kevin Saunderson of Inner City, so he could get to work on it. Things were getting exciting.

Neil Rushton *"I turned up at my local wine bar No.7s in Burntwood one Thursday night and Neil Macey was DJing there. I had just taken Neil on at Network and was also managing Kevin Saunderson and Juan Atkins while licensing tunes from Detroit. So there I was in this provincial place, which had quickly become a beacon for the emergence of acid house. I was introduced to Mark Archer and we got talking. It seemed a perfect marriage. He was releasing what I was releasing and so I decided to get Mark into the office. That was Nexus 21 and that was where it all began... I wanted the perfect UK techno group to put out some tunes and Nexus 21 were sublime."*

Network would take us out for meals and stuff and we'd get to hear all the latest music in Neil's car on the way to meetings. One morning, he put this tape on and it was a Kevin Saunderson mixtape. I'm sitting here listening to all these tracks from raves when he suddenly mixes Inner City with the Nexus 21 record. I was speechless. One of the blokes, who was perhaps the major reason for me wanting to make records, was playing one of my tracks on a mixtape! And he obviously liked it, although it was a blatant rip-off of one of his releases. Not long after, Kevin Saunderson did a remix of *(Still) Life* alongside mixes by Carl Craig and Marc Kinchen. Three Detroit producers all on the one 12". Kevin wasn't mad keen on the vocal on *(Still) Life* and so he got a girl from Detroit called Donna Black to re-record it.

I had gone from buying these records and being really influenced by these people, to suddenly being in the same world. They were on tap at *my* record label, sending in tunes and mixing bits and pieces. I was genuinely gobsmacked. I could easily have been making sausages at that point.

"Ten Things You Already Knew About Nexus 21"

1. Nexus 21's first LP *The Rhythm of Life* (recorded for a local label) is no longer available, but it has been bootlegged and fetches upwards of £30.
2. A 12" DP promo of the original mix of *Self Hypnosis* was bootlegged in London recently on the 'Dance Classics' label. The culprits are now clapped in irons.
3. Their last single *(Still) Life Keeps Moving* was a startling piece of progressive pop music.
4. Nexus 21 and their travelling techno circus are available for weddings, funerals and bar mitzvahs. Call Neil Macey on the number below.
5. Mark and Chris have worked on other Network releases by Kate B and Cyclone.
6. Mark and Chris are trailed by some strange people. One devoted fan recently claimed that after listening to *Self Hypnosis*, it had a strange effect on him. 'It made me come in my pants,' he said.
7. The *Self Hypnosis* remix is to be taken seriously. An advance tape of the track has so far destroyed two sets of speakers at Network.
8. Parts of the bassline are only audible to dogs and other domestic animals.
9. Mark and Chris were both recently made Freemen of the City of Stafford.
10. The remix of *Self Hypnosis* is entitled "The Mr Whippy Mix" due to its alarming similarity to the sound of an ice cream van. Bob's Ices, based in Stafford, have adopted the computer refrain from *Self Hypnosis* for their fleet of 25 vans. **John McCready, Network Records**

CH. 7

Stafford Techno City Versus Detroit Techno City

8 Of The Best: Detroit Techno

1. Reese – *Just Another Chance*
2. Model 500 – *Off To Battle*
3. Rhythim Is Rhythim – *It Is What It Is*
4. Suburban Knight – *The Art of Stalking*
5. Rhythim Is Rhythim – *Beyond The Dance (Cult Mix)*
6. Reese & Santonio – *The Sound*
7. Psyche – *Elements*
8. Model 500 – *The Passage*

Was Stafford the new Detroit? Was it fuck! But it was fun for a while to pit this sleepy West Midlands town up against the might of the Motor City, the creative powerhouse that had produced some of the finest soul, proto-punk rock and heavy metal the world had ever heard. The West Midlands also had a history of producing cars of course, and was the *home* of heavy metal, but Stafford was not Detroit. There will be no *8 Mile*-type movies trawling the dark and moody streets of this quaint English town, famous for having four Wimpys and some pretty major road connections.

A major player in Stafford's quest for world domination, however, was Network's press officer and hilarious scouser John McCready, who got journalists into Nexus 21 from the off with some great tongue-in-cheek press releases. *"There are two things you need to know about Stafford. The first is the quickest way to get out of it. The second is that this town – stuck to the side of the M6 – is the home of UK Techno…"* John worked well with Neil Rushton and between the pair of them, they gave Nexus 21 a real identity. John's press releases were highly amusing as well as clearly daft, but there was always a grain of truth in there that had people fooled for a while. John was a talented journalist and worked for magazines such as *NME* and *The Face* and he had a natural gift for creating hype.

Neil Rushton *"I first met John when he was sent over by Virgin to do press for the Techno! album. I instantly thought of him when it came to Nexus 21. He really wanted to get involved and he loved it. He was so bizarre, in a nice way, so it was a good combination. So John did their press and got them all over the world. Mark and Chris were so funny and ready and willing to go along with all the nonsense, which helped a lot!"*

Neil Rushton was a Northern Soul DJ and many of his peers got into house quite early on. I think Neil was often out in Detroit looking for Northern Soul tracks, trying to find a super rare record someone had 50 copies of in their garage; people will pay a fortune for these gems. He was out there sometime in 1987/'88 when someone played him techno and took him to some clubs to see what was going on. Neil loved the techno sound and saw a chance to make a connection between Detroit and the emerging rave scene back in the UK.

Neil Rushton *"I loved house music. I packed in a pretty good job as a newspaper reporter to get back into music. In the late seventies I was a promoter of soul all-dayers and an importer of soul/jazz/funk records. I owned Inferno, which was a Northern Soul re-issue label. I loved my newspaper job, but got more and more into house music and in 1987 packed the job up to start a label. A lot of the Chicago labels already had alliances in the UK, but I was very much into the Detroit releases (nobody called it techno then) and so when I did the Virgin Techno! compilation that spawned Big Fun I went after the rights to the releases nobody else was going for."*

Three people were credited with inventing Detroit techno: Kevin Saunderson, Derrick May and Juan Atkins. Following that trio came the second ring of Carl Craig and Eddie Fowlkes et al. Neil Rushton signed up the main three and licensed tracks for what became Kool Kat. Neil ended up managing Inner City after putting together *Techno! The New Dance Sound of Detroit*. Kevin Saunderson suggested putting a little 'vocal thing I've been working on' on the album and that became *Big Fun*, which went on to be a monster hit.

Neil and the Network lads were really down to earth, but full of crazy ideas. They would just fire them off at you. 'We can do this! Get such-and-such to mix you. Work with so-and-so in Detroit...' All the way through our time there, Network were great. I don't think the future would have panned out the way it did with any other label. The pranks, the media hype and the support was all brilliant.

John McCready *"I met Neil Rushton whilst I was working for NME on a trip to Detroit to cover the techno story. We got on and bonded over record collecting and he invited me to handle press for Network. I knew of Nexus 21 before Network and was aware that – like 808 State – they were true UK trailblazers.*

Mark and Chris were lovely people who were dead serious about music, but really fun to be around. I think the sleeve-notes to the first Bio Rhythms compilation started life as a press release. The stuff about raves in launderettes was daft and utterly unconvincing. They were innocent times though and we loved it when people took them at face value, but it was never a given!"

Although Blue Chip had released a Nexus 21 album we had no idea as to how well it did. But by hanging out at clubs we met many people who said they loved *The Rhythm of Life*. A few people claimed that our album was the reason they started making tunes. I just couldn't believe what I was hearing.

In 1990 Network and Warp were at the forefront of UK techno with the bleepy bass thing and John McCready did some great press releases that pushed the hype to breaking point. John made up an underground techno legend called Kid Persil who ran an illegal club in a launderette where he synced the spin-speed of the machines to the tunes he made, to make them hypnotic. This was for the *Bio Rhythms* compilations Network put out. There was always an edge of truth to a lot of the things John invented and people often fell for it. After all, *Bio Rhythms* sounded like a washing powder.

Chris and I were asked to remix some of the new Network releases as well as working on our own stuff and so we were grafting away at Network, which was just the way we liked it. We remixed Frank De Wulf's track *Kate B* and remixed the old Paris Grey tune *Don't Lead Me*. We had also written a Nexus 21 track called *Self Hypnosis* in a Derby studio (Square Dance) after Chris had come up with the riff on a tiny little keyboard. I don't think the keyboard was meant for studio purposes at all, but it had a midi socket on the back so you could control it from the computer. The riff was played on what was called 'electronic piano', but sounded nothing like it. Chris brought a computer disc with that pattern on it to my house one day and I added the drums. I now had a Roland MC-202 at this stage and so we were slowly building up a stockpile of gear.

Chris and I were never friends as such, but it was cool. There were things about him I wasn't mad keen on, such as the smoking which was by now causing me severe migraines every time he sparked up. I was scared of the cops, something Chris definitely wasn't. Once, after recording *Self Hypnosis* over in Derby, Chris got followed by the police on our way home. Chris had an old Cortina and it was 2-3am. The police car followed us for a bit and then the lights went on. Whereas I would have been 'What's up officer?', Chris wasn't having any of it. Eventually we pulled to a halt and they came over for a chat. 'You alright, lads?'

- 'Well, we were until you pulled up.'
- 'What are you doing at this time of night?'
- 'What's it to you?'

Then I got involved. 'Come on Chris, answer the bloke and we can go.' It was completely unnecessary. Chris wasn't mad keen on the police for whatever reason and had no respect for authority. Maybe I had too much, I don't know. We were just very different people, I guess. Eventually the police let us go, but I think they were just curious as to why we were out at that time of the morning when the roads were dead quiet.

When we did *Self Hypnosis* – which Network released as a single – Chris's mad bleepy riff got pigeonholed as the 'ice cream van jingle'. Whenever you heard that track played out, it would get to that riff and everyone would wiggle their fingers in the air. Chris was dating a friend of a friend of Karen's and I remember Zoe once telling us that she was seeing an ice cream man and I think that guy was Chris. So when we remixed it, we called it the *Mr Whippy Remix* which was possibly one occasion when the Network press release contained some shred of truth.

Network recorded loads of tracks for this *Bio Rhythms* compilation album that featured Derrick May, Rhythmatic and Nexus 21. There were also two remixes we'd done and the C+M Connection track. It was Italian on side one and techno on the flip. So we had four tracks on the 10-track album surrounded by the likes of Carl Craig, Marc Kinchen and Derrick May. That was a massive honour.

(Still) Life... was remixed at Network with Donna Black replacing Diane Grey and was mixed by Kevin Saunderson. It was also the first track Carl Craig mixed for release when it came out on KMS as *The Detroit Mixes*. We would record on two-inch tape, but just for my listening pleasure I would get a quick version down on cassette. You had mute buttons on each channel so you could bring in the breakbeat as when you wanted it, taking it down and stuff. We did a rough mute mix of our track *Flutes* (by C+M Connection), a very downtempo track with fluty bits and pads, but we never finished it off. The mixing desk had a Commodore 64 as its computer and it would read this SMPTO tape. Then, as you ran it through and pressed these mute buttons, the computer would remember the order in which you pressed them. Every time you played it, it did the mix the same.

When Network asked for more stuff, I played them the cassette and they loved it, so we recorded it straight on to DAT for the second *Bio Rhythms* album. The quality was tape-to-tape, but it was sent off and pressed; it had so many fuck-ups in it. We were trying to emulate what they did in Detroit, but we didn't know how to do it and so we did the best we could, which was a whole other ball game.

Neil Rushton sat us down one morning and hit us with a bombshell. 'As you're making and mixing Detroit techno we're going to send you to Detroit. You're going to work with the people out there.' WHAT!? I was speechless for about a week after that. I couldn't believe it. These people were, and still are, my musical heroes. I was off to work with Derrick May and Kevin Saunderson. I was totally wired. Detroit might as well have been the Moon.

Neil Macey *"Neil Rushton had been back and forth to Detroit a lot and it was his idea to take Mark and Chris there to work with Kevin*

(Saunderson) and Marc (Kinchen). Indeed, (Still) Life Keeps Moving came out on Kevin's KMS label in the US."

Karen and my parents didn't seem to share in my excitement at all. It was like I'd said I was going to the chip shop. I was going to Detroit to meet Kevin Saunderson. It was to be only the second time I'd been on a plane. I was buzzing.

It felt like I'd been promised the trip of a lifetime and I didn't want to miss a thing and so we got a video camera to document the journey. The problem was that Chris started filming the minute we got in the car from Burntwood to Birmingham when there was absolutely nothing to see. Chris then left the camera running as we went through security and so there's a sideways view of an X-ray machine on the tape. By the time we got to Detroit the battery had virtually run out and Chris hadn't brought a charger.

We got to Detroit and checked into this motel. I couldn't believe the size of these people. I knew that Americans ate a lot, but standing in the foyer of this hotel was the fattest man I had ever seen. He had a stomach so big and firm it looked like a bouncy castle. Remove your shoes before jumping on.

We ventured out that first night and took it all in. It was April and so it wasn't that warm. Detroit was a big, busy city and we felt suitably small. We were walking down this avenue when this geezer stopped his car in front of us and popped the hood. He asked us if we wanted to buy some gold chains. We were just in awe at how different people were there. Very direct. I politely declined the offer of some iffy-looking jewellery and we walked on.

There was a slight language barrier in Detroit, but Chris was just plain stubborn about it. He would constantly ask people where he could buy 'fags' knowing that it meant something quite different over there. Chris seemed to look for trouble sometimes. I was really scared of the cops over there, of course; they had GUNS!

I just couldn't get my head around Woolworths in Detroit as it had a pet department that sold parrots. Everything was slightly distorted compared to back home. Parrots! Earlier that morning we went down for breakfast and were asked what we wanted. 'Corn Flakes with sugar, please.'
-    'Don't you mean Frosties?'
-    'No. Corn Flakes with sugar.'

I was asked if I wanted my eggs 'sunny side up'. I had no idea. First time someone says 'over-easy', you're like 'What?!' There were a few hip hop tracks that mentioned eating collard greens and later that day I asked Marc Kinchen what they were, exactly. He thought I was taking the piss and wouldn't tell me.

- 'But we don't have them in the UK.'

We found a jar of collard greens in Woolworths, but it was just full of green stuff. Was this language changed simply out of spite?

To make sure I didn't forget a thing I helped myself to all sorts of keepsakes. I kept the room key, envelopes, invoices and whatnot for my scrapbook, because I honestly thought I would never come back. It was quite surreal and dreamlike. I am Mark from Stafford. This is Detroit.

A week alone with Chris was enough, though. We just didn't gel as friends really. Chris had this thing back home where he would phone me up and then not say anything. I'd say, 'How are you doing?'

- 'OK. What are you doing?'
- 'Nothing.' And that was it. This would go on for ages.

Being with Chris 24/7 was very hard, but the anticipation of meeting – and working with – these Detroit legends stopped me getting too tense about it all. We'd been thrown together by Kev Roberts and were making a pretty good fist of this music malarkey and so it was sometimes best not to think too much.

The first proper morning we were there we went to meet the guys. Neil Rushton, Chris and I entered Kevin's studio, which was beneath Derrick May's apartment and my face went as red as a cherry when I clocked them. Kevin Saunderson had his own studio in a corner building on Gracio Avenue, in Belleville, Detroit. The 'Belleville Three' of Kevin, Juan Atkins and Derrick May – credited with starting techno – were all there. They were all just really friendly. Juan was pretty quiet and Derrick was loud, but he shut up shop when it came to talking production techniques with me. They all seemed to have this really great vibe; all part of something unique. I could not believe this was happening. Chris was totally oblivious as to the significance of this trip as he had no idea who these guys were. To Chris, they were just some dudes doing the same kind of music as us.

So we spent the day in Kev's studio with his engineer Chris Andrews. Marc Kinchen was also there to show us how to give the percussion that authentic Detroit feel. The percussion was all about using a Roland TR-

727 and sampled sounds on an Akai MPC60, pieces of gear we didn't have and there was a certain programming style that the Detroit lot had. Neil Rushton knew we didn't have the equipment back home and so it was good to see how it was done, even if it was a case of trying something different back in the UK. Donna Black was then drafted in to record some vocals. We were then told that we were to perform a PA later that night, at Club Taboo where Inner City were playing.

Eddie Fowlkes was DJing and Chris Andrews did the sound check in the early evening while a hip house video was being shot – hip house was massive over there at the time. Our video camera finally died – I'd been saving the final few minutes in case of emergency – the moment Kevin appeared on stage. We had five minutes of footage from this incredible journey. 'Why are you having a go at me?' Chris moaned.

-   'The battery's gone because you filmed the rain in Burntwood.'

We had never performed on a stage before, but I was more excited than nervous. The PA required us to mime behind the keyboards while Donna sang, so it wasn't too taxing. After we did the sound check, we walked back to the hotel for a rest. Walking down one of the avenues we saw a roadrunner, right in the middle of Detroit. Now I expected one in the desert, maybe, but it seemed so odd. We walked into the centre of town, searching for the hotel, clearly looking confused. A guy outside a hotel came over. 'Are you guys lost?'

-   'We're looking for our hotel.'
-   'What are you guys doing here?'
-   'We're playing a gig at Club Taboo tonight.'
-   'What are you called?'
-   'Nexus 21.'
-   'No way. I know you guys!'
-   'What?!'

We were not known in Gnosall, never mind Stafford, and yet here we were getting some respect in Michigan!

The gig was nerve-racking. I was standing there behind the keyboards – set out in an L shape – looking like some multi-instrumentalist from Emerson, Lake & Palmer or something. Then this geezer clambered up behind the keyboard and asked, 'What's that beat?'

-   'It's a 909.'
-   'No what's that beat?'
-   'It's just a Roland 909.'

I didn't realise that 'beat' was slang for the name of the tune.

Donna Black was amazing and had such a great voice. My abiding memory of her, though, was when her boobs fell out of her basque top as she spun around on the floor. We hung out backstage after and met loads of people. The first wave of Detroit techno – Kevin Saunderson, Derrick May, Juan Atkins, Eddie Fowlkes and Blake Baxter – were all there, chatting away. Even the second wave of Detroit techno were there: Carl Craig and Jay Denham. Jay Denham was a huge bloke, really tall. 'Yo dog! Wasupp?' I just didn't get the whole dog thing. I was so out of my depth language-wise. I was puzzled. 'Dog is like friend, it's cool,' said Jay.

I really wanted a 909 drum machine and Jay said he had a friend in Chicago selling one for $600. 'Do you want me to get him to drop by?' I just nodded. Anyway, this dude drove from Chicago to Detroit to sell me it.

I assumed the 909 was going to be full of techno drum patterns, but there weren't any. Instead, it was full of hip house; stuff like Fast Eddie and Mr Lee. Even the people from Detroit loved hip house. I couldn't get my head around it. 'But techno is much better. Why are you loving hip house so much? Techno is ace!' So I had to start my techno drum patterns from scratch, but still, I was sitting in a Detroit hotel that night with a 909 on my lap that Jay Denham's mate sold me. This wasn't happening!

We had some great times with the Detroit lot. When the recording session finished in Kevin's studio, we went through the mic booth and into his house. Kevin was sat there with his family and they had some Nintendo game on that had a dance mat. 'Right Mark, you're up next. You're racing against Kevin.'

There I stood. 'Ready, set, go!' Suddenly I was running on the spot. My legs were going like the clappers and all I'm thinking was, 'Oh my god, it's Kevin Saunderson!' There was no way I was going to win. I just couldn't concentrate on this game. My head was blown for the entire week.

We went to see Juan Atkins in his studio too and met this guy called Darren Mohammed who had come over to work with Derrick May. Darren had scored a massive acid house tune for MCA with Adrenalin M.O.D.'s O-O-O. I was sat in Juan Atkins' studio as Derrick May mixed a track and all the hairs were up on the back of my neck and all along my arms.

We all went to watch the Detroit Tigers baseball team with the crew that night and there was a massive fight involving all the players, who ran at each other and started scrapping. I had a camera with me and snapped Kevin and Derrick in the stands. Those photos are very special to me. I also got everyone to sign my autograph book while I was there, including Paris Grey of Inner City. Kevin's wife Ann was a member of a group from the UK called Kaos, with her sister Judy Nanton, and we hung out with them too. Kaos had a great tune called *Definition of Love* which I knew really well. We also met New York producer Andrew Komis, who was in Detroit that week.

We recorded quite a lot of material in Detroit, some of which has never seen the light of day. Donna Black supplied vocals for an idea we had involving a bassline, top line and rough kick. The track was *Don't Do It Like That, Do It Like This* and we wanted Donna to record a sultry spoken vocal. There we were, sitting in this big studio and she's standing there in the mic room trying to be sultry and we're all sitting there getting giggly like kids, in the control room. She's like, 'I can't do this with them laughing away.' So I had an idea. 'Tell you what: turn all the lights off, so we can't see you and then you don't have to worry about us.' She seemed happy with this and so we turned all the lights out. My word, she nailed the vocal, making all these sexual noises and stuff. Then suddenly 'WWOOAAHHHH!!!' We all looked at each other in shock. What the hell was going on in there? She was screaming like she was being attacked by a rabid coyote.

Well, Donna didn't know where the light switch was and apparently someone had left the door ajar to the mic room and Kevin's Saunderson's cat had wandered in and brushed up against Donna's leg. She totally freaked.

We did a remix of *Don't Do It Like That, Do It Like This* and got Kevin in to do a spoken word bit at the end. We recorded Kevin saying the title of the song in an authentic Detroit voice; after all it would have sounded crap with a Midlands accent – we had done this in the past and it was lame. Chris shouted 'mental' on one mix and I had said 'logical progression' on another and it hadn't sounded Detroit at all. It was totally Stafford.

Neil had been in a club in Detroit prior to our trip when they played our track *Real Love*, which sampled Derrick May's *Wiggin* wholesale. We nicked the bassline and kick drum, sampled and looped them and put a drum over the top. Derrick May heard this and was very angry.

'Who sampled my tune? I'm going to break their fucking legs!' Neil had to calm him down.

- 'It's cool, it's cool. They're with us.'
- 'Well, bring them over, then.'

We smoothed it all over when we met him and assured him that we wanted to do proper Detroit techno that wasn't just a rip off. We wanted to learn how to do it properly as lots of people classed our records as Detroit techno.

The Detroit lot were really friendly. I've not seen a lot of them since, but I can still message them and they talk like it was only last year that we hooked up. I still can't believe how lucky I was to be out there mixing with them. If that didn't keep me on the road I was on, then nothing could. I thanked all of them for their kindness and hospitality to two berks from the West Midlands. It was sad leaving, but at least I had my 909. We got back to the UK and the whole bleep thing was happening. The UK was getting very bleepy.

Neil Rushton *"Mark loved the idea of going to Detroit and recording at Kevin Saunderson's studio (KMS) and ended up hanging out with Kevin and his wife Ann and Derrick May and his girlfriend and Juan Atkins. That was surreal, you know what I mean? It was a great opportunity for them, to visit Detroit and do some recordings at KMS studios. Not a bad start to a career."*

Neil Macey *"Mark and Chris came back to the UK with these recordings and they sounded fantastic and these were what made up the Self Hypnosis EP. I remember the anticipation and excitement we had when we put out records like that. It felt like we were at least at the beginning of the curve, if not slightly ahead of it. It was never really about the money. We just wanted people to be as enthusiastic about our records as we were."*

CH. 8

Knob Twiddling, Russian Long Wave And The Doors

"Hailing from a music capital like Stafford, it's sometimes hard for Nexus 21 to shine through. Stafford has now established itself as Techno City UK. Its bars and clubs are thronged with techno victims keen to have their ribcages rattled by the dubsonic sound of the new computerised pop. Everybody wants to talk about Stafford and its growing music scene... local techno outfits 3 Pin Plug, Electric Kettle and Stafford Bastards also record at their studios. The Stafford scene is growing, but not however, as fast as Nexus 21." John McCready, press release for *Progressive Logic EP*

"Self Hypnosis is a stunning mix of stop-start electronic beats (and 'bleeps') and vague, unobtrusive vocals. Hear it once and you're charmed. Hear it twice, you're considering gluing it on to your turntable..." Barbara Ellen, *NME*, August 1990

The *Progressive Logic EP* was released in August, 1990. The original version of *Self Hypnosis* came out on *Bio Rhythms* as a promo, but because of the increasing influence of sub bass and bleeps we did the *Mr Whippy Remix* for the EP. *Together* was a Detroit production that featured on the EP as did the *Strings of Life*-influenced *Techno Symphony*. *Real Love* was the highlight for many at Network. The title of the EP was a nod to the *Technological* tune we did as Bizarre Inc, which Nexus 21 moved on as *Logical Progression*.

Network ran a club night called Bio Rhythms, just off junction 10 in Walsall and Neil Macey from No.7s – who first introduced me to Neil Rushton – was the DJ there. I got chatting to him one night, and he said, 'Why don't you do a Nexus 21 PA?' It made total sense. I had a chat with Chris and it was agreed that we would hit the stage.

That initial PA we did at Bio Rhythms was the most shambolic performance ever. Thank God we never performed under the influence as that would have been unlistenable. Because we actually played live and Chris's new Atari could only load one song at a time, it was a stuttering spectacle. You had to load up the samples and the songs every time you finished the previous tune and it took an eternity. So you played one track, and then you'd had to have a noodly bit to afford you time to get the next one loaded. It was a highly irritating experience for us, and presumably the crowd. The mixing desk wasn't earthed or anything and so it was picking up Russian long wave radio and we had no idea how to stop it. I shouted to the sound guy, 'Make it stop!' It was humming. These loud Russians talking about God knows what to the good people of Walsall.

We managed to do the PA, however. Chris was good in these situations as he was the more technical. I was the very nervous one on the mixing desk playing with the toggle switches on all the channels as everything came out at the same time. Chris was positioned with the keyboards, operating the computer and he wasn't anywhere near as shaky. The PAs were going to continue, though, and so we needed a rethink over playing live.

Adamski had a couple of tunes out using just a drum machine and this particular Ensoniq SQ80 keyboard, and this gave us an idea. Chris got hold of an Ensoniq and with my 909 from Detroit, we demoed up the live set and stored it in this keyboard, which had a built-in sequencer, bassline, acid patterns and chords. We would then add some plonky piano over five or more tracks. Chris could then shuffle through the different patterns. I would have a drum pattern and roll for each song on my drum machine, which controlled the tracks. So I would press 'start' and a bassline would play and then Chris would scroll to the next pattern and add some chords before I brought in the kick drum and hi-hat. That was how we did live PAs. It was really unspectacular to look at. Just two geeks twiddling with their knobs.

We did a PA at The Dome in Birmingham in 1990 and they actually projected us on to the screen behind us. God, talk about magnifying the knob-twiddling. Karen came to the gig, as did one of the Stafford breakdancers, Jon McDonald, who brought his mate Paul Rosson. I came off stage and asked what they thought. They said it sounded great, but 'looked really boring. Heads down looking at the equipment and pressing buttons'. Nowadays people are constantly clicking on their laptops and checking their emails during dance PAs, but back then people wanted a bit more.

December 1990, Nexus 21 were asked to perform on *Dancedaze*, a Channel 4 music show. The recording was at the Brixton Academy on a massive revolving stage and the headliner was Adamski. You'd start off behind this false wall and then the music would start playing and you'd rotate to face the stage. It was filmed during the day and there was no audience, which was weird. It was an impressive venue, though. As the stage revolved, these horrible little kids – not sure what they were contributing to the show exactly – stuck their fingers up at me and Chris. 'Fuck back up north!' That was nice.

I was behind the drum machine during this performance, but there were no wires, as we were miming. Chris was behind his keyboard and MC Man Parris from Coventry was on with us with two of his friends dancing. We played two numbers including *Together*, which C4 wrongly credited as *Self Hypnosis*. It was a really fun experience, though. 'Look Mum, I'm on telly!' It was proper.

We did the performance, came offstage and were ushered upstairs for interviews. Someone came up and started putting make-up on us, which felt really weird. We were rather warm from playing under the lights and were now caked in foundation. So we started the interview and Chris kicked off by chatting about Dire Straits and Kylie and Jason and stuff, and it was from that point on that I knew I had to seize control in these situations. Because Chris wasn't into house and techno he didn't know the background to what we were doing and so he'd veer off on silly tangents. So when someone asked him a question he just burbled utter rubbish. I always found doing press really difficult because I was so shy and it could be quite intimidating having someone firing questions at you, but I slowly got used to it. I wanted to sound like a producer from Detroit, but I was actually still living with my parents in Stafford.

We never really knew if anyone was buying Nexus 21 records, but the PAs and TV gig had us feeling that we were getting somewhere. Hacienda DJ Mike Pickering had sent back some more positive DJ reaction reports on our stuff and although we got the odd bad review –

'Detroit techno is done and finished' – I was astonished by the positivity we received. It was nice seeing press as well as adverts for our releases and appearances in the various charts. A relatively big moment for me personally was seeing that Teletext had given *Self Hypnosis* a great review. 'We've made it!' I recall scrolling through all these pages before chancing upon it. 'I'm on Teletext!'

***

We played these nine tracks we'd done at Blue Chip – during its last few days – to Neil Rushton and Dave Barker and they really liked them. 'They sound a bit like Nexus 21, but there are more influences,' Neil explained. We had hip house in there as well as Belgian techno and the tracks soaked up lots of styles right across club culture. 'We like it, but we don't want to call it Nexus 21,' Neil added. 'We want Nexus 21 to remain Detroit techno. Can you think of a new name?' Chris and I had a brief meeting about a possible name for this side project. When Chris was at school he had been in a rock band called Alienate and we both quite liked that. So Alienate it was. These decisions were often very quick as we were so busy. We forgot about Alienate for a bit and carried on mixing.

I remember getting sent a tape at Network from some guy called Geoff Hibbert (from Leicester) early 1990 and I was well worried. It was ace! Every week, Neil Macey would vent: 'Fucking hell! It's brilliant!' I was a little scared that this guy would usurp us. Anyway, Chris and I were asked to spend some studio time with Geoff to help get his material polished and so off we went to a Nottingham studio. Geoff's original track was *A Place Called Bliss* by Cyclone, and it was only two-and-a-half minutes long, as that was all the sample time he had on his home keyboard. It was a great two and a half minutes though.

So, we got as far as Geoff had got with the demo and he said, 'That's it! That's all the ideas I have!' It turned out that he'd poured everything into those two and a half minutes and so we stretched it out a bit and finished it off for him and did the B-side as a dub version. It appeared on a Network side label called One After D (get it?). Geoff went on to do the massive old-skool classic *Break of Dawn* by Rhythm On The Loose. He's a good mate, Geoff, and he was one of the first acts we helped along in those early days. So, as well as

Nexus 21 and the work we did with other acts, we now had an official side project too: Alienate.

Neil Rushton *"We got them in the studio and a couple of months later Mark and Chris turned up with what became known as the eight-track 12" and we pressed maybe 10,000 copies of it. It was really good, but it wasn't Nexus 21. This was something quite different. I don't know if it was a little naive or whatever, but we saw Nexus 21 and the new material as two distinct things, and so we agreed that the sampler would be the first release of a new band called Altern 8. I liked the name Altern 8 because it summed up the irreverent, non-conforming attitude of the songs, which were where my heart was at the time. I remember them coming in with the eight tracks and there was some mention of Alienate. I said no, I prefer Altern 8."*

It was decided that we would do an 'eight-tracker' and instead of a DJ promo, Network would press it up and start selling. As it would retail at the same price as a normal 12" – with normally only one or two tracks on it, we thought that eight tracks for the same price represented great value for money. DJs would buy it straight away and there were already examples of these multi-trackers coming in from the States by the likes of Frankie Bones, Tommy Musto and Lenny Dee. Frankie Bones and Lenny Dee had released a multi-track 12" called *Looney Tunes* and it was excellent DJ fodder. So a couple of weeks later, moments after a meeting at Network, this box turned up. We opened the parcel and lifted out the first release by Alienate. The sleeves were orange and silver, which were generic Network designs. There was a sticker at the top that said 'Altern 8'. We were like, 'That's not what we're called.'
- 'It's a little late now,' Neil explained, 'because the record has been pressed. So you're stuck with it!'

So we had eight tracks on an EP by a band with an '8' in its name, but that wasn't borne from a conscious decision. It wasn't a thing we had decided upon at all. This was the *Overload EP* and Network expected it to do well.

This was a strange time really, as Nexus 21 was our primary concern and Altern 8 was just an experiment. Altern 8, was at that stage, a way of selling some older material. We would go to clubs in Birmingham in late 1990 and would hear Altern 8 and Nexus 21 tunes played back to back; no one realising that the same people were behind them. The *Overload EP* was duly released and charted at number 99. We'd cracked the Top 100.

Neil Macey. *"Around 1989/90 Mark was continuing to go out clubbing and it was at this time he heard the new hybrid rave sound developing; more breakbeaty, stabby, more aggressive. More English. This new sound was an amalgam of styles, rather than straight Chicago, New York or Detroit. Then Mark came in with this record he'd done which was the white label promo of Overload, his answer to this new emerging scene. As Self Hypnosis hadn't sold to everyone's expectations, Overload actually ended up helping Network out of a cashflow crisis."*

So, there I was living at home in Gnosall, with my parents and very little money. But we were learning so much at Network, with lots of remixing work and meetings. Then came the live shows, which started putting much-needed cash into our pockets.

The PAs were getting better too, but we were still fairly green. At Shelley's (in Stoke), March 1991, we were asked if we wanted a mic set-up by MC Man Parris who had played with us at Brixton. Chris said yes. Now, I hadn't got the voice and certainly didn't have the bottle to MC, but was frankly quite surprised that Chris wanted to step up. During the PA Chris kept motioning to the soundman to turn the microphone up, so he was turning all these mics up and it was causing massive amounts of feedback. So all this noise was going off and Chris was shouting, 'Nothing's coming out!' Halfway through the PA he realised he'd switched the mic off, so he turned it on and loads of feedback blasted out. They eventually turned the levels down, though and Chris was left standing there, staring at this mic like he's going to say something. For ages. And you're willing him to say something, and then he finally goes, 'Woaaaahhh!' After all that? That was it? No more MCing for the rest of the PA.

Another little addition to the live production was a black banner Dad had painted 'Nexus 21' on to. It was a massive piece of canvas, painted black, and as Dad was a brilliant signwriter, he painted our logo 'free hand' on to the backboard. It looked professional having some branding behind us and took some of the attention away from us.

In a way, my differences with Chris worked quite well, but it was odd. I loved everything connected to dance music and yet my partner had no interest in it at all. A typical PA would see me get there early to set it all up, whilst Chris was sat backstage. We would do the PA, then get changed and he was off, whereas I couldn't wait to get onto the dancefloor. I was so influenced by all the clubs and they were the reason I started the whole thing off. But on the plus side, Chris wasn't trying to sound like a certain band or style and that gave us an original edge when we worked in the studio.

Chris wasn't a mate, but we'd have a laugh. Our relationship didn't start off strained, but we did start to annoy each other a bit. For example, I would often pick Chris up on the way to meetings, and yet get to his house to find he was still asleep. I'd be banging on the doors, shouting: 'Get up! We have a meeting at Network!' He just seemed to operate in a completely different way to me. We wouldn't go out for a drink or anything after work and had little in common. The smoking was a real source of tension between us, especially if we were in the Transit van on our way to a gig. I remember getting sick at Raindance in London and it was only the adrenaline of playing live that got rid of the pain, but once we were offstage, it all came back. Boom!

Raindance was disastrous for us. One of the tents got blown down and the set started badly. The rave was in the middle of some housing estate in London. I gave the DAT to the sound engineer and all he had to do was press 'play', but somehow he'd managed to pull the tab across and accidentally recorded over the first track. There were always cock-ups live. When we played Sudely Castle some months before, the promoter demanded that we do *Self Hypnosis*. 'I really want you to play that track. I will get the DJ before you to play it and then you can come on,' he said. It was Daz Willot who was on before us and he had the promo of the *Bio Rhythms* album, but the labels were stickered to the wrong sides, and so instead of *Self Hypnosis* he mistakenly played this party killer of a tune by Paris Grey, which was really slow and moody. A terrible way to kick off a gig.

You always had people coming up on stage with requests as well. We played Great Yarmouth in 1990 at this massive venue and while we were on stage – a live PA with no MC – this lad climbed up onstage, walked right up to me and asked if I had any Public Enemy. I was trying to explain that I wasn't DJing. 'This is a gig!' We hadn't realised quite how spannered people were getting out there. There I was trying to have a chat with him during a show.

I remember this geezer at Shelley's with long curly hair who climbed up onstage one time and I had no idea he was off his nut. He started staggering about and messing a bit with my 808. I was like, 'Can you not do that?'

- 'Why, what are you going to do about it?'
- 'C'mon, it's expensive kit.'
- 'Do you know who I am?'
- 'No…'
- 'Ever heard of The Doors?'
- 'Yes.'
- 'Well, I'm Jim Morrison.'

Even though I'd met Derrick May in Detroit I still didn't have the bottle to say hello when we shared the bill at Quadrant Park, Bootle. Derrick had Jay Denham with him and it wasn't exactly a rammed night. Very quiet. Chris brought the video camera with him to that too, but surprise, surprise: the battery died after filming us driving around Bootle. Neil Rushton wasn't there, like he was in Detroit, to bridge the gap between us and the techno kings and so I just kept looking over at Derrick and Jay, hoping to catch their gaze.

Shelley's, Dead Fish And Only For The Headstrong

8 Of The Best: Bleepy Techno

1. Q – *Mental Cube*
2. Forgemasters – *Track With No Name*
3. Ital Rockers – *Ital's Anthem*
4. LFO – *LFO*
5. Rhythmatic – *Take Me Back*
6. Nightmares On Wax – *Dexterous*
7. Ability II – *Pressure (Dub)*
8. Project One – *A Few Dollars More*

1991 saw the dance scene really start to split. Hardcore was very different to house and garage. The term hardcore was first used to describe those who stayed until the end of the night rather than the music itself, but soon it applied to the faster, harder-edged tunes. Back in 1988 the UK was into New York acid house, garage and deep house, but by 1989 Chicago, Detroit and the European influence started spreading. 1990 saw lots of different styles getting played out: London's Soul II Soul, Frankie Bones from New York, Italian piano and techno from Detroit and Belgium.

The music sped up a lot in 1990, often with frenetic breakbeats on top. I remember hardcore dancing on the spot to 808 State's *Cubik*.

'This is savage!' That track came at you like a chainsaw. You could see the split in clubland perfectly in Stoke. Freetown was a well-dressed club that played Kym Sims, Crystal Waters and the slower rave stuff, whilst Shelley's would go for the frantic stuff, or hardcore as it was now known. Many of my generation look back on 1988 with a great fondness as everything was getting played, everywhere. By 1991, you were being forced to choose from a scene that often wasn't static for longer than a weekend.

Neil Macey *"Musically, things were changing so quickly back then. This new UK sound – that developed into hardcore and jungle – was very aggressive. Late '90/'91 raves could be rather unpleasant places with harsh music preferred. I was still getting booked as a DJ, even though I played the housier stuff, as there just weren't that many DJs around.*
I got wrongly programmed one night at Starlight, which was run by a gang of Birmingham City lads. I found myself sandwiched between Simon Bassline Smith and Micky Finn, both of whom were playing at a pace; just very fast records I hadn't heard before. 'What the fuck am I going to do? Is there anything I can blend from this?' I was still playing Detroit and New York, but this crowd wanted mean and moody music. I decided to go the opposite way. I had just received a promo for Orbital's Belfast and thought 'Fuck it, I'll start with this!' Simon Bassline Smith finished and I left a bit of silence and kicked off with Belfast and its syncopated arpeggio melody. There was uproar to begin with, but then there was this massive lift out of the aggressive onslaught that had no real breakdowns to speak of. Then Micky Finn placed himself just in front of the decks, stepped back and knocked the record, causing the needle to slide. So I gathered myself together, put the needle back and started again. It went down like a lead balloon, though. Ha ha! It was not what these people wanted."

I started going to Shelley's in Stoke at the beginning of 1991 and it had a great atmosphere. Amnesia House from Coventry's The Eclipse had taken over the weekend residency at the former roller rink. Based in Longton, Stoke, Shelley's attracted many from Manchester (fleeing gang violence) as well as Birmingham, both of which were both only an hour or so away. Shelley's was very busy and would go on to break Sasha who DJed there on a Friday night, as well as Dave Seaman and Carl Cox. Amnesia House were the most successful in getting Shelley's up and running after a few false starts from previous promoters, and their nights at The Eclipse in Coventry were legendary. We would often go to The Eclipse at weekends.

The Eclipse was an old bingo hall with more than one floor and it was a fantastic venue, very much like Shelley's. I took Jon McDonald, Paul and Karen there when we got booked to play as Nexus 21. I had expanded the PA by then. I had a sampler that logged all the vocals that were triggered by this little Yamaha drum machine. So, I had an 808 and a 909 with drum machines triggering the samples. Chris had the SQ80 and a Casio CZ1000 keyboard and so we had so many more sounds at our disposal. Because clubs were so hot, we started lugging a big box of Mr Freeze ice pops about as well, so we could throw them out to the audience. It was a little gimmick, but the audience loved it. I loved sucking on an ice pop while dancing.

Nexus 21 joined the Warp/Network UK tour at the start of '91 on the same bill as LFO, Nightmares On Wax and Rhythmatic, going up and down the country from London to Scotland. We were playing 100% live at this point, but we soon saw the error of our ways, as everyone else on that tour was using DAT. You plug in a keyboard, drop some noises in over the top of the DAT and that way your songs sounded like the records. Meeting other bands can be great for picking up tips etc. 'Ah, they're using that sampler… or this drum machine.' We made up a few tracks and tried *Together* and *Self Hypnosis,* but somehow they just didn't sound like the records.

We had a real laugh on that tour. We were down to do two London dates at Subterranea, but a food fight between Nightmares On Wax and LFO had upset the promoter; so much so, they cancelled the second night. It was a moody crowd, which was odd. Everyone just stood there, arms folded, looking at the stage. 'Go on then, impress us!' There was a real north/south divide going on back then. Actually it was more of a London/everywhere else divide.

The tour manager was having real problems with the money side of things and some of the cheques were bouncing. We'd lost one of the dates because of the food fight as well. The manager also had problems driving the minibus. When she picked us up in Stafford, having already picked up the other lads in Leeds, she pulled up on to the motorway by driving up the rumble strips. The thing is, she had no intention of leaving the strips and the noise was deafening. But she just carried on. And on. I told her that she was driving along the rumble strip and she turned and thanked me. 'I wondered what that noise was!' I stared out of the window, more than a little worried. 'She's driving us all the way to Scotland!'

There was a massive fish tank built into the wall of the Vertigo, Glasgow, with some absolutely massive creatures in it. Big as dinner plates. We all did our sound checks and bearing mind the deep sub bass of LFO at the time, it was perhaps no surprise that every single fish in that tank snuffed it. They often joke that there's a note or a musical 'bottom end' that will cause you to fill your trousers, but there's clearly a bass level so low that it kills fish. The vibration was horrendous. Poor sods.

Gez Varley (LFO) *"Growing up in Leeds in the eighties was a great time for music and culture; breakdancing and hip hop. Then we all slowly got into house music and techno around '86-'88 (Nightmares On Wax, Ital Rockers, Unique 3 and Juno). Around 1988, we started going clubbing in Sheffield as our mate DJ Martin (from the original LFO line-up) was playing out there. So about five carloads of us would go over and hang out with people like Winston Hazel at Cuba. Then LFO got signed to Warp and we were hitting the road ourselves.*

Our first ever tour featured Nexus 21. We didn't quite know what to expect from the experience really, which was totally hit and miss from us. Ha ha. But we had a really good laugh though and it was an amazing learning curve.

The second night at London's Subterranea (Notting Hill) got cancelled after an argument with one of the guys working there about the food. We ended up throwing pizza at him, which was awesome! Loads of stuff kicked off all the time, thinking back. We also had a huge food fight on the tour bus and the driver refused to take us until we cleaned it all up.

Mark was a lovely guy, but we didn't know him so well back then, although we knew and loved his music. But our paths were to cross quite a lot after that."

The first time I heard *LFO* by LFO was with Neil Macey from Network. Neil got on well with the Warp lot and he had a promo copy of the single. He was still DJing at No.7s at the time, when he shouted 'Archie! Have I got a track here! You just wait till you hear the bass!' There was that bit where the normal bass came in and I was like, 'Yeah, that's heavy, but nothing to lose sleep over.' And then the real sub bass came on. No.7s was a chintzy wine bar and full of little mirrored tiles and a racking system with glass shelves that stored all the wine glasses. So when that bass came on, the glass shelves all started rattling and the glasses started dropping off the bar. It was like an earthquake. The bar manager was screaming at Neil 'Make it stop!' As soon as the bass dropped we realised there were another seven minutes to go and so the bar staff were grabbing all the glasses they could to get them somewhere safe. What a track.

Neil Macey. *"Network were very aware of Warp and were fairly jealous that they had their own sound: that unique, bass heavy, very electronic thing. So Neil Rushton had the bright idea of doing a spoof. Neil was a real talent at coming up with pranks. Neil knew Mark Gamble from Rhythmatic and played him a load of records and asked him to 'do something like this'. Take Me Back came out as a promo 10" on 0742 Records, which was the dialling code for Sheffield back then. Rob and Steve who ran Warp's record shops were completely confused. 'What the fuck is this?!' That record sent everyone buzzing in Sheffield. 'Who did it? It must be someone from Sheffield!' It was us."*

My mate Jon McDonald, from the breakdance days, was at university in Sheffield and he was raving about this pirate radio station up there; so much so, he started sending me tapes. SCR (Sheffield Community Radio) was wicked and we didn't have anything like that around Stafford at all, so I was eager to hear these shows. These tapes were so exciting and the vibe was infectious. My favourite DJs by far were Astrix And Space and they played some amazing tunes. It was odd because you'd get all this crazy hardcore techno and sub bass and then on the hour, every hour, there were adverts for hairdressers and local Caribbean restaurants, which I guess were funding the station.

Astrix was a guy called Chris Duckenfield and Space was Richard Benson. This pair sounded like they were having a real laugh on these tapes. There was one intro, which led into *Dance Tones* by Hypersonic (an early Danny Donnelly track) where Chris said, 'Yeah, check this next track out, you've got Astrix And Space. Watch your bass bins, I'm tellin' ya!' Then on came the sub bass. It was so brilliant I sampled it off the cassette and saved it to disc. I had to do something with it.

We were asked to do a remix back at Blue Chip Studios in March 1991 with 23-stone engineer Mike Bell or 'The Fat Controller'. We were booked from 2pm-2am and by the time we finished our work we still had four precious hours left and so we thought we'd try some new stuff out. I really liked the hardcore genius of *Pure* by G.T.O. and it had these mad crowd noises at the beginning. *Pure* was a big tune that drew on loads of different influences. The way I saw it was: people like acid and people like breakbeats and sub bass from Sheffield, so why don't we put all the ingredients together? So that's what we did. We then added the Astrix And Space intro too. The track was to be called *Infiltrate 202* which was to lead the forthcoming *Vertigo EP*.

We used a crowd sample from a Depeche Mode live CD, but it wasn't a rave audience and so we got some air horns and went into the mic room and blasted them off as samples. We made some horns a bit quiet and others a lot louder, to make them sound like they were recorded in a big stadium; yes, the whole crowd thing was made up. There was a journalist for *Record Mirror* called James Hamilton and he had a unique style to his reviews and we got him to review a record down the telephone, which we sampled and added to the end of the track. At the end of *Infiltrate 202* it says: 'Instantly classic rave stomper made in Stafford. This track has enough power to destroy the most expensive washing machines.' We then recorded *Infiltrate 202* on the Wednesday night.

The following Saturday we were booked as Nexus 21 for Shelley's and we were hanging around with our girlfriends, wearing some natty black long-sleeve tees with the Nexus 21 logo on, that someone had made for us. There I was, dancing away to the tunes when this lad called Mark Butler from Sheffield came up. 'You with Nexus 21? My mates love your stuff! Hey, Darren, stay there, don't go anywhere and I'll go get them.' I said to Karen, 'Darren?! We've got a right one here.' I didn't think he'd come back, but true to his word he returned with these two lads.

'Nexus 21, meet these two top DJs from Sheffield. They're called Astrix And Space!' I was gobsmacked. I was like, 'Oh my God! I just sampled you on to a tune four days ago. That's the spookiest thing ever! By the way, I'm not called Darren.'

I started hanging around with the Sheffield lot quite a bit. I would go up on a Wednesday and stay at Benson's flat. Mark Butler was often there with various mates and girlfriends. There was also a lad there called

Michael 'Booty' Boot who took supplies up to Astrix And Space while they were on air. 'Where's Booty with the booty?' they'd ask. Booty was often at Shelley's dancing next to Stevie P 'The Atmosphere Controller'; a real Shelley's regular who danced on the back of a chair. True to his name, Booty once travelled to The Eclipse from Sheffield... in a car boot.

I eventually asked Benson if he fancied MCing for Nexus 21 and he said yes. At this point Nexus 21 was still the main focus really. Jon McDonald from Stafford also agreed to dance for us, as did a guy called Bob Head, who actually had long curly hair. It felt good to have more of a show to put on when playing live. Having this lot doing their stuff added so much to the live experience.

Jon McDonald *"I met these two DJs Astrix And Space when I went to Sheffield. They had a show on Sheffield Community Radio that I used to tape for Mark because there was bugger all in Stafford. SCR kept Mark in touch with all the latest tunes. Astrix And Space were very excited when Mark sampled them for Infiltrate 202."*

Richard Benson (Astrix And Space, RAC) *"Chris (Duckenfield) and I were working on a pirate Caribbean radio station called Sheffield Community Radio and we were well aware of Mark from his Nexus 21 work on Blue Chip. We thought they were big things as far as British techno was concerned and we played them a lot on SCR.*

I remember going to Shelley's in March 1991 and I was a bit worse for wear, to be honest. Then this mate of mine said that Nexus 21 were standing over by the bar and that we should go and meet them. Chris and I were in awe of them and yet there they were, stood right next to us. Mark was a straight head and hadn't partaken in anything and was very polite. 'I'm Mark Archer from Nexus 21; someone said you'd like a chat?' I had instant respect for him. Anyway, we were chatting by the dancefloor and it was great getting caught up in the moment. Then Mark turned round and said, 'Have you heard of these two pirate DJs from Sheffield called Astrix And Space?' I stood there wondering if this was a wind-up.

- *'Say that again?'*
- *'My mate is at uni in Sheffield and he's sending me these tapes from these guys called Astrix And Space and in fact I love them so much I've just sampled a bit of their show on a new project I'm doing.'*

I was looking directly at him thinking, 'Holy fuck, this is unreal!' So I said to him, 'I do know Astrix And Space, mate. I'm one of them!' We didn't remember half the things we said on air, never mind a quote, cos we'd always take a couple of acid tabs before the show and so we couldn't remember Chris's line about the bass-bins. But it was clear that this line had affected Mark as he was telling us the release date for this track due out on Network that included the line. 'C'mon, give over!' It didn't feel real. How much of a coincidence can that be? So we exchanged contact details and agreed to keep in touch."

808, Infiltrate And Altern 8

808 State want us to play Brixton with them. 808 State! Brixton Academy! And us!

Nexus 21 – complete with dancers and MC – hit the Brixton Academy in April 1991 as guests of 808 State. Now 808 State were the big dogs at that time, with a career that had already provided some legendary moments in dance music history. A credible act with chart success too, Graham Massey and the boys were in demand and we were bowled over when we were asked to join N-Joi as support to the Madchester legends. The Brixton Academy was an enormous venue with a capacity a smidge under 5,000. These would not be festival ravers, happy to dance to anything or clubbers completely unaware that you're on stage. Brixton would house 5,000 people who had paid to see a show.

MC Tunes was performing with 808 at this time, after a few chart hits with them, and he had a real bad-boy reputation. In fact, the fuckwit smashed his own dressing room up that evening after having a fight with *himself*. We were next door and heard Tunes and all his hangers-on shouting and knocking stuff over. We were a little intimidated by all this uproar and when Chris came out of the dressing room with his cheekbone bright red and swollen we thought Tunes had had a swipe at him, too. Turned out that the telephones in all the dressing rooms were high up on the walls and one had come loose and fallen straight onto Chris's cheek. Neil Rushton was there that night and, never one to miss an opportunity for a story, he decided to tell the press that MC Tunes had smacked Chris one. 'Tunes just chinned Chris!'

We went on after 808 State had done their thing, which was an amazing performance. They had big keyboard risers, loads of lasers and a dancer who held a mirror ball that shot the lights back off it as it spun around. It was a proper show. N-Joi were good as well and told us that they were influenced by us, so that was nice to hear as they were big news at the time. As we were booked at the last minute we didn't feature on any of the posters, which was a shame, but it was a top gig and a real honour. Nexus 21 weren't big at all and Altern 8's *Infiltrate 202* had just come out on promo.

There was a Manchester DJ at Brixton called Nipper and we gave him a copy of *Infiltrate*. There I am up on the balcony with Darren, Andy and Graham from 808 State, chatting away, when our promo comes on – complete with keyboard pads from 808 State's *Pacific State*! It got to that bit and I suddenly thought, 'Oh shit!' and they just looked at me. 'I'm sooo sorry!'

'No no, that's cool.' No suing was mentioned. In fact, they loved it and came to see our set.

Daz Partington (808 State, Spinmasters) *"Without a shadow of a doubt the Spinmasters were playing Nexus 21 out as we were well aware of that Chicago/Detroit thing that had come through electro. We just instantly connected with it. We could basically hear ourselves in Nexus 21. We had the same upbringing and were drawn from the same cloth, musically. Electro, New York hip-hop; you can hear all that in Nexus 21 as well as British hip hop and electro of the eighties and Chicago house and Detroit techno. They took the same wonderful path we took as the Spinmasters.*

Nexus 21 was an amazing apprenticeship and Mark cut his teeth there. Messing around with machines is what this kid was born to do and he got a lot of respect from our peers in America. He might have been in awe of the pioneers from New York, Chicago and Detroit: the Marshall Jeffersons, Frankie Bones and the Derrick Mays, but Mark was gifted with the same ears. Mark was still a punter on the dancefloor. He would have a boogie even when he was DJing later that night.

We supported him back on Sunset radio, the black urban community station, and would play the whole back catalogue of Network. It's nice to be able to turn around to people and say, 'You're just like us.' They dug what we were doing and vice versa. We then talked about doing a US tour together, but it didn't happen, although Nexus 21 did play Brixton with us.

Brixton was a combination of the right music, the right people, the right time. It was a perfect night. Nexus 21 were not a support; they were a natural fit with what we were trying to do. That was the quality of Nexus 21. It wasn't slapdash, 'We're trying to emulate house.' It had its own sound. It was well crafted, intelligent house that had that stamp of authority. Class.

We were getting a lot of supports thrown at us, but we sorted that out ourselves. We had people with the finance of major labels wanting to get in on it, but we handled who was going to be on that bill, by inviting people we respected. We had Moby touring with us, before he blew up, and people like Darren Emerson and that was important to us. We had that platform. There's no documentation of that gig, which is a shame as it was a top night.

Not many people could have gotten away with sampling our stuff. Infiltrate 202 had the Pacific sample on it and we were absolutely fine when we heard it. Mark treated it with a lot of respect and took it on with that in mind and he knew we would listen to it. We respected him for that. We've had people absolutely annihilate our stuff over the years. A lot of people won't even touch our work, but we trusted Mark with our kids. You don't let just anybody babysit your children, do you? I have a lot of respect there.

I know DJs in Japan who play Mark's stuff. Your music being spun by some Japanese kid in a dingy Osaka club is amazing, isn't it? Quality always prevails. Mark has cemented his position in the 'house nation', our family, and is a fully paid-up member, constantly bringing out amazing stuff. He set a precedent with all this quality from the off. Mark could read where the scene was going. We could see things happening in the press and thought 'the lad is smashing it!' It was refreshing to hear feedback from mates who had seen them. I knew he was going to be around for a long time."

We had two little keyboards in the middle of this enormous stage, with no risers. Dancer Jon McDonald had borrowed Chris's winter coat and got a pair of glasses with torches attached to either side. He was doing this rave dance, swatting flies, and didn't want anyone to see his face as he felt so embarrassed. Benson absolutely smashed it too. We went down so well. It was one of the biggest gigs at that time and we were really nervous beforehand.

Jon McDonald *"The first time I danced for Mark was at Brixton Academy as that was the only way I could blag myself in. So I found this coat and some weird glasses with laser eyes and suddenly I was a dancer, on stage at Brixton Academy. It was mad.*

I had no stage presence because I wasn't a great dancer or anything close. Nexus 21 played live which was a STUPID IDEA, considering that everyone was using synths, decks and DAT. Ha ha. We were all in love with N-Joi's singer Saffron who went on to front Republica and we kept gawping at her although she totally blanked us.

Brixton was the first real, proper venue I played and it was amazing. The dancefloor at Brixton sloped and was massive, as was the stage. I was incredibly hot out there as I was wearing this bloody Puffa jacket. I'm amazed I didn't pass out from the heat. I never really had time to get nervous, though, as I didn't know I was going to be dancing until 10 minutes before. It's interesting because you can't really see anyone in a crowd; you can only really see the first ten rows.

It was a steep learning curve. I realised that, as a dancer, you have to overcompensate your moves, so you can't just walk offstage, you have to bounce away. It doesn't look good if you shuffle like an old man, so you have to accentuate every move you make. What a night, though!"

***

June 1991 Nexus were booked to play this big outdoor gig called Perception, at Long Marston Airfield. We were on the same bill as Rhythm Section, who came wandering over before the show. I was totally starstruck. 'God, one of them doesn't half look like Magnum!' said one of the lads. It was really funny as one of Rhythm Section had this massive moustache and a white vest. Magnum was spot on. Even though the dance scene was so associated with drugs I was still so oblivious to it all. Chris seemed to like the odd smoke, but he never seemed to do anything harder. But working with Benson opened my eyes a little.

Security wouldn't allow Benson on to the stage at Perception as they thought he was a spangled raver. He was babbling away to security and we had to go over and sort him out. As soon as the gig finished we packed the stuff away in the red Vauxhall Cavalier – I'd got rid of the Mini and got an estate to act as our tour bus – and Butler, Benson and Bob Head were all sat in the back, chatting away. Just as we're about to leave, Benson said, 'I'll leave this for you.' Benson then placed something on the car seat.

- 'What's that?'
- 'It's half a pill.'

There was no way I was going to take it. Who knows, my whole career could have been different if I had, but Benson just couldn't understand it. People still find it hard to believe, but I just wasn't willing to go down that road. Benson was baffled. 'You being a musician, how do you make these records, without doing stuff? When you're off your nut, there's always a little bit of a record that you tag on to and that becomes *your bit*, and it's amplified when you're off your nut. It could be a cowbell, or a hi-hat or a little keyboard noise. All your tunes have got them bits in, Mark and yet you don't do drugs. How do you know to put them in?' I didn't know what to say as I didn't know the answer myself.

I was so innocent in these things. I remember a rather strange aroma at one club and had no idea what it was. It was around the time of 8-ball suede leather jackets and I nudged Neil Macey and pointed to this raver who was sweating his balls off in this coat. 'He stinks!'

- 'That's poppers!' said Neil, 'Not BO!'

Put it this way, I thought people pulling faces while dancing was simply a reaction to the music or 'putting your bass face on'. No one believes me but honestly, I was that naive. If there was a rave going on, I'd be there from 9pm till 6am, having had nothing stronger than a bottle of water. I was there for the music.

Richard Benson *"My recollection of Perception at Long Marston Airfield is a bit hazy. It was a massive super rave and security wouldn't let me onstage because they thought I was just a raver. I was heavily into using drugs at the time, which became a distraction to what I was supposed to be doing, really. I was just walking around trying to split an E with my mate when I was meant to be on stage. Ha ha! We did some mad Nexus gigs. There was this underground tunnel venue in Bath and it was very dark. Nexus 21 went down a storm there and I looked over at Mark doing his thing and just felt this great vibe. Afterwards, this bloke came up and asked, 'Are you Nexus 21? You are amazing! Mark's amazing! I wondered if you would kiss my girlfriend?' He then put this rosary thing round my neck and started stroking my neck. Then he did it again and urged me to get off with his missus. Mark was just shaking his head. Those gigs were really good fun."*

We had started recording a new Nexus 21 album to follow up *The Rhythm of Life* and it was a bit bleepy, klonky with a dollop of sub bass. Two tracks had break beats and rave stabs, but we had problems with licences for the vocal samples and decided to shelve it and the album never came out. But as the workload for Altern 8 started to increase we found it hard to keep both projects bubbling anyway.

Chemical Warfare, Men In Masks And Radio 1

I wasn't sure if I was losing my mind. I sat and looked at the outfit laid out on the bedroom floor and wondered what I'd done. Would people buy into this? What must Gene Simmons have thought when he first saw that KISS make-up? I put the costume on and looked in the mirror. Well, at least they won't see my receding hair and unlike the drummer of KISS, I wasn't a fucking cat…

We got a call for another gig at The Eclipse in Coventry that July, but this time it wasn't for Nexus 21. They wanted Altern 8. It was quite a coup to get a booking off the back off a solitary single and a promo. DJs like Grooverider had given *Infiltrate 202* a lot of love and clearly this had built up some interest in the new project. The only problem was that I was a little worried that anyone who had attended the Nexus 21 gig at that very same venue might be miffed to see the same two guys doing something else, but under a different name: 'Oh, it's them again!' I'm not sure if I was right to be so concerned, but I was, so I started to cook up something new for what I assumed would be a one-off gig.

I talked to my brother Paul about the situation and he said he might have the answer. Paul was working for the RAF at that time and was able to 'borrow' all sorts of gear and equipment. 'I've got a couple of these NBC suits,' he said. NBC suits protected the wearer during nuclear, biological and chemical attacks and had drawstring hoods. The green suits were meant to be worn with respirators and whatnot and they looked really distinctive. The dance scene had just started getting a little darker and more industrial and druggy and these suits somehow tapped into that. The NBCs came vacuum-packed and were thick and heavy. I liked the look of them and so spent an entire night cutting the charcoal lining out of these costumes as we'd have died on stage with that kind of protection. I cut my fingers to ribbons and on some occasions the suits themselves, but after a few tweaks here and there, they were perfect. The only thing was that when you pulled the toggles on the hood you looked like a trainspotter and so to finish the whole look off, we added the DIY mask. I was really into the whole UV thing and had covered many T-shirts and hoodies with luminous paint for trips to Frenzy. So I bought another tin and covered the masks with fluorescent yellow.

The NBC suits had chest pockets and I wrote Altern 8 onto an area I had already Tippex-ed white. I then drew around it in black and filled it in with a highlighter pen. It stayed like that for a while until we had to finally wash them and the logos cracked and crumbled.

We showed Network the idea for the new look and they were cool with it. It was wacky and brilliant. Techno was always being accused of being 'faceless techno bollocks' so here we were with our own little twist on it. That was the great thing about Network; everyone was up for whatever.

It was weird wearing the suits because people treated you so differently. We acted differently too. I suddenly felt less shy and embarrassed with this mask and suit on. It felt like protection. As a result, my onstage activity got much more lively and dynamic. The hood also covered my bald head. My granddad never had hair, nor did my uncles on my mum's side, who had very thin hair. Mum had very fine hair and so I was always very worried, 'Am I going to lose my hair, Mum?' Dad combed what he had right back. So at last I had a hood with which to cover my increasingly shiny skull.

Neil Rushton *"I think we had conversations about the masks and the chemical suits when they came into the office with this set-in-stone idea. 'This is what we're going to do.' The whole thing took off so quickly, with myself and press officer John McCready, that no one really questioned it. Ha ha!"*

We didn't know if The Eclipse gig would be our one and only appearance as Altern 8 and as the gig would require so much equipment to play these songs live, we decided to mime. We borrowed a quarter-inch tape machine from Dave Barker at Network and recorded *Infiltrate 202* and a couple of tracks from the *Overload EP*. The engineer at the Detroit studio had taught us how to splice tape and perform reverse edits, which came in handy. Reverse edits are where the beat goes backwards, so as soon as one track finished playing on the beat, it would go straight into the next. We demoed up a couple of little tracks just to play out with no intention of releasing them, one of which was a tune called *Say It Y'all*, which would reappear the following year under a different name. It had a basic breakbeat, bassline and stab with a vocal sample. We also had *Give It To Baby* and a demoed *Activ 8*. I did them all completely on my own and recorded them to this quarter-inch tape to play at the gig.

We got to The Eclipse before anyone else and set up the gear. The crew from Sheffield – Richard Benson, Mark Butler and Bob Head were there as well as Karen and Zoe. Benson's girlfriend turned up with her mate Carrie Barker and we asked her to mime the vocal for us, which she was fine with. Mark Butler would be dancing with Bob Head while Benson MC-ed. Ian from Delta Video filmed the entire set.

Richard Benson *"Just as Infiltrate 202 was coming out, Mark came up to Sheffield and spent some time with us and we struck up a real friendship. It was quite surreal. I was just 20 and caught up in the whole scene at the time. Things started to explode a little bit. 'How do you feel about doing the Infiltrate video at The Eclipse as part of Altern 8?' asked Mark. 'You can MC for a bit and bring some kids with you.' My flatmate at the time, Carrie Barker, ended up miming the vocals on the video. Mark had a soft spot for her I think. I wasn't very good at MCing really. I just swore a lot, rather than busting bars."*

Chris and I sat in the dressing room before the show – in full costume – just staring at each other. 'We must be mad!' The idea was to film the PA and use it as the video for *Infiltrate 202* and so Ian was walking around with his camera. We took to the stage and noticed fractal images of Chris and me being bounced around a projection board. Bob Head's brother Little Bob Head was right down the front dancing away with our friends and partners. It felt as if something good was about to happen.

Chris and I started to change our stagecraft that night. I think that gig at The Eclipse was the first time we started pointing at the crowd and karate chopping the keyboards. Basically, if you saw someone going bonkers you would point in appreciation and nod your head. The crowd at The Eclipse didn't quite get the gist of what we were doing and thought that a 'point' meant 'join us onstage'. Before long we had a full-on stage invasion. It was a top night, though. When we played *Infiltrate 202*, the place went off! We were buzzing, trying to work our way through the crowd at the end. I bumped into Homeboy from A Homeboy, A Hippy And A Funki Dredd and he said 'Ay, nice one!' Such a rush.

We finally got to the dressing room after the show and we both just looked at each other. 'No way! That was brilliant!'

We packed the suits away not knowing if it was the last we'd see of them. We didn't bother washing the suits either, but they were definitely humming. We agreed that it would be a shame if the Men In Masks never reappeared as it felt as if we'd hit on something. We had such fun on stage and everything seemed to fall into place. However, there was no way of influencing more bookings back then as they came in through the label or an agency, and things moved very slowly.

Network wanted to release *Infiltrate 202* that July and so the footage from Ian at Delta represented the best solution to not having a proper promo video. We got all the footage together and spent four hours editing the £400 promo. I went round Ian's while he was making it, firing questions at him. I think I must have irritated him a bit. 'Can you do this? Can you do that?' As the video wasn't made in a proper studio, the soundtrack was really quiet and not quite 'broadcast standard'.

A Nexus 21 gig at Batley, West Yorkshire quickly followed a show in Sheffield, but the gig wasn't exactly what we'd hoped for. There were only about seven people at Batley and they were terrifying. The whole rave thing hadn't really caught on with this crowd. Benson's girlfriend got spat at and the whole night had this nasty vibe. But we were doing more and more gigs and so we didn't dwell on it too much as we were busy demo-ing more tracks to play out. The next night we played Bath followed by a night at The Eclipse on the Saturday. That was a heavy week.

Richard Benson *"Batley was an awful gig, like something off Shameless. We were all buzzing and up for the gig yet the venue was home to these proper Yorkshire rednecks. The women looked tougher than the men. You could feel that they were not ready for what we were about to do.*

One woman started spitting in my girlfriend's hair. It was shit. An awful mess. We ran out of there, worried for our safety. I doubt they could even spell 'peace, love and unity!'"

We played an Altern 8 PA at the Dome in Birmingham and Radio 1 DJ Mark Goodier told us that *Infiltrate 202 (Vertigo EP)* had a mid-week chart position of 44. Mark was really excited that it would go Top 40! That sent my pulse racing. Sometimes you feel that things are out of your control in music. You control so much of how things sound and whatnot and then there are those times when the tune is out there, finding its audience. It's quite a mad feeling, but a good one.

We did this Dome gig with Cookie Crew and I was a little starstruck as I had bought some of their records. Yet here they now were in the next dressing room. Right Said Fred were on too. Carrie couldn't mime the vocals at this gig and so we got Bonnie from Rotherham, who was a friend of Astrix And Space. I remember waiting in the corridor and Cookie Crew walked up to us, looked us up and down and said, 'Are you Right Said Fred?' We didn't say anything and just pointed at the two bald dudes in spandex.

Mark Goodier was very excited about *Infiltrate 202* and was the only person at the time who was playing our stuff on Radio 1, which must have been massive help when it came to the final chart positions. I had watched *Top of the Pops* avidly since the seventies and always listened to the Sunday rundown and so come the end of the week I was buzzing to get the news. When it hit, I felt winded. We were number 40! We had a Top 40 hit! It completely blew my head apart. 'I am in the Top 40!'

Mark Goodier (Radio 1) *"During the early nineties I was given the opportunity to try something original on weeknights for Radio 1. I wanted to get something new and exciting that was resonating with the audience that wasn't currently getting aired. Jeff Smith, who invented The Evening Session, and I wanted to play a bit of everything. We were not interested in being elitist and staying within one scene and so anything that was interesting was in. So we would play a Perfecto remix of U2 by Paul Oakenfold or Happy Mondays or whatever felt exciting at the time. What Altern 8 were doing was great, and so it was decided that bands like Altern 8 and Prodigy would feature on our shows too. The era was rave culture, Ibiza, Seattle – and the Sub Pop bands – and what was turning into Britpop.*

Radio 1 started doing live gigs on the radio called Sound City and we had Prodigy on the first ever line-up, live from Norwich, and they totally fitted into our world view of what music was. When I saw Prodigy I thought they were a rock band; Liam was doing his interpretation of rock music and when you look through that particular prism, you can see how they went on to be the band they are. Altern 8 were also great and theirs was a music that they kind of invented and what they did definitely resonated with the Radio 1 audience.

That time was good for playing records we loved and we really celebrated Altern 8 getting into the charts. It wasn't a reflected glow, just a great feeling to be able to put them in front of an audience and for that chemistry to work.

The Radio 1 Roadshow was one of the first events to put multiple acts on the road. We had SL2, Blur, loads of people and I definitely remember Altern 8 turning up. We would often mix the pop acts with the more underground. You might have Take That and their hordes of fans, as well as The Wonder Stuff, Jesus Jones or Altern 8."

Nexus 21 and Bizarre Inc had reached the Top 100 before, but in my mind even number 41 didn't count; you had to be in the rundown on the Sunday. *Top of the Pops* ended up playing our video, but as we expected, the music was really quiet – twice as low as any other tune. But who cared?! We were on *Top of the Pops*! We failed to finish the video in time for the *Chart Show*, who instead cobbled together some of C4's *Dancedaze* documentary, but at least we got a snippet played.

The following week was even more mental. We went up to 28. As well as support from radio, raves contributed greatly to record sales too. Millions of people went to raves each week and if only a small percentage bought your tune, you were in the charts. So gigs were just as vital for dance acts as they were for rock bands. I have always been in favour of the charts. I have never felt that you are selling out by getting into the Top 40, as long as your music isn't designed purely to chart. Popular is very different to commercial.

As the big stores like Woolworths stopped stocking it, *Infiltrate 202* soon bombed out of the charts. It seemed that those types of stores just weren't keen on this whole rave thing that they had no control over and were never that keen to supply the demand for it.

It was with Altern 8 that Network and its maverick press officer John McCready came into their own. The press releases and stunts were great and they knew that Chris and I would always play ball. We were always larking about at the Network offices. I would often pull up alongside the office windows in my car and we would wave to all the staff, before edging forward a bit and then back, for another wave. We would sometimes do this for half an hour or so. There was a great vibe at Network. Network's plan was to get us, and keep us, in the papers. Some of the stories they hatched were very funny. We designed our own disco biscuits for one magazine, but rather than being drugs they were actual snacks. We also told journalists that Chris and I met whilst working as deckchair attendants in Ibiza. There were loads of daft tales, all designed to keep those masks in the public arena.

John McCready *"Musically, Altern 8 were of their time. Looking back, it was a gag that got out of hand, really. In musical terms, both Mark and Chris were capable of so much more, but it was impossible to ignore the significant impact of their crackpot cartoon diversion.*

At the time, if you had a record in the chart then the tabloids were hungry for any old crap you could come up with. I don't think they were fooled by our nonsense for a minute; we were just making life easy for them by filling up gaping column inches.

I can still see Mark and Chris from the window of Stratford House, reversing backwards and forwards, fully togged up in the suits, seemingly having driven from Stafford in them."

8 Of The Best: Hardcore

1. SL2 – *DJs Take Control*
2. Liquid – *Sweet Harmony*
3. Bizarre Inc – *Playing With Knives*
4. The Family Foundation –*Express Yourself*
5. Acen – *Trip II The Moon (Part 2)*
6. Manix – *Feel Real Good*
7. Nebula II – *Flatliners*
8. Yolk – *Music 4 Da People (Original Mix)*

No Sleep Till Telford, Bye Bye Benson And Let's Get Activ!

Suddenly, one song blew us into the big time. We had no idea when we recorded it as to the effect it would have, but this one tune took us into a whole new dimension where Michael Jackson, Bono and Kurt Cobain lived. We didn't write songs with the sole intention of achieving 'success', but we weren't going to cry ourselves to sleep over it either. We strapped ourselves to the side of this rocket and closed our eyes...

Infiltrate 202 hitting the Top 40 caused rumours of a *Top of the Pops* appearance and this wasn't what Benson wanted at all, as he felt we were taking the tracks somewhere they shouldn't go. So that was the last time we hung around with Astrix And Space. Which was a shame. Benson and Chris were getting quite a lot of attention themselves and they felt that it could be damaging to follow us into the overground. I still love their mix of *Infiltrate 202 (The A&S vs Altern 8 Remix)* which they did before signing to Warp. They're good lads. So, needing an MC we approached Benson's friend Mark Butler and he was well up for it.

Altern 8 were getting lots of bookings since hitting the charts. I remember Telford Ice Rink as I was out dancing for ages before I realised my feet were freezing. 'Yeah we're in an ice rink!' Karen informed me.
-    'Oh yeah.'

It was weird how different raves boasted about more and more things on their flyers at this time. The Telford Ice Rink promised 'fresh fruit'; how many ravers were partaking of their kiwis and grapefruits I have no idea. This was around the time that flyers had changed too from hand-drawn, lo-fi leaflets into computer graphics of robot women and fractal images. Raves were becoming big business and if fresh fruit and pictures of bikini-clad robots got people in through the doors, then so be it.

I remember the MC at Telford kept asking people to close the fire exit to 'keep the sound in!' I think he was just cold. At one point, the MC asked if anyone had an inhaler and if so, to bring it to the stage. Quick! The gig carried on and a bit later the MC returned: 'Quiet! Keep the noise down. You all thought we had a casualty on stage, but don't worry! It was nothing but an epileptic hardcore raver!' Apparently the guy had a fit owing to all the flashing lights. When the crowd heard he was OK, the place went mental!

Jon McDonald *"When Altern 8 really kicked off we got more and more bookings. My nickname was J-Bass as I loved dancing to tracks with loads of heavy bass in. I'm a big fan of The Egyptian Lover and loved it when Mark sampled that.*

I was not that into the techno side of things so much, but it was OK. Mark was obsessed with the Detroit sound of Strings of Life and all that. Dancing for Nexus and Altern 8 was sometimes tricky. I would often realise halfway through a song that Mark had changed the track again and if I was expected to do the vocal bits, I never knew when to come in. Ha ha.

We had some amazing times though. It wasn't really about drugs and all that, it was about being in that minivan speeding about all over the country to these gigs. Dance events were semi legal around 1991. They had venues, but were often lacking licences. It could still be a little dodgy, to be honest. Someone attacked the alarm system with an axe at Starlight in Birmingham, so I'm guessing some corners were still being cut. We had a friend who raved with us and his uncle was in charge of the West Midlands 'ravepolice' and he would tip us off as to which raves would be raided that weekend, which was handy as you knew which parties to definitely avoid."

Network needed some new press pics to keep up with the demand for all things Altern 8 and I'm sure we did some round the back of Shelley's because we couldn't get in during the day. We took some in front of Shelley's and then round the back near some beer crates. Chris was sat in a shopping trolley or something. Peter Walsh was doing a lot of our photos at the time. We also went to Meeford Power Station, which is no longer there. There was no one working there at the time as I think the whole station was more or less closed down. We went there with Peter and Mike Bell the engineer and there's one shot of all the dials and I'm pointing at something or other. I don't know what the various levers and dials did, but I assume they represented all the different areas where the power went and one was called Stafford North, so I was pointing at that. There's another photo of us inside the lockers that had little porthole windows on them and there's one where you can just see my face.

We'd not long been with Network when we had photos done at this place called the Custard Factory, which is pretty famous in Birmingham now; there are loads of events going off there now and it's home to loads of really cool units and shops. Network ran their distribution from the Custard Factory for a while. We did the photoshoot when it was completely derelict. It was the old Bird's Custard Factory and there were piles of rubble in all the rooms and the ceilings were falling down. It was quite eerie in there with water dripping from pipes and pigeons flying around. There were dead birds all over the floors. We managed to catch some great images of corridors with sun streaming in through the windows, casting nice shadows on the floor. A music magazine ran the A-Z of techno and N stood for Nexus 21 and the picture they used was us on the window ledge about four-to-five feet up. It was quite precarious up there and we were hanging onto these pipes trying not to look like we were worried. One of the panes of glass between us and the outside had been smashed out and if you look carefully through the crack you can see the Rotunda; a really famous building in Birmingham. Photographers are great at spotting those angles you didn't often notice until later on.

Richard Benson *"Due to the success of Infiltrate 202, Altern 8 were due to appear on Top of the Pops and this marked my departure. Mark was clearly excited about Top of the Pops and called me up in an overwhelming wave of excitement. But I didn't personally share that sentiment although I was proper made up for them. I didn't want to be in the mainstream and I felt that Top of the Pops was taking them – and us – from where we needed to be. We said they could use some cardboard cut-outs of us, but that joke fell a bit flat. It wasn't a personal thing; it was purely us trusting our instincts.*

While Infiltrate 202 was going on Chris and I had quite a following in Sheffield; unbeknown to us. We had a cult show, which was a big thing I guess, but we didn't really know. This led to Warp records wanting to put us in the studio. Warp were setting up a new label called Nucleus and were looking for new artists; more underground, experimental. Warp wanted to sign us to the label to release EPs under the name RAC (Richard and Chris). Warp was a well cool label. We did a remix of Infiltrate 202 for Mark, though. Chris (Duckenfield) did the original 'Watch your bass bins!' but he really distanced himself from it at this point and so I said the new line on the remix and we were really pleased with it. I remember Grooverider and Carl Cox loved it.

Mark and I never really fell out and he replaced my MC work with a friend of mine called Mark Butler. Mark couldn't understand where I was at back then and I didn't know what was going on half the time. It was a crazy period and our relationship took the brunt of that and we ended up not speaking for nearly 20 years."

Autumn 1991 saw the new line-up get some really big gigs, which were great for getting our name out there. We played Amnesia at Donington Park in Derby to over 10,000 people and it was so weird looking out at all these thousands of people, dancing to music you'd made. It was an amazing privilege. It was the culmination of everything you'd done and why you were doing it. Moments like that made me realise that I was right not to take that job at the butcher's. We also had a new single coming out that we felt was some 'next level shit'. Although Benson had left due to the prospect of *Top of the Tops*, it never actually happened, although we hoped it wouldn't be our last chance.

Donington was a top night. Man Parris and Grooverider were on, as was Keith Suckling, who did a lot of the Midlands raves. Donington also had hygienic toilets, which was always a bonus. The only glitch was a delay from the soundman who took an eternity to press 'play' after the MC introduced us. Still, *Infiltrate* went down a storm.

I saw lots of faces backstage, but I still had this crippling shyness. I just didn't have the bottle to speak to them. I remember the first time I ever saw Slipmatt and just watched Mark the new MC go over and chat to him. 'No way, that's Slipmatt!'

***

It was around this time that Karen and I started to think about getting our own house. I had saved up a deposit of a couple of grand and Karen applied for the mortgage as she had a full-time job. It's weird looking back because we were so young – I was 23 – and I had nothing to compare our relationship to. I'd had such a bad time with the bullying and was so bad at reading signals from women I simply held on to this relationship as tightly as I could. Karen kept me in my place and I never considered any kind of life outside of what we had.

I recorded *Activ 8* and *Give it to Baby* on my own around the time of *Infiltrate 202*. I wanted *Activ 8* to be bigger than just a home demo, though and so added an acid line, stab noises and vocal bits. For a hook, I took some strings off *2 Hype* by Kid 'N Play (*The Dancin' Danny D House Mix*), which was huge in Stoke. I borrowed a copy from DJ Pete Bromley who worked in the Stoke branch of Lotus Records.

We had *Activ 8 (Come With Me)* demoed up and went to the studio to add this violin part. *Charley* was out by Prodigy and it had this little Public Information Film cat on it (Charley) and Neil was determined to have some little gimmick in our track that would make it stand out. As press officer John McCready was from Liverpool he would often refer to 'Billy Anfields' or ravers, who would say, 'Top one, nice one, get sorted!' Neil thought that this phrase would strike a chord with people and so we ended up recording his four-year-old daughter Clair saying the vocal. *Activ 8* started life as a different mix, with sampled noises from Belgian tunes. The stab noise is quite long on *Activ 8* and to give it energy we shortened the notes. At the end Clair said, 'John McCready in the house. Nice one!'

We were doing this photoshoot for the *Activ 8 (Come With Me)* sleeve and everything just seemed to come together. We had a proper typeface for the logo and some props: cardboard cut-outs of two big 8s – for the 1988 acid house thing – and pegged these numbers to a makeshift clothes line and stood in front of them. We were covered by a white parachute and got all tangled up in it for the front cover. We also did a massive thank-you list featuring nods to Astrix And Space and MC Man Parris. We sampled Jeff from the Amnesia gig during a Derrick May set. Everyone from the Sheffield and Stoke crews had that hallowed tape. Derrick May started off with a reel-to-reel moody track that has this weird intro. This noise was really harsh, but it soon faded into floatiness. Then all of a sudden *Strings of Life* came in. 'Did you hear that, man?!' says Jeff. 'Did you hear that bugger?! Get mental in the house!' I sampled that for *Activ 8* and checked with Jeff and the record label first as I wanted to do everything right. The line was from a rave tape sold by Amnesia House and so no one got paid other than the DJs, who were making a little money on the side.

We did all four formats: 12", 7", cassette and CD, and I had a really good feeling about it. *Overload* was good value as it had more than one track you could play out and *Infiltrate 202* really built up interest. This was the third in line and we were promoting the hell out of it.

People never really picked up on our drugs references at all. There's a child – Neil Rushton's four-year-old daughter Clair saying, 'Top one, nice one, get sorted,' and at one point in the track Chris shouts 'Rushin'!' Getting a child to do the 'top one' line was genius. John McCready told the press that Clair was a rapper from New York called MC Crazy Clair and people were actually trying to sign this four-year-old.

Neil Rushton *"Getting my four-year-old daughter to do vocals on Activ 8... yes, that was probably my idea, but it was a democratic process and so it could have been Mark, Chris or John who came up with it. It's the kind of thing I would have thought of, but I can't claim credit for it. Clair is 29 now. That bit took maybe two or three hours, as she wouldn't do anything until John McCready got there."*

I loved Clair's vocals and was totally cool with it. I looped it over this acid patter and the mix was better than the original. We decided to play it out for the first time at Shelley's on a Saturday night. MC Man Parris stopped all the tunes and gave us an intro. 'We've got the new Altern 8 tune! They're always at Shelley's and are a part of the Stoke-on-Trent crew and this is the first time it's ever been played in a club!' They dropped *Activ 8* and because it had the Kid 'N Play sample, which was such a big tune in Stoke, it went right off when it got to that bit. It got an incredible response. You could just feel that things were getting interesting with this track.

It seemed natural to film the video at Shelley's too as we always got in for free and got loads of support from the club. We wanted to give something back to Shelley's and we were rewarded in kind with what proved to be a rather momentous night...

Carbon Monoxide, Raving Robots And Smells Like Vicks...

Kurt Cobain was in a bad way. He had lost his voice and wasn't going to waste his vocal chords talking to us. I wouldn't have guessed that I was hanging around backstage with someone who would become as big as he did. He just seemed shy and rather uncomfortable at having to appear on Top of the Pops. Maybe he was just trying to avoid talking to Phil Collins...

People would often stand around their motors in the car park after Shelley's, just listening to music. There were no big booming systems, just little speakers on the parcel shelves and really tinny rave cassettes. This got me thinking. 'Why don't we keep the party going by turning up with a big sound system to give them what they want? This would provide amazing footage for the *Activ 8* video.'

The idea for the *Activ 8* video was signed off by Network and we were off. Chris's uncle owned a lorry and so that was sorted and one of the guys who did van sales for Network 'DJ Stan The Devil Tune Man' could get hold of a sound system. Anthony Johnson was Bizarre Inc's manager and he accidentally let slip to a few industry people about what we were up to although it was meant to be a surprise. So we knew there would be a healthy crowd. We parked up this lorry in the Shelley's car park on the Saturday afternoon so we were parallel with the club. With the tarpaulin down we set the sound system up before disappearing into the club. Just the thought of pulling off this gig was getting the heart racing.

We hired a video company (Status Video Productions) from Congleton to film parts of the night. This was to be the last time Jon McDonald would dance for us as he couldn't get any more time off uni. We decided we needed some sexy girls to dance in the video too and so one of the film crew went to Freetown to get some friends of his.

At one point in the evening we were all sat backstage in this really tiny room, sucking on ice pops, while the film crew captured some footage. There are bits in the video that are a bit pervy, to be honest. The cameraman did a few up-skirt shots and there were some sweaty legs in there too. A rumour has it that there is a very risqué clip in the video and I would like to put this to rest: yes, it's true. There are a couple of frames – and you can't see them unless you're looking – where, if you pause at the exact right moment, you can find a girl deep-throating a bottle of Sol, before proceeding to wank it off. Classy!

There are some real characters in that video, including local drug dealers, and the bloke holding a giant inflatable banana is Crez who would go on to become one of our dancers. Crez was a real regular at Shelley's. Another character, who would stand next to a big mirror near the DJ box, was Stevie P (Ptak) who everyone knew as The Atmosphere Controller. Stevie P would perch himself on top of the shelf area above the seats where they attached to the walls and wherever you were in Shelley's, you only had to look over to the mirrors to see him in his dungarees, no top on, doing 'the dance'. Stevie P just willed the atmosphere up.

It got to the point in the evening where we needed to go outside for our set and so we waited 15 minutes inside that lorry just waiting for the explosion; it seemed like forever. We had the keyboards set up and long UV tubes lined the front and sides. There were a few ravers already outside in white paper suits and DIY masks, which was cool. Jon had a special suit too, which had As and 8s all over it. I had put fluorescent spray squiggles over anything in sight.

The idea was just to get some footage, so this wasn't strictly speaking a PA although it would have to be pretty close. So everyone piled out of the club and waited for the tarpaulin to go up. There were floodlights and everything. Butler then explained what we were doing and the crowd went mad. It's quite funny looking back, but we gave them this whole monologue about what we were doing and why, but just imagine how 'out of it' the crowd must have been. I don't know why we thought they'd give a shit. Ha ha. Dominic Green, a local freelance reporter for BBC Radio Stoke turned up with a portable DAT machine and microphone and he recorded the entire set. That car park was packed and there was rumoured to be three times the normal crowd at Shelley's that evening.

So we started playing *Activ 8* as the cameras rolled. We didn't actually know Dominic Green was narrating at the time. *'So the tarpaulin on the side of the truck is up, people are gathering around in anticipation... the atmosphere is electric and people are dancing on top of cars. They're going mad! This is the moment they've all been waiting for! This is the sound of Altern 8!'* It was an incredible night.

'Want more?!' I had to take a DAT out, rewind and then fast forward and so there were huge gaps in the show. Then off we'd go again. We were playing a different version of *Activ 8* just as the police turned up. Shelley's was not in the most built-up area, but there were some houses about. For publicity reasons the label phoned the police from a phone box to get some good publicity: the struggle between the ravers and the police. 'Come on, that's enough now,' said the copper. 'Stop it!'

-    'No no. They want some more!' We played one more.

'Seriously, people will get arrested.' So, suitably chastised, we stopped. Neil Rushton had to go to Stoke police station and have a chat with them about what we'd done, but we had all the footage we needed.

Jon McDonald *"The Activ 8 video shoot at Shelley's was a funny one. One of the last gigs I did with the lads I think. I had trouble keeping on my feet, which could have been due to the carbon monoxide I was sucking in from the generator. I ended up being sick all night. But what a way to bow out!"*

The following day we travelled to Trentham Gardens in Stoke to get some more footage. Basically, the Shelley's segment was Altern 8 'at night' and the shoot in the historic public gardens was to represent the day. Trentham Gardens was full of families wandering around the old grounds on a lovely sunny day. Halfway through the *Activ 8* video we jumped over into this surreal world of Altern 8, all filmed during the day. The Victorian gardens were meant to complement the violin samples on the tune.

We wanted to paint a giant Altern 8 logo on to a wall and as all the hideous magnolia paint was cracking and coming off this certain stretch, we just got on with it. I had a can of green fluorescent spray and designed an Altern 8 logo – the A with an 8 behind it – while no one was looking. You see this big green logo on the wall, two girls dancing either side of the doorway on podiums and then it cut to the violin from Kid 'N Play and Chris and I 'air violining'. We actually tried to play the violins as we mimed, but the sound was awful. A real screech. I also had the 303 I took from Blue Chip with me and Chris had his 101. We were walking towards the camera with this robot geezer behind us, covered in silver paint, tottering about on stilts made from air-conditioning pipes. Roboman had attached himself to Altern 8 and had started turning up at certain gigs in this bizarre get-up. We never really questioned these things too much.

Jon the dancer couldn't make the daytime shoot due to carbon monoxide poisoning, which was a shame, but Neil brought his daughter Clair for the vocal mime. Then the video team went away and put it all together. They filmed my logo on the wall before the park keeper came up and started having a pop. 'You are going to get rid of that, aren't you?' he said, holding a tin of magnolia paint and a roller. I had to undo all the damage or he'd call the police. Still, we had a great promotional video.

There is a scene at the end of the video where we are back in the car park and as joyriding was in the news at the time, we pretended to break in and joyride our own car. Just to cause a stir. This being Altern 8, Chris had a sign on the dashboard of the untaxed car that said 'Tax in the post!' Chris started the car up and tried a wheel spin, but the car stalled. However, owing to the power of wonderful editing it looked like he revved it up, but you can clearly see that he stalled it. We screeched around the carpark as the tune played out in the background. At the end of the video someone from the petrol station called the police as we performed doughnuts and handbrake turns. The police then took our details and gave us a ticking off.

The video was filmed in September 1991 for a November release so it was quite a quick turnaround to be honest. We had a massive shock when the track finally came out. It went straight in at number 12! I was lost for words when we got the phone call giving us the midweek chart position. Gobsmacked. 'What do you do? Who do I tell?' I promptly went to Lotus Records in Stafford and bought some tunes.

***

Vicks was strongly associated with rave, owing to its alleged rush-inducing relationship with MDMA. We played Rezurrection in Newcastle with LFO around the time of *Infiltrate* and the ravers there were covered in Olbas Oil and Vicks. That place absolutely reeked. But we didn't start using Vicks until we did the *Activ 8* video shoot at Shelley's, when we all started getting carbon monoxide poisoning from the generator. After that we smeared it inside our masks to give us something nice to smell. The masks got incredibly pongy after a gig and the Vicks stopped us passing out from the stench. But we played along with its association with drugs when we released *Activ 8 (The Vicks Vapour Mix)*.

Ian Bland (Dream Frequency) *"My first experience of rave was at the Park Hall Club in Preston, which was a Sharon and Tracy place. This guy started playing this thing called house music in 1986 and it sounded great, but it hadn't morphed into any rave scene whatsoever. Later, we started going to The Hacienda. I soon went from being a clubber to wanting to make house music.*

In 1990 we started going to Shelley's and the illegal Blackburn parties and from there I started Dream Frequency. I became lucky enough to earn a living from it and left the RAF where I was working as a technician. I then cut a record deal with Citybeat (which later became XL Recordings) through Nick Hawkes who signed Prodigy.

I remember chatting to Mark in Blackpool after a Nexus 21 PA, which was very good. I didn't realise that some of the tunes I'd been playing out were his and then the penny dropped. Mark then went on to start Altern 8. The funny story I always tell him is that we dodged that legendary gig after Shelley's, where they played in the wagon. My friends and I were there that night, but we were just partied out. I came out of Shelley's and thought, 'Should we hang around? Should we fuck!' Ha ha. That was the Activ 8 video. Looking back, we should have stayed."

The night of the *Activ 8* video shoot was Jon's last as our dancer, as uni was demanding more of his time and so we enlisted John Parkes from the Stafford breakdance crew and Crez, who appeared in the *Activ 8* video with the giant banana. I bumped into Parksy that night at Shelley's and he said, 'What are you doing here?' I hadn't seen him for two-and-a-half years, but he was a really good dancer. 'We need a dancer for Altern 8. Would you be up for it?'

-       'Can my mate come too?'

Parksy's mate Crez would turn into our version of Prodigy's Leroy or Happy Mondays' Bez. Crez perfected a great stage persona, pointing at people in the crowd who were going for it and scowling if they weren't. With the mask on, I could act like a complete dick too as no one knew who I was. I didn't have to be embarrassed. I didn't have to be shy. That get-up totally allowed me to be stupid and larger than life.

Being told that *Infiltrate 202* was Top 40 felt ridiculous, but when *Activ 8* went straight in at 12 my head was totally scrambled. There I was at Sandon Road in Stafford, in a two-up-two-down with a beat-up car and a record in the Top 20. People assume you're minted at these points, but that was definitely not the case. But number 12! We were within a whisker of the Top 10.

Altern 8 were cartoon characters and people loved them. We got the call on the Monday morning following the Sunday charts. It was the BBC. *Top of the Pops* wanted us to perform *Activ 8*. What a rush! There I was pretending to perform on *TOTP* as a kid, and even later on Dean and I joked about who would do what when we appeared on that legendary show and now it was actually happening. *Top of the bleedin' Pops*!

Chris and I were both in the musicians' union, but Crez and Parksy had to join or they wouldn't be allowed to perform. Parksy was the kind of guy who would hand you a form and ask you to fill it in as he couldn't be bothered and so it was no surprise when he said, 'Can you do it? I know I'm going to fuck it up.'

Crez was more sensible although he completely fluffed his up. The union asked, 'Which instrument do you play?'
-   'I don't play an instrument. I'm a dancer.'
-   'Well you can't join the Musicians' Union then, can you?' Great.

So we had to pay a dancer from an agency as Crez couldn't do it. His mum had even packed him a bag to take with him to London. Crez was proper gutted. So we had a dancer from agency we had worked with before and then it was me, Parksy, Butler and Chris. We had heard that Rozalla was going to be there, as were Nirvana, Phil Collins and Tina Turner.

The Monday after the charts is when the pluggers try and get your record on to the show. If it was something that hadn't been done before it could be quite refreshing, but two blokes behind keyboards wouldn't carry it and would probably force them to show the video.

The producers insisted everyone sang live at this point, which was a massive smack in the face for dance music owing to the samples; you often couldn't get the original vocalist. Well, this dancer Sarah McNeil looked like a vocalist and so we got her to carry the vocals. All the time the producers are asking Sarah, 'Are you going to sing?' and she's like, 'I'm saving my voice for later.' We'd heard Sarah sing in the van going to gigs and so we knew she could. We had a name tab that slid into the dressing room door like at a doctors' surgery. Sarah had a different dressing room to us, which was next door. She said she wanted a little tape player so she could practise singing the song prior to the final performance and so there I was knocking on the door, but no answer. Now, I knew she was in there as there was nowhere else she could be. So I knocked again, but still no answer. So I went to open the door and someone put a foot against it. I just managed to poke my head half way round the door when I realised what was going on. Sarah and Butler were certainly excited by the thought of being on the BBC, judging by the panting. I was well embarrassed and simply said, 'Here's your tape player' and closed the door.

We did the rehearsals and the dress rehearsals without the live vocals and then it was showtime. There was a great big light next to us and we were proper hot. There were cameras all around. On your final performance they'd film it as it was due to be shown, so if you fucked it up, it depended on how famous you were, as to whether you got another go. Tina Turner fluffed a couple of words and was able to re-record as she was on a major label.

The *Top of the Pops* studio was a strange oblong room, with a stage at each end and down each side; so while Rozalla was on one stage, we were on another, ready to go. As Rozalla was finishing, the chart rundown would start and all the crowd moved from her stage to ours. There were not many people there, I might add. So on came the start of *Activ 8* and we were off! The camera zoomed in and I pointed to the camera, eyes wide open, tongue firmly in cheek, in that 'I'm off me nut' kind of way.

One problem with gigs and PAs is when the crowd don't clap in time and they did this during *Activ 8*. When it broke down to the acid bit in the middle and 'Top one, nice one, get sorted,' the audience were clapping too quickly. It was just like watching someone who can't dance and suddenly you can't dance either. All I could hear was the beat of the tune and then all these people clapping out of time and so I came in on the offbeat. Butler kept with it though and banged in perfectly. Sarah really froze and she was clutching the mic like it was going to save her and as she looked up you could see the fear in her eyes, 'Please get me off here!' She was singing slightly out of key and it was getting worse and worse and then down, down, down. We came off and I was gutted. 'That was shit!' The runner gave us a thumbs-up though. 'It's a take!'

- 'You're joking me. Did you hear that? It was shocking.'

I was not happy, but we went up in the charts that week to number six. I was still not happy with the performance, though; something Steve Wright picked up on when he started up a comedy segment on his Radio 1 show where they played a ravey tune with someone singing out of key over the top. Oh well, it was still an amazing experience and we got to meet Rozalla and Nirvana and as it was filmed in the same place as *EastEnders* we bumped into the Mitchell Brothers in the canteen. Ricky Butcher was bang into all the rave acts and so he would sit there watching the performances. I also got wedged into a cubicle door as Prince Be from PM Dawn tried to get out of the toilets. 'I'm real sorry,' he said, heading for the taps.

People often ask me about Nirvana. It was weird because they were a grunge group from the States and no one knew what was going to happen to them. They were just another group. Kurt was a little low as he had a sore throat and was due to play Wolverhampton or somewhere that night. So Kurt wanted to save his voice for the gig, rather than what he obviously saw as a fake/corporate TV show. So he stood on stage, not even miming, with his hand completely flat on the guitar like Windy Miller or something. He had the mic in his mouth and he was mumbling, 'Wooaahharrghh!' It was a terrible performance. There were a couple of grunge kids in the crowd and they got on stage and kicked the drums all over the place. My dad was made up though as I got Phil Collins' autograph for him.

CH. 14

Puddings, DIY And A German Sausage

"I don't think you should be dropping Christmas puddings from a hot-air balloon. Do you know the damage a pudding can do from that height? Think about it!"

Activ 8 was flying. We had gone from number 12 to six, which really surprised me due to the poor performance on *Top of the Pops*, but then we went up to four and finally number three. We released our single at the same time as Michael Jackson's *Black And White* and Vic Reeves and The Wonder Stuff's *Dizzy*, so for us to get to number three at that time was amazing. You don't beat Jacko.

I wondered whether Kev Roberts from Blue Chip was watching the charts because two of his former acts ended up in the top five in the very same week. Bizarre Inc's *Playing With Knives* was battling it out with *Activ 8* to be Stafford's biggest tune, which added a nice element to a lot of the press. Chris's brother Ade was MCing for Bizarre Inc at the time and was nicknamed MC Badmouth because he couldn't stop swearing. He did a PA at The Place on a Sunday once, which was broadcast live on local radio. 'Whatever you do, don't swear!' they told him. The first thing he said was, 'Make some fucking noise!' He swore all the way through. Badmouth was a spy in the Bizarre Inc camp though and he told us a rather interesting tale, although we don't know if it's 100% true. Bizarre Inc were on their way to a gig, listening to the Sunday chart rundown, when it got to the Top 5. Their tune was number four and as there'd been no sign of us, they assumed that Altern 8 had bombed out of the charts. 'And number three is… Altern 8 with *Activ 8*.' There was a deathly silence apparently and then someone turned the radio off.

We never really had a proper rivalry with Bizarre Inc. I certainly have flyers with both our names on and so we weren't avoiding each other. There were rumours that Prodigy had a beef with us too, but again it was probably dreamed up by journalists. Rivalries sell papers.

So Stafford ruled rave. At least for a week. The biggest thing musically to have hit the town before us was The Climax Blues Band. The weird thing was that Blue Chip had opened up as a studio again around this time and we went back there to record when Derek Holt, the bass player from The Climax Blues Band, took it over. It's a small town.

Andy Meecham (Bizarre Inc, Chicken Lips, The Emperor Machine) *"In 1988, I went for a job as a keyboard player and engineer at Blue Chip Studios. I walked into the room one morning and there were Dean Meredith and Mark Archer, making music. I didn't know Mark, but I know he recalls me and Dean making mixtapes and stuff like that.*

Kev Roberts was a nice guy though and really put the effort in. Kev brought back lots of records from America that we could sample and stuff like that and he was a really up-for-it fun kinda guy.

Rhythm Mode: D was Mark and Dean and I played keyboards on some of that. I remember they were sorting out the artwork one day and we all went out into town to get these moody photos taken.

Chris and I played some synths and Mark did a lot of the engineering himself on Bizarre Inc. Eventually, Mark and Chris left to do their own thing, leaving Dean and me to do Bizarre Inc.

Dean and I used to send demos out almost every morning after Blue Chip closed; we were determined to find another label. It got quite ridiculous. It's quite funny, looking back. We would start every morning by saying, 'Right. Who should we get to tell us 'no' today?' It was John from Vinyl Solution who finally phoned us back. He invited us down to London and got us a deal.

It was quite interesting really when both Bizarre Inc and Altern 8 made the top five in 1991; they got one place higher. It all happened so fast. I guess we were in the right place at the right time. Our paths crossed sometimes, but not very much to be honest. I can recall a friendly rivalry between the bands, piss-taking that went on, but nothing more than that. So Kev Roberts saw two of his former acts in the Top

Five that week. I still have my contract from him: 2% was the deal. Wasn't good, really.

It was a magical time. My happiest memories of that era were of coming home to my parents' house – after a gig – in the early hours of the morning with a big chunk of cash. I can still remember my dad letting me in. 'Did it go well?'

- *'Yeah it did!'*

I'd go upstairs to my bedroom and roll loads of money into the bedside drawer. I had thousands of pounds in that cupboard. I was living at home, no mortgage, no responsibilities, having lots of fun. We went on Top of the Pops five times too, which was great. It was a magical time."

Our second performance on *Top of the Pops* was much better. We used one of Lisa Stansfield's backing singers as we weren't going to get the piss taken out of us by Steve Wright again. Crez missed this performance once again and so we had a female dancer teaming up with Parksy.

We were treated a little differently after *Top of the Pops*. We started to get dressing rooms and whatnot. Although when we played Donington that autumn we had to get changed in the corridor whilst Shades Of Rhythm had a dressing room – with a toilet! But that was how it was sometimes. That said, I always felt very lucky to be playing in front of 10,000 people. Each time something happened it just got bigger and bigger. Even the mother-in-law was proud of me. Up until then she'd hoped Karen would dump me, but I guess she wanted what was best for her daughter and there I was messing about in the studio. But now, something had come of it. I was on *Top of the Pops*. I was in *The Sun*!

We did *Dance Energy* with Normski on C4 whilst *Activ 8* was out. I first knew Normski as a photographer from the early days of the rave scene who had also done a track with Juan Atkins, which he rapped on. It was shit, but the tune was good. The stage at *Dance Energy* was odd. The studio was all white and bright and the walls were covered in squirly murals. It was weird being in a club with all the lights on. They didn't want an MC either, so Butler had to dance. 'I'm not a dancer!' Butler was not happy.

The vocals on *Activ 8* were actually done by a man, but we got Sarah McNeil to mime. There were loads of breakdancers from Leeds and Sheffield there who knew Butler and when the violins came on and the electro drum beat started, they formed a circle and started doing their thing.

Martyn 'Crez' Cresswell *"I used to see Mark round Stafford quite a lot with the guys from Bizarre Inc. I would also see him walking around Stafford high street with Karen a few years later, both wearing bubble jackets. Mark had fallen out with Dean Meredith at the time and was going clubbing and releasing stuff as Nexus 21. I then heard about this Altern 8 group and was there when they did the infamous Activ 8 video at Shelley's. I saw Mark in the car park later that night and he gave me a couple of DJ promos he'd just played, one of which was Activ 8. I still have that copy. A few weeks later at a gig my mate John Parkes said, 'I'm gonna be dancing for Altern 8 at the Queen's Theatre in Burslem!'*
- *'Cool. Get me in.' I was always trying to blag my way into a gig.*
- *'No, no. Mark wants you to dance too.'*
- *'No way!'*

So, we cobbled some outfits together and performed at the Queen's Theatre. The following week, we did 10,000 people at Donington. That was a bit of wake-up call and then it was off all over the place.

I can't dance even now and I never was a proper dancer; I was just into clubbing, although I was well known for dancing by the DJ box at Shelley's. I was nervous as hell before gigs and used to chuck up before going on – a mixture of chemicals and nerves. Ha ha.

It was fun on the road in that minibus with the whistling window. Oboe The Troll drove us all and we'd have a right laugh on the road. You'd go off on a Friday night and not come back until Sunday. Just young guys having the time of our lives. We all had nicknames of course. 'You're gonna give it, you gotta give it to The Cresswell' or 'The One Deck Wazzock' because unlike Carl Cox 'The Three Deck Wizard', I couldn't DJ for shit. Butler was Midget Gem as he was always whipping his little penis out. John was 'The Chicken Strangler' as he was always wanking away.

Mark was married to Karen at the time and a lot squarer than he is now. Mark was very reserved back then, but we made up for it. I used to hang around Stafford a bit playing Laser Quest with Archer. We were obsessed with Laser Quest and I was always 'top gun'."

***

This was a time of constant promotion. We did all kinds of gigs: outdoor and indoor raves, townie clubs and under-16s discos. The under-16s discos were mad. The noise down in Redruth, Cornwall was Beatles-esque. You couldn't hear the music for all the screaming. Parksy always proper fancied himself, but even he couldn't go to the front of stage because the girls were trying to grab his trouser leg in order to pull him off stage. We were constantly being propositioned: 'My mum and dad are out tonight, so you can come round if you want.' It was well dodgy. We did another under-16s at Shelley's and they made a real din. It was 5-9pm or something like that and so it was weird coming out of Shelley's and seeing a load of parents waiting. It was light too and not the early morning variety.

The press department at Network went into overdrive and we engineered loads of daft stunts to keep pumping the oxygen into this beast. We went along with all of it. We took part in a stunt for a short-lived dance magazine called *RAGE* where we gave out branded Christmas puddings from a hot-air balloon.

We bought some puddings from Sainsbury's and mocked up labels that said 'BRAND-E' and 'The Poor Know The Score!' The weather was too bad to take the hot-air balloon up, though, and so that put paid to that. 'Anyway, if you drop a Christmas pudding from a hot-air balloon, it's likely to cave someone's head in,' the photographer piped up. We hadn't considered that. Now, that's not good. It could have been a bloodbath if we'd launched those puddings.

But we needed some shots for the magazine and so the photographer hatched a plan. We drove up to Shugborough Hall (Lord Lichfield's house), a massive stately home I'd worked on when I was at Fisher Decoration. I recall meeting a scientist who was studying the Lord's walls and he revealed that the original paint had been made from cow shit. I wrote my nickname 'Mega' all over the walls prior to painting, only for Lichfield to walk in. 'Cover that shit up!' he barked. I felt like a right tit.

So the photographer lay down on the floor in the gardens where our hot air balloon was now located. He then shot up at us standing in the basket, leaning out into the lens holding these Christmas puddings so it looked like we were up in the air, although there was actually no balloon at all. I'm sure many will be disappointed to hear these revelations, but we had to get the job done.

So off we trotted to Stafford to give the puddings away to the townsfolk, who would clearly be receptive to some free scran. Only they weren't. Stafford is a small, quiet town and the locals didn't quite take to two blokes wearing chemical warfare suits trying to give away weirdly labelled puddings. This wasn't the norm. I'm not sure I would have taken one. One old lady took a pudding and posed for a photo, though. Which was something. Not long after we gave up and took the puddings home. I ended up selling one of these £3.60 puddings for £100 on eBay. Who are the fools now, eh Stafford?

John McCready *"The conceptual balloon 'pudding drop' over Stafford was popular, even though it never actually took place. But don't forget: 'The poor know the score!'"*

Activ 8 really got us noticed and we were in the local and national press. Local photographers were always the cheekiest, though, as they just didn't get the whole mask thing. Our first shoot with the *Wolverhampton Express And Star* was a bit moody. The photographer was proper vexed when we turned up in our gear. 'Come on lads, we need to see your faces!'
-   'But that's not what this is about.'
-   'But people want to see your faces!'
-   'No they don't!'
We often got bullied into these things as it was hard sticking to your guns. They took 30 shots with the masks on and one without, and used the one without. You give people pantomime and they want the boring truth. *Smash Hits* didn't want the masks either and so they shot the back of mine and Chris's heads. It was beyond me as to why they did this. I remember *Smash Hits* wanting to print the lyrics to *Infiltrate 202* which was funny as it was just a repeated sample all the way through. 'We can't print that!' they said.
-   'Well, we did try and tell you.'
We tried to wear the masks for interviews and shoots, including this one in London that was filmed. We kept our masks on all the way through the filming and Shut Up And Dance – who were involved for some reason – were not happy about it at all. A couple of minutes into it, they were like, 'OK, you can stop being dicks now and take the masks off!' We just shook our heads.
It's weird how we were treated in France, though. We did a press evening in a hotel when we played a gig in Paris and had interview after interview and every single journalist smoked like a chimney and I already

had a migraine from the flight and the taxi straight to the hotel. These chain-smoking French journalists were desperate to get to the *meaning* of Altern 8. 'So what is the message behind the music?' As there was a language barrier and absolutely no underlying meaning to our music, we just made stuff up. There were hundreds of these interviewers and they were all hyper-positive and so you had to really match their enthusiasm although you felt like crap. 'There are no conspiracy theories. This is not political music. We want you to dance to it. That's it.'

***

Now Altern 8 were a popular act we felt we needed to push the live experience a little more too. We certainly didn't want to go back to the static stage presence of Nexus 21. We were having a real laugh on stage at the time. We had a settled line-up of dancers (Parksy and Crez) and MC (Butler) and had also swapped to DAT, which made playing live easier, as one track spliced into another in a continuous mix. We also mimed away on the Jen SX1000, which I'd bought for a fiver.

I had taken a load of wood flooring from Blue Chip when it closed, which had been worn thin from wear and tear and had an idea when I came across it at home one weekend. I wanted to make some giant 'A' and '8' keyboard risers to give the stage show a little more impact. So I made a square with the top corners off and a block in the top and middle. It had two hinges and a desk lid, so it was all hinged. You could stand it up and stick a keyboard on it. It was rock solid. The Cavalier came into its own at this point, transporting the A and the 8 to all the gigs, although we couldn't take the signs abroad. These signs couldn't be missed on stage once I'd painted them fluorescent green. Altern 8 was a happy mixture of accident and DIY. From the name and the suits down to the stage props, we did virtually everything ourselves. We even got some stage costumes for the dancers and Butler, which consisted of grey long-sleeved tops with the A8 logo on them. The logo I designed.

We had some great times travelling to and from gigs in that Transit van we used for longer trips. Butler's nickname was the Mardy Sleep Monster because if you ever woke him up he'd be in the worst mard ever. 'Fuck off you bastards!' He would often take up a whole row of seats and fall asleep, so everyone else was cramped together. We once found some bale string and tied him up and so when he awoke he couldn't move. 'Fucking bastards!' Chris's brother Ade came with us too. He was a lovely lad and would do anything for a laugh. There was a rumour that he had nicked a spider or something, but I never got to the bottom of that. We went to this service station once and the owners wanted to know if we were ravers. 'Nope.'

-   'Well, that's OK, then.'

We all sat down and someone picked a massive bogey and put it in a sandwich. Ade was like, 'I'll eat that.' Ade was younger than Chris. He once nicked a wheelchair I think. Ade was always doing daft stuff. He was never malicious though, he just liked a laugh. Ade ate every last crumb.

***

We did a little mini tour of Paris and Germany at the start of December 1991 and actually had a tour bus this time, previously used by Iron Maiden. I remember Crez sitting behind me slapping his chops like a monkey all the way to France as he was off his face on wizz. I didn't really cotton on, though. 'Crez! What are you doing with your face? Have some chewing gum.' He'd stick his head between the two headrests and listen in on our conversations, chewing like a mad cow.

The European jaunt was called Speaker Damage and we invited *Select* magazine to come and join us. Although *Select* was an indie/grunge magazine they had taken a liking to us, primarily due to journalist Andrew Harrison, who wanted the music monthly to reflect the more interesting elements of the dance scene. So we invited Andrew to come and join us, label mates Rhythmatic and the whole Network crew.

Andrew Harrison (Rage, Q, Select) "I first encountered Mark Archer through Nexus 21 and Network more than anything. I loved their stuff and would play anything that came out on Network. I loved the sound and even the artwork, which was all done by designer Trevor Jackson. Nexus 21's Self Hypnosis EP was a massive deal for us. We played that out at little parties and it would blow the speakers. Nexus 21 were very Detroit techno and it helped that Network was linked to KMS because it meant that the actual Detroit scene got involved. Then Altern 8 came out and it was silly with lots of bass. I loved the original Infiltrate 202 and played it out a lot.

Once I'd started work for music magazines I was always looking to increase the coverage of dance. I worked for a magazine called Rage for a while and it was a fringe title that didn't do very well; it was Robert Maxwell trying to get into the youth market. We couldn't get the big artists, but we could get the people we liked and so we did a piece with Altern 8 where we flew a hot-air balloon over Stafford to drop Christmas puddings to the poor; puddings that were meant to contain a certain little something, which they obviously didn't. It was a big con. My mate, designer Steve Hicks, made the labels for the puddings: 'The poor know the score!' There were lots of things that made me and my mates love Altern 8. Obviously the tunes were fantastic and the whole approach to rave culture was fun. I really liked the press releases by John McCready, too who wrote some great pieces for The Face; you always looked forward to getting his mail-outs.

I then joined Select magazine. Rave was a massive subculture and although the nineties keeps getting regurgitated, as if it was just Blur and Oasis, rave was equal to and probably bigger than Britpop and Mixmag was outselling a lot of rock magazines. Select covered the living hell out of Britpop, but there was a small percentage of dance music content. We covered clubbing as well as The Wonder Stuff. If it was all just The Wonder Stuff it would have gotten so boring, so we battled with the publishers to get what we liked into the magazine. So the time had come to do a proper feature on them and the first reaction was, 'Why are you putting all this stuff in? Aphex Twin etc.?' But the battle was positive and the right thing to do actually, because a magazine full of DJs would have been too much.

I convinced Select that we needed to do Altern 8 and so we covered their dates in Paris and Cologne. LFO turned up to the night in Cologne and we dressed them up in Altern 8's chemical warfare suits and snapped Chris and Mark in their normal clothes, trying to strangle them.

I remember MC Butler running around on stage in Cologne shouting all sorts of rubbish in English because the fans couldn't understand it. They then decided there wasn't enough entertainment on show and so they got this giant moveable ladder and made me climb up and down it during the show while Butler shouted, 'Ladder Posse, where are you?!'"

We got the journalist Andrew Harrison and Neil Rushton to sit on these giant step ladders in Cologne. As you were looking to the left hand side of the stage you could just make them out holding their pieces of cardboard that said 'Ladder Posse' on them. Butler kept shouting out to the Ladder Posse. There was an element of danger to this and no one had really thought about what might happen if the ladder toppled over and killed an editor of a major magazine *and* the boss of our record label.

There was a photo of me in *Select* with my shirt off. Don't ask me why, as I should have been the last person to take their top off, although I was quite trim back then. I wasn't even drunk.

The promoter took us all out for a meal with the record label the night before the gig. We managed to get our girlfriends along too, which was nice. Some of the lads were not the most cultured and we had been warned to be respectful when dealing with traditional food. They brought out a plate of sauerkraut, traditional sausage and all that and a couple of people started turning their noses up. I could see the promoter starting to get upset. When someone left their sausage untouched it was quickly wrapped up in a napkin and pocketed. As I have said, I was green when it came to drugs and so when someone offered me half a disco biscuit, I crumbled it up into a powder with a key fob and sprinkled it into one of the label boss's drinks. I realise now what a stupid thing that was. I had no idea as to how powerful drugs actually were. The middle-aged man complained a little later in the evening that he had a stomach ache and needed a lay down. He was OK though, thank God.

The stolen sausage soon re-appeared when we got to the venue. Commando-style I moved across the stage on my front as the club was going off and placed the sausage in the bulldog clips of the mic stand. When the MC came out to get the mic there was this bratwurst sitting in the stand. Then Dave, the guy who had the powdered E, jumped up on the stage, stole the sausage and placed it inside his open flies. We were not invited back.

Gez Varley (LFO) *"LFO became Altern 8 at one gig. We were in Germany, working with Karl Bartos in Düsseldorf when we heard that Mark and Chris were playing in nearby Cologne, so we went down to see them. We ended up getting dressed up as them for a photoshoot, which featured Nexus 21 strangling Altern 8 (LFO)!"*

There was a lot of silliness around this time and all good fun. We bumped into LFO in Cologne and got them to wear our suits for a photoshoot we were doing for *Select* magazine. We wore our Nexus 21 T-shirts and were photographed pretending to strangle ourselves. It was a great idea, but was this an omen?

CH. 15

Big Apple, Special K And A Monster In The Loft

Parksy sat in the giant throne dribbling, whilst the hipsters and weirdos of New York's dance scene jigged away below. We couldn't move him. 'Wake up! Parksy! Wake up!' Parksy had popped something very different to E. 'For fuck's sake Parksy, wake up!'

Karen and I finally got a two-up two-down in Stafford, which allowed me to leave Mum and Dad's and finally get some independence. I was leaving sleepy Gnosall behind for the bright lights of Stafford Techno City.

We had a budget of £29,000, but many places were bare shells for that price, almost derelict. You could move in, but there'd be a hell of a lot of work to do. But if you went up to £35,000 you got a totally different range of properties. We found this house on Sandon Road, Stafford where you walked straight into the front room. The decor would be considered a bit tacky and chintzy now; there was a dado rail and patterned wallpaper that matched the sofa, which they left. It was very cosy and the kitchen was as big as the front room. There were two rooms upstairs, but they partitioned one into two. There was a very small bathroom.

The studio was a very small room, especially once my equipment was placed against two of the walls. You had to walk into the room and turn sideways to get in. If you had a bunch of mates in there it was total chaos and very warm. I had quite the set-up by now.

The walls were that thick in these really old houses, it really helped soften my work, although the property had problems with flooding.

There was a brook that ran along the bottom of the garden over the brick wall and the road always flooded at that point when there was a storm. The fire brigade once pumped water from the road into the brook, until it burst its banks and raw sewage flooded into the back garden.

Karen would go off to work in the mornings and I would go downtown to Lotus Records in Stafford with my gig money to see what was new. White labels, imports, I'd go through them all. You'd sometimes get sold a complete load of shit, though; the staff knew exactly where to place the needle for a tune to sound good.

There was an assistant at Lotus called Yvonne who always went to Freetown in Stoke. She knew I was into the harder stuff and so she'd always play some great tracks. Lotus really supported us when we had records out. They once covered the shop window with our record sleeves and we even did a signing session there. There was always a level of local pride that we were from Stafford.

Just before Christmas 1991, we landed a gig at the legendary Limelight Club in New York; Neil used the trip to meet up with a few record company people out there. We met Lord Michael, Andrew Komis and Joey Beltram.

The Limelight was a converted church and just before it changed into a club it was, rather ironically, a drug rehabilitation centre. The Limelight had a real punky vibe about it and people were actually moshing at the front. It would go on to further its reputation when, five years later, it was the location for a notorious clubland murder that prompted the Hollywood film *Party Monster*. New York was ace. We had our picture taken – in full costume – riding one of those horse and carts that trot around Central Park and we climbed some traffic lights for another shot. The locals couldn't quite work us out.

We went out for a meal with Lord Michael and Joey Beltram in New York and that was amazing. I remember looking over to the other side of the table and thinking, 'Blimey! That's Joey Beltram!' Butler chatted with them, but I was far too shy. Beltram's *Energy Flash* and *Mentasm* were classic tunes. I was more than a bit starstuck as *Energy Flash* was a major inspiration. Joey was actually turned on to R&S Records in New York because of Nexus *21's Logical Progression/Techno City* that they licensed from Network earlier that year.

The Limelight was mental. There were go-go dancers in cages and the crowd was a real mix of straight and gay. It was a crazy vibe. Crez,

Parksy and I were in the DJ box while Lenny D was playing – I had bought his records back in 1987 – which was amazing.

We were so naive. Parksy and myself were sat opposite these two girls and you could see that he was about to crack on, when one of the girls turned to the other and they started snogging. 'We were like, wow! This doesn't happen in Stafford!' This was porn going on, right next to us.

Joey Beltram was playing right before us and the last tune he played was *Move My Body,* the original from our *Overload EP*, which was to be the first tune of *our* live set. 'Fuck! Why has he played this?' He was scratching over it, just vibing and playing over the top. Of course we didn't say anything as everyone looked dead hard and would have kicked our puny British asses.

Cathy Dennis from D-Mob was there, along with Madonna's producer Shep Pettibone. The gig was really hyped and was a well strange venue. There were these big beams, mad arches and a giant throne in the middle of the stage, covered in gold and red velvet. Parksy had discovered something odd too: Special K. I rather innocently thought all drugs were the same, but K was definitely not E. Special K was ketamine and was designed to tranquillise horses and, true to its word, it had Parksy slumped in this throne with the lights well and truly out. When it was time to go, Butler tried to wake him, but he was still comatose in the throne like something that had been shot at the Grand National. We ended up shouting at him. 'Wake up you fucker! We're in New York! You need to sort your shit out!' But the tranquillised Parksy couldn't hear us. Eventually we picked him up and carried him out to a cab.

It wasn't long before ketamine cropped up at Shelley's and in my humble opinion, it was not a club drug. If bouncers saw you out of it, they'd throw you out of Shelley's, so you had to act like you weren't spangled when you needed a pee. Parksy took some ketamine at Shelley's later that year and said to Crez, 'I need to go to the toilet, but my legs don't work. Don't make me look like I'm off my head.' I would always know when Butler was on it as his eyes would close right up like little raisins, but he'd carry on talking. 'How on earth can he see?'

The dancers and MC always partied harder than Chris and I, which was fine. In fact, it worked quite well as nothing would have gotten done if we were all away with the fairies. They still got into a few scrapes though. We were doing a gig in Scotland once and Parksy had another turn. Parksy was the sort of person who would swipe anything he saw in a room. If you left a packet of crisps on the side, Parksy would start eating them. Well, Parksy was right on it at this gig and when Butler – who was feeling under the weather – decanted his cough mixture into a Lucozade bottle to take on stage with him, Parksy took the bottle and put it into his bag, thinking it was Lucozade. Feeling a little cotton-woolly in the mouth department Parksy – after a little wizz – necked the bottle of cough mixture. Parksy loved the attention of being recognised at gigs and so he soaked up the atmosphere on the dancefloor for a bit before feeling a little sick. He then went as white as a ghost and sat by a speaker. 'I can't dance. I feel like shit.' I said he had to try to put in a performance and to be fair he did although he spewed up once he came offstage. We always had wicked crowds in Scotland and that was no exception. We got back to the hotel and Parksy was still in a bad way and eventually a doctor was called to come to the hotel and inject him in the arse. I was loving it in New York though, and I hadn't been tranquillised. Joey Beltram had been playing our music and we'd just played one of the most hedonistic rave venues ever.

It was December and New York was freezing so I bought some baggy jeans, hoodies and Timberlands. A shop owner threw some hot water on to the sidewalk and it froze before it reached the kerb. It was Baltic out there. It was such an honour being able to visit other countries *and* get paid for it. It is a blessing. The flyer for that New York gig was amusing, proclaiming us 'Manchester's Altern 8!'

Although I was jetting off to New York and appearing on *Top of the Pops*, life couldn't be any more humble in other respects. Lying in bed the night I got home, back in our two-up-two-down, I was awoken at silly o'clock by a series of thumping noises from the loft. Boomp! Boomp! Boomp! 'What the hell is that?!' After a while it stopped.

The following morning, I went to take my suitcase back up to the loft and soon realised that something was amiss. Karen and I had received a set of luggage as an engagement present, his and hers suitcases essentially, and it was instantly apparent to me that Karen's suitcase was missing as I climbed into the loft with mine, the following morning.

Because we lived on a row of terraces, each loft space had the triangle bit up to the roof, which didn't go all the way up. You could basically squeeze in and climb over the wall and get into next door's loft. 'Karen! Have you taken any of the cases down?'

-    'No!' That was when it clicked.

The nextdoor neighbour had climbed into our loft and nicked our luggage; a problem I'm sure Rod Stewart didn't have to deal with. I phoned the police. 'It's our nextdoor neighbour, he's stealing from our loft.'

- 'You can't cast aspersions like that without any proof,' said the police.
- 'But there's only two ways into our loft. One is from our house, or along and through the loft.'

It turned out that the police had been keeping an eye on this geezer for quite a while. Eventually, the police went nextdoor and recovered the cases. Apparently the bloke thought they were his. Easy mistake to make I guess. Not.

This was not the first time we had a run-in with him though. One morning at 4am he woke us up by repeatedly playing Madness's *House of Fun* at full blast. Now the walls were quite thick, but in the middle of the night this music was making an absolute din. So, I threw my dungarees on – essential rave wear – and walked out into the pouring rain. I'm not a confrontational person at all, but I started kicking his door when he failed to respond to the doorbell. Still, nothing. The song ended and then four or five seconds later it started up again. The situation was somehow made worse by the jolly nature of the tune.

I stomped back into our house, got a piece of paper and the only thing to hand that I could find to write with was a thick crayon. So, in a rather angry, manic style, not helped by the thick red crayon, I wrote, 'Turn this fucking shit off!' I then marched round, banged on the door and pushed this note through the letterbox. He must have seen the note because that was the end of the music for the night. I was actually quite proud of myself for intimidating someone. It must have been the crayon.

***

Birmingham City Council wanted Altern 8 to play a major role in its new year celebrations, which was doubling up as the official start of the city's year (1992) as European Capital of Culture. *Activ 8* had peaked at number three in the charts, and dropped down, but it stuck around in the lower reaches all the way through to December before it started to climb again.

I had assumed that this gig would be in a town hall or something, but the four-grand fee (for 15 minutes) did raise an eyebrow; it was considerably more than we were used to getting. We were due on at 9pm after which we'd pack up and go do a gig at Wigan Pier at 1am. It was common practice for DJs and dance acts to do two or three gigs in a night.

Come the morning of the gig, it was just a normal day really. We had two gigs planned and one of them was fairly local. Easy peasy. Then Dad phoned up. 'You know this Birmingham Council gig?'

- 'Yeah.'
- 'Well, I'm watching the news. There's 45,000 people in the middle of Centenary Square!'
- 'Holy shit!'

I had played to 10-20,000 at raves before, but this gig was major. The whole of Centenary Square had been cordoned off. They had this massive stage and the line-up included UB40, a male voice choir and loads more bands. It was a family thing really, yet right down the front were two or three thousand hardcore ravers waiting for us. It was a sea of heads and when this blue light panned up and down, there were people as far as you could see. All these people at the front were shouting 'Altern 8! Altern 8!'

The compere said hello to all the mums and dads and children and yet again, all you could hear was 'Altern 8! Altern 8!!' I have to say, I was trembling as we waited for our cue. Then the compere asked the crowd, 'Is everyone ready to get active?!' Boom! It just went right off!

Parksy would often get quite precious over 'his' stage and he wasn't happy with things that night. 'I'm not dancing on that! Wipe it down! I also need security to help keep the stage safe!' What a prima donna. We had also instructed Butler not to swear due to the family nature of the entertainment and consequently I have never heard somebody say 'wicked' so many times during a set.

The opening seconds were amazing. Crez and Parksy came out and did forward rolls and the crowd went mad. 'Woooaahhh!!!!' I couldn't quite get why the crowd were getting so excited about two forward rolls, but I kept karate-chopping the keyboard like a man possessed. Then the crowd roared again and I could see why. Behind us was the giant robot guy again, only this time he was on stilts. Body-popping! We did 15 minutes and it was really good. All you could hear was 'Altern 8! Altern 8!'

So we all bundled into the van after and went up the motorway to Wigan Pier. That Birmingham gig was next-level and totally mainstream.

That was when we realised how far we had come since that night in Coventry – just six months before – when we first donned the masks. Holy shit!

So 1992 started in Wigan; now that was a sweatbox of a venue. It was so hot in there my DAT machine got soaked with condensation and my nose was dripping like a tap behind the mask. The DAT machine then started to malfunction and I had to wrap a load of towels around it, so it would stay at a certain temperature. Still, it was another brilliant gig and what a way to start a new year. I couldn't quite believe it.

***

Neil Rushton phoned to give us the details. 'You've got a Peel Session!'
- 'What?!'
- 'You heard.'

Now John Peel was a proper legend and actually quite partial to hardcore techno and so to do a Peel Session was mad. It was so weird to think that someone like Peel liked our stuff enough to do a session. I was speechless. So we made our way to London with all the gear. The engineer was Dale Griffin, who was the drummer with Mott The Hoople, and he really stamped his foot when we arrived. We were meant to have brought all our DATS with us, but we thought it was a 100% live session. So Dave Barker brought all the tapes down from Birmingham as Dale huffed and puffed. As Dave was transferring the music across the engineer said, 'You do you realise it's in mono, don't you?' *Frequency* was made in the bedroom of my parents' cottage; just six samples and another noise and that's it. *Frequency* really angered the engineer, though, which put a downer on things plus we didn't get to meet John Peel either, which was a shame.

CH. 16

Armoured Cars, LA Riots And Altern 8 For Government

We got compared to The KLF a lot and at the time they were the biggest-selling dance act in the world. But we never tried to be them, we just loved their sense of fun. We were often called the Budget KLF and if they bought a submarine, then we would hire a tank, which was considerably cheaper.

I looked out of our living room window and saw an XR2i drive past the house with the Altern 8 logo covering the back window in green insulation tape. The logo was done perfectly. I saw that car a lot around Stafford. Altern 8 were in the daily papers, monthly and weekly magazines as well as popping up on TV and radio. Bookings were coming in fast from all over. The Men In Masks were everywhere. I wasn't loaded, though, although I did invest in some new latches for the loft.

So what do you do when you have a public demanding a follow-up to a number-three hit? You go back underground, of course. The dance scene is very precious. Once you've gone mainstream, a certain portion of the scene turns off. 2 Unlimited went down a storm at Shelley's and yet as soon as *Get Ready For This* charted, no one wanted to know. Yet, if Ray and the boys had hit back with an underground tune, they might have retained their original following. Instead, they released the same single again and the Great British Public bought it. But because the pop-buying fans have the attention span of a goldfish, once you've done that so many times, they move on to the next thing. Then life gets hard because you can't go back underground. Neil Rushton was very clever with how he managed our profile. He knew when to go for the money and when to hold back.

We decided to release *Frequency* – the track that angered John Peel's engineer so much – on a new side label called Stafford North. Dominic Green's original Shelley's interview during the *Activ 8* video shoot appeared on the *Activ 8/Frequency (Live Outside Shelley's, Longton)* B-side. We did it as a limited edition to try and raise some eyebrows. There's a bit on the live version where Butler's on stage shouting, 'I'm still on one!' and this got his mum asking some rather difficult questions. 'What does this mean?' she asked. And then they had the whole drugs talk. *Frequency* was quite a sought-after tune and was massive when played out live.

I did *Frequency* on my own, as I did with a lot of the tracks, but Chris and I agreed on a 50/50 cut, to prevent any arguments. *Armageddon*, *Give it to Baby*, *Re-Indulge* and *Frequency* were all written by me. *Frequency* and *Give it to Baby* featured on the second 12". On *Frequency* I assigned samples to the actual pads and then recorded the drum patterns that would play them. So, the stab pattern in *Frequency* was four or five individual pads that would play the tune. Then you had a drum loop on another pad. *Frequency* was essentially six samples and a high-pitched noise from another keyboard that went out into a four-channel mixer. I couldn't pan anything either as I had no effect units or EQ. These were straight samples into my mixer and DAT. I had no Atari computer at this point.

The *Frequency* sleeve was bright blue with pink writing and was limited to 10001 copies, all individually numbered. 'It doesn't matter which way you look at it, it's 10001 copies,' because even if you turned it upside down, it was still 10001. This move annoyed a lot of people as it could have been a hit if we'd pressed more, but I stand by it. We might have been cutting our noses off, but it wasn't made for the chart. So effectively we stopped ourselves from having another hit straight after *Activ 8,* but it *was* a nod to the underground that quietened down talk of 'cartoon ravers'. For a bit. John McCready and Neil Rushton were very clever. I didn't quite get it back then, but now I can see it. However, if you go quiet for too long, you simply don't exist.

Network kept us in the mainstream press even when our output was underground. The joyriding in the *Activ 8* video was leaked by us and it added to the growing phenomenon. Some elements of the rock press sneered at us a bit, and there was a lot of mickey-taking, but the dance magazines were fantastic. Altern 8 made for great copy and pictures and so our trip back underground wasn't for long. The press was brilliantly managed. If we were offered a big gig and yet we were already booked to do another, we would tell the papers that we had chosen to play a recreation ground rather than a festival and they lapped it up. We said we sacrificed the DAT tape of *Frequency* on a bonfire just to enhance the limited-edition run. I still have that DAT at home.

It was a dream come true, early 1992, when we were invited to review the singles for weekly music magazine *Melody Maker*. One of the tracks we were given was TC 1991's *Berry*: an Italian tune, which got very big. This tune wholesale sampled the entire bassline from *Technological*, the Bizarre Inc track. As I liked to break a track down to the bassline – often my favourite part of a tune – it did leave things open to plundering. Towards the end of *Technological*, the drums and everything faded out and it left just the bassline on its own. Well these dudes had nicked the whole bassline and did a track around it. I looked at Chris, he looked at me. I was gobsmacked. 'No way!'

- 'What?'
- 'That!'
- 'What do you mean?'
- 'The bassline!'
- 'What about it?'
- 'You played it!'
- 'Oh yeah.'

I couldn't even play keyboard, but I spotted Chris's riff, so how the hell did he not recognise it? Back in 1989, when we were doing Bizarre Inc, Chris replayed that bassline every time he started up the keyboard. When Chris was experimenting with riffs that was the bassline he always started playing around with. That riff was something he'd made up at home and he loved playing it, so it came as a bit of a surprise when he didn't even recognise it. We ended up making *Frequency* Single Of The Week. 'But you can't pick your own tune,' they said.

- 'But it's the best one here!'

In the end they called it the Disqualified Single Of The Week. We always had a mischievous thing going on and were always trying to pull a fast one.

So, finally the time had come to follow up the number three single with something just as big. We needed to continue with the head of steam we'd built up with *Activ 8* – although *Frequency* had bought us some cred – and so we hooked up with Derek Holt back at Blue Chip. I'd recorded a demo called *Say It Y'all* a while back and so decided to expand upon that on as I wasn't the greatest keyboard player. The track was in distinct sections that we filled in with various noises. We could then flip back to the bit with that noise. The noises wouldn't overlap if they were in different keys, but the track worked OK in sections and so I used my original bassline and drums and Chris did a vocal stab pattern. We wanted another big old-skool hook like *Pacific State* on *Infiltrate 202* and Kid 'N Play on *Activ 8* and so we used *Strings of Life*. I loved *Strings* and it was a huge influence on me. Network contacted Derrick May and asked him if he was cool with it and he said fine, as long as he got a percentage. We also wanted to do some original vocals for this one.

P.P. Arnold was a big star of the sixties and had done a few rave tracks – the 'ahahaha' for KLF's *3:A.M. Eternal* and others – and she agreed to record a vocal for us. Neil sorted all this out from his connections. P.P. Arnold had worked with The Beatmasters in 1988, and was used to housey stuff. She was also used to better treatment, which was clear when I picked her up from Stafford train station in my beat-up Cavalier. We were on a budget, but she had the right hump.

We needed a title and a vocal for the song that would take an '8' and so we tossed a few ideas about with The Fat Controller Mike Bell. Someone suggested *E-vapor-8*. It seemed OK, with an E and a nod to Vicks in there, but it was totally meaningless. It was at least a notch above *Masturb8*, which always got suggested two or three times. We then added the lyric: '*Don't Make Me Wait.*'

When we got to the studio, someone was already booked in and so we offered them some money to let us jump the queue, which they agreed to and we filmed the sessions as footage for the video. We placed the much darker *Armageddon* on the B-side, which was much more hardcore and underground; it was receiving some great DJ reaction reports. Doc Scott loved *Armageddon* and it still gets props from the underground, which is very nice. We then recorded some more crowd noise, but added some original wolf-whistles. We also got

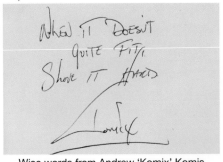

Wise words from Andrew 'Komix' Komis
(R.I.P.)

Derrick May

Jay Denham - thanks for the 909

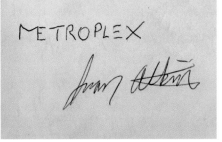

Juan Atkins - The Godfather of Techno

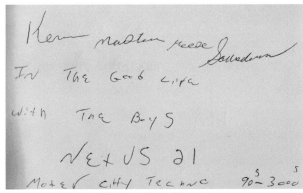

Kevin 'Master Reese' Saunderson

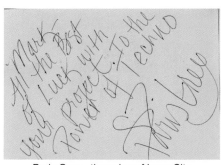

Paris Grey - the voice of Inner City

The Innovator - Derrick May

Trying to look natural whilst being totally star struck by your ultimate musical hero, Derrick May

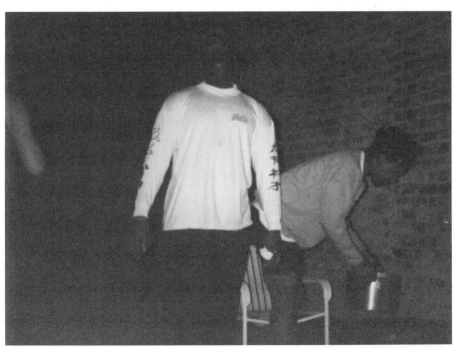

As if I'm at a barbeque at Derrick May's house

Playground twist: Chris (L) and Mark look out for the next Southern trend (spit)

Nexus 21 photo shoot, 1990

Bio Rhythms club night,
Walsall, 1990

Nexus 21, *Record Mirror*,
1990

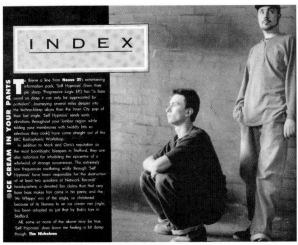

Nexus 21, *Record Mirror*

Nexus 21, live at Quadrant
Park, Liverpool, 1990

Can U Steal It?

Altern 8
'Overload'

Eight Track Extended Pleasures Of Technology

The sticker that sealed the name - Altern 8

The first Altern 8 release

Phoenix Leisure™ Presents
The Real Sound of the Underground!

introspective

Every Friday 10.00pm-2.00am at the Leisurebowl
Commerce Street, Longton, Stoke-on-Trent, Staffs Tel: (0782) 321611

— Friday 5th October 1990 —
2 for Joy (P.A.)

— Friday 12th October 1990 —
Nexus 21 (P.A.)

— Friday 19th October 1990 —
Awesome 3 (P.A.)

— Friday 2nd November 1990 —
Guy Fawke's Revenge
Indoor Pyrotechnics (controlled explosions)

— DJ's —
Buck ● Justin ● Bromley Jr

— MC —
Ragga Juddah

— Attractions —
Laser Effects ● 10K Sound Systems ● Strobe Flowers
Neon Flowers ● Ambience Room ● Film Show etc, etc

Be early to avoid disappointment. Introspective is for Phoenix Leisure
members and their guest. Proof of membership required

For Complimentary Membership complete and return below (with I.D.)
Name _____
Address _____
_____
Telephone _____ Date of Birth _____

Admission £4 before 11 - £5 thereafter

Introspective, the Leisure Bowl, Longton,
Stoke, 1990

ASTON VILLA
LEISURE CENTRE

SPECTRUM ENTERPRISES PRESENT
'TIME'
MONDAY 31ST DECEMBER 1990
DOORS OPEN 8:00PM SHOW TIME 9:00PM
EVENT RUNS FROM 8:00PM TO 7:00AM
STRICTLY NO ADMITTANCE AFTER 2AM
(BUS SERVICES FROM CITY CENTRE TO ASTON
STATION NO'S 65,67,104 & 114)

£22.00
+ BKNG FEE

TICKET NO.
00018

OVER 18'S ONLY
RIGHT OF ADMISSION RESERVED
INFO LINE - 021 454 2967
(THIS PORTION TO BE RETAINED)

Time at Aston Villa Leisure Centre, 1990

Le 8 Dec. à partir de 21h. au Parc des Expositions du Bourget

THE RAVE
MAXXIMUM POWER ZONE

NETWORK ET WARP Records Présentent 'ON STAGE'
NIGHTMARES ON WAX - RYTHMATIC - L.F.O. - NEXUS 21
plus DJ NEIL MACEY
WEST BAM - DJ EDDY DE CLERCQ
MAXXIMUM 'GO BANG' SLAM JAM
power featuring FREDDY B.
DJ LAURENT GARNIER

004419
P.A.F. 80 Frs

Navettes (GRATUITES) entre la Porte de la Chapelle @ et le Bourget

A trip to France with the Warp/Network tour,
1991

in association with *e-zee*
PRESENTS promotions

"THE WEEKEND OF LOVE"
(All Nighter)
FEATURING
NIGHTMARES ON WAX
L.F.O.
NEXUS 21
RHYTHMATIC
Plus
THE BANG CLUB DJ'S
(JACQUI, JIM and ELVIS)

16K sound system - special lighting efx - food-juice
bar - tickets £16.00 available from 1. up Aberdeen
642662 - groucho's Dundee 28496 - goldrush Perth
29730

STRICTLY TICKET ONLY EVENT
(To avoid disappointment, tickets must be
purchased in advance)

SAT 9th FEB
BEACH BALLROOM, ABERDEEN
10p.m. till 6a.m.

The Warp/Network tour hits Aberdeen

Nexus 21 live set-up (with a few bits of LFO's gear), Warp/Network tour, 1991

Benson and Bobhead visit the cottage, 1991

WILDMAN PROMOTIONS
PRESENTS

NEXUS 21

FRIDAY 14TH JUNE
PLAYERS CLUB, 7 NORTH PARADE, BATH
9 TIL 2 ADMISSION £3.50

forthcoming wildman events at players
IZIT friday 21st june
NIGHT TRAINS friday 28th june
DESCARGA friday 12th july
INNOCENCE friday 26th july

PLAYERS CLUB
TEL:0225 422030

Nexus 21 playing live and looking boring,
Warp/Network tour, Scotland, 1991

Nexus 21, Bath, 1991

Very early Altern 8 photo with the Tippex name badge

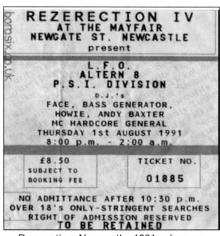

REZERECTION IV
AT THE MAYFAIR
NEWGATE ST. NEWCASTLE
present

L.F.O.
ALTERN 8
P.S.I. DIVISION
D.J.'s
FACE, BASS GENERATOR,
HOWIE, ANDY BAXTER
MC HARDCORE GENERAL
THURSDAY 1st AUGUST 1991
8:00 p.m. - 2:00 a.m.

£8.50 SUBJECT TO BOOKING FEE	TICKET NO. 01885

NO ADMITTANCE AFTER 10:30 p.m.
OVER 18's ONLY-STRINGENT SEARCHES
RIGHT OF ADMISSION RESERVED
TO BE RETAINED

Rezerection, Newcastle, 1991, where we discovered Vicks

We used to follow SOR around the country

Altern 8 photo shoot 1991 before the change in masks

DIY props, 1991

Shelley's car park gig. Live from the back of a truck

The Activ 8 acetate that was played at Shelley's

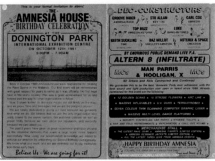

Amnesia House, Donington, one of our first really big gigs

The pot of Vicks on TOTP, 1991

Altern 8's evil acid smiley, nicked from a flyer, 1988

NYC, 1991, climbing up lampposts

A bit windy in Times Square

We had to pay the cab driver for this shot

Limelight flyer, our first trip to New York, 1991

Dominic Green to re-record his commentary from the Shelley's car park shoot, as Neil loved it so much, but incidental noise meant we couldn't use the original.

We wanted to do something different for the *E-vapor-8* video. Now, we had been the subject of constant comparisons to the KLF, but we didn't mind being the Budget KLF. There was a rumour going round at that time that KLF had bought a submarine and so we decided to hire some armoured tanks for our video. The storyboard for *E-vapor-8* was very comical; basically a 'day in the life of Altern 8'.

So, it started with Chris and I waking up in bed together, in full costume, whilst reporter Dominic Green did his intro. But Dominic didn't show up to the video shoot and so his intro was portrayed on screen by a rubber Boglin creature and this really pissed him off apparently. His intro followed the Joey Beltram-style *Mentasm* stab of our alarm clock that roused us in our teenage bedroom (Neil Rushton's son's).

It then cut to the kitchen where we're eating breakfast, shovelling Corn Flakes into our masks. Then P.P. Arnold appeared with the vocals whilst Crez danced. It was during the filming of the recording session, following breakfast, that Derek Holt completely lost his shit (after we paid off the previous occupants at Blue Chip). It was so awkward being there, as he was going off his cake. P.P. Arnold was ushered out as Derek was effing and blinding behind us. Not a great vibe.

We hired three tanks and a tank transporter and took them to a field in Cannock for a rave, as you do. It cost a lot of money to hire those, what with the drivers and fuel. We then put on a Shelley's style-PA in the field. We were worried that people might not show, but they did. Shitloads. It was very cold and everyone was just standing about. The 'plot' hinged around a battle between our robot and the tanks, which represented the authorities that were trying to shut the rave down. Pyrotechnics were going off everywhere as the tank trundled past with smoke bombs exploding. Thinking about it now, it was absolutely mental. A clod of earth flew up and hit one of the tank commanders in the face.

Earlier that day we'd all bundled into an amphibious vehicle for a quick jaunt around Stafford. There was me, Chris, Butler, Crez and Parksy in this open-top amphibious vehicle, driving through daytime Stafford, going round and round as Crez danced like a loon. We had a banner that said: 'Hardcore – you now the score!' We were meant to be the Pied Pipers of rave and were told to go through town and gather up a load of ravers for the gig. One local legend caught on film with a tambourine was a homeless geezer called Russian Rob. I'm not sure if he had a clue as to what was going on.

Another scene featured the acquisition of the personnel carrier. So we turned up at a car dealership and walked along the cars shaking our heads. Dave Barker played an Arthur Daley-type in a sheepskin coat trying to flog us a motor. We walked along the cars, shaking our heads, until the car dealer had a bright idea. Ding! A tank, priced £808. The last scene had us driving towards this big lake. We were proper nervous as this amphibious vehicle entered the water. How many tonnes of tank was this? It drove straight in twice, one shot with us, one without, so that we could *evaporate* in the final shot. Put it this way, we didn't make much money from this single, although it got to number 7. Fun fact: did you know that such was the influence of this tune, that there is now a sports sock called the Evapor8? Eh KLF, how about that?

Roboman started showing up at all sorts of different gigs and was well into the whole rave thing. I guess there were always people at raves who juggled fire and attached things to their bodies and so it fitted in on that level. I think his first appearance was at The Eclipse in Coventry and Neil Macey from Network spotted him. It was quite a sight when you were off your kipper to see this robot walking past you. It blew everyone's heads from the summer of '91 onwards.

Roboman later came to the States with us and she – Bill is now a woman – went down a storm. Roboman was so tall the cameramen had a job fitting her into their shots. I remember she modified these mad helmets at one point and had bolts sticking out like Pinhead from *Hellraiser*. She also put mirrored tiles all over them so when we pointed a laser at her, they pinged off into the crowd. If you'd looked directly into the helmet you'd have burned your retinas out. Bill was bang up for anything though and looked ace on stage.

Tanks, robots, masks and suits – we had travelled about as far from away from Nexus 21 as it was possible to get. The stage act was really tight now and while we karate-chopped the keyboards during these big stabby riffs, everything was accentuated. Butler was jumping up and down whilst Crez and Parksy did their routines. It was proper powerful. Then, when they needed a rest, the robot would come on. The PAs got longer and longer, starting at 30mins, then 45 and finally, an hour.

As we were achieving a certain level of success we thought it might be time to change the costumes a little. The paper masks had served us well, but one of them had been damaged during a Hacienda gig. The first time we played there we experienced technical problems, which delayed the set. Then halfway through *Frequency*, Sasha just stopped it without warning, so he could get his start time bang on, so there was no big ending for us. So we went off stage in a sulk and threw our masks down and the bus driver promptly sat on mine. The masks were from B&Q and were squashy and painted with white emulsion, so they were hard. They were so tough you couldn't breathe in them so I punched some holes in the top. But the driver's arse had cracked the paint when he sat on mine and the mask was fucked. Designer Peter Walsh said he wanted to do a picture of some masks for the *E-vapor-8* sleeve and so we used this opportunity to get some new ones. We thought we'd go for foam masks that were thicker, with a smoother surface. The problem was that we couldn't breathe in them and were close to fainting while performing. Then Chris left his on top of a gas fire and it melted, so those were fucked too. So we went back to the paper ones. The eagle-eyed fans might notice the slight difference in that the grooves went across the front of the mask and not down, like the original ones. We also bought balaclavas and a big great plastic sheet with a hood on it from army surplus for this sleeve shoot. We put an A and 8 on front of the green cape and it caused quite a stir. Network got a call from *Mixmag* asking to do a piece on the new get-up for a full centre spread. It seemed our profile really was growing. We bumped into Inspiral Carpets up in Manchester and we said, 'No way it's Inspiral Carpets!'

- 'No way it's Nexus 21!' they replied.

We really didn't expect them to know who we were.

Techno was quite a thing by now and even kids' TV was picking up on it. A kids' current affairs show called *Ipso Facto* took us to Alton Towers to discuss whether techno was boring. I'm sure we were interviewed at Chris's house and they had to make it all dark so it didn't look like a bedroom. This host asked us a few questions, nothing too in-depth and we had to explain why 'techno music' wasn't boring. I guess it was just to dispel preconceived notions that you just pressed a button, so the computers could do the rest. We then spent a day at nearby Alton Towers in full costume, having a top laugh with Crez. We also linked up with Mark Goodier again on Radio 1's *Evening Session* where we made a song, live on air, with the help of listeners. This woman called in to say the vocal part and really kept mucking it up. It was a bit embarrassing really. 1992 also saw us do quite a bit of mixing for some class acts like Yellow Magic Orchestra and Pet Shop Boys. Our stuff didn't really suit Neil Tennant's voice and so we sampled an old house vocal for the Pet Shop Boys and put the vocal through a vocoder to make it sound robotic. We were getting offered a lot of progressive house stuff at the time too, but it wasn't our kinda thing.

***

I preferred *Infiltrate 202* and *Activ 8* myself, but the song that everyone seemed to rave over was *E-vapor-8*. We recorded Butler shouting 'evaporate' at the end of this gig at Aintree in Liverpool, to appear on the track. Butler wasn't happy. 'It doesn't mean anything!' Everyone thinks it says 'Move out of the way' and to this day I still get that shouted at me in the street. 'Move out of the way!' I had no idea as to why they were doing this, for years, until someone said, it's from *E-vapor-8*. 'Move out of the way!' We were no longer just a rave act, we were a part of pop culture, getting played along Right Said Fred's *Deeply Dippy* at 'Sharon and Tracy clubs', which of course wasn't so great on many levels.

Top of the Pops was getting easier, though. We knew *E-vapor-8* was going to be a hit purely by the pre-sales and so TV beckoned once more when *E-vapor-8* entered the charts at 10 before peaking at 6. Crez was able to join us this time plus, in P.P. Arnold, we had a proper singer. P.P. turned up in a crushed velvet catsuit – very Austin Powers – with Marigolds on. She then took a piece of silver foil from a chewing gum pack and stuck it to her lapel because it apparently looked 'techno'. What?! P.P. Arnold really belted out the vocals, which was a massive relief.

A music magazine wanted to do an interview with us at *Top of the Pops* and they followed us around for a day as we had sarnies and went to Boots and other exciting capers. As we were standing in the corridor they asked me: 'What do you think of *Top of the Pops*, then?' I explained that although it looked like a proper gig, it was nothing of the sort. Everyone was herded about and an Akai sampler played crowd noise. 'It's a bit crap really innit?' We didn't really think it was crap; we were just giving an insider's point of view. However, they took that quote and made it massive on the page. So we got banned from *Top of the Pops*. We went to Network the following week and were told the news. I felt like a proper dick. I know all publicity is good publicity, but we had shot ourselves in the foot. Majorly. As much as you could brush it off, we were banned from *Top of the Pops.*

***

I was watching the LA riots on TV. The violence that swept through South Central, Los Angeles that spring – following the acquittal of the four LAPD police officers who beat Rodney King – seemed so shocking, sat at home in Stafford. These scenes were hitting home particularly hard as Altern 8 were booked to play LA and the day of our departure was not far off.

We landed in LA just 12 days after the LA riots and you could just feel the tension on the streets. You could tell some major shit had gone down. Something wasn't quite right and I didn't feel that safe outside the hotel complex that was home to a number of celebrities. The hotel was a safe haven at that time.

We took Roboman and all the usual crew with us, and the lads were all besotted by Stacey Smith (Paul Young's wife) who was sunning herself by the hotel pool. She was stunning. We were all sucking our stomachs in as we walked around her. I was losing my hair by that point and so I doubt I represented much of a threat to Mr Young. Axl Rose was there too and so I can safely say that I have had breakfast with Axl Rose. Well, I saw him up at the bar getting some cereal, if that counts.

We were told that you shouldn't dive into the pool, but Butler had found a set of steps that led up to a roof terrace and he started bombing into the water from a flower bed. Then someone produced a camera as Butler got his cock out. The camera disappeared inside Butler's pants, as he giggled away. 'Hey, Midget Gem! Why do you keep getting your dick out?'

Crez was impressive in that he would just get up at the crack of dawn and go out investigating, no matter where he was. He just became a native wherever he went. LA riots? 'I'll just go for a wander.' Butler and Parksy would just sleep all the time. Parksy once slept for 24 hours after one gig. Looking back, we were all so young and daft. Those moments are gold-plated really. Getting paid to go to LA and play some music and hang around a hotel with Axl Rose; what's not to like? When I say 'hang around a hotel with Axl Rose', I mean, he was sometimes within a few yards of us.

The gig was at a festival in Orange County and I wasn't sure if we were going down well at all. It was a different crowd from what we were used to and I had a slightly skewed perspective from being jetlagged. It honestly looked like no one was dancing. 'We're going down shit here!'

Then some geezers wearing chemical suits ran across the front of the stage and jumped back into the crowd before the bouncers could catch them. The US label bosses were freaked out that the crowd were wearing masks and suits, considering that we were totally unknown over there. 'How do people already know your stuff? How is this possible?' We weren't signed to anyone over there so it was a bit of a shock to them. The US promoters really went to town with the flyers, which had a coin taped to them. They also gave away a square flexi-disc single of *Infiltrate 202*.

Normally, at the end of a gig Parksy and Crez would come to the back of the stage to get Chris and me and we'd walk to the front and bow, but because I wasn't getting good vibes from the crowd, although the robot was doing her stuff, I refused to do the 'thank you'. I didn't want to ask for appreciation if it wasn't going to come. I just shook my head and left the stage. But Parksy took massive offence at this.

We were back at the Winnebagos getting changed, whilst talking to a woman who was interested in signing us, when Parksy came steaming in. 'What the fuck was that all about?!' Parksy was proper going off his cake. The label boss was freaked and obviously found the whole thing awkward and cleared off. This was a key moment in our careers and we'd blown it. It also spoilt the rest of the trip. Parksy was sharing a room with me, but he took a bed in Butler's room after the spat, which represented a minor mutiny of sorts.

It was a really weird trip in that I later found out that we had gone down really well that night and we actually got fan mail from LA from fans saying how that gig had completely changed their lives. We blew their minds which is why everyone was just staring, motionless. Oh well.

Marci Webber at NCT management was looking after us in the US and she organised a sit-down to try and smooth things over between Parksy and me. I tried to explain what had happened and how I felt but the upshot of it all was that I had to apologise to Parksy – and offer him a pay rise! I apologised to John, but said I felt a little isolated, like everyone was ganging up on me. Chris didn't take sides and Crez was always cool with everything, but I felt like it was always up to me to make everything better.

The lads had a good time over there however, getting up to all sorts. You could tell that something had gone down in LA. There was anger in the air. Still, I spent an afternoon record shopping down Sunset Strip and so I was happy.

Crez *"I would always say I was into ladies' trousers at the time, as that was my day job. I was a purchaser's assistant and used to buy the zips and threads and all that for M&S. Weird to think I was buying zips one minute and in LA staring at Paul Young's wife the next. LA was a great trip although not long after the riots. Stacey Smith was by the hotel pool and we all fancied her. Axl Rose's wife was there too, as was Robbie Coltrane who was doing the Coast to Coast show. LA had a real air of menace about it at that time. I remember sitting around the Sunset Bar and The Viper Room. I was chatting to this girl from Wolverhampton when this big black guy came over. 'Who's this?' There was lots of tension. I'm from Stafford and she was from Wolverhampton, both 5,000 miles away from home, and yet some dude had the major hump with me.*

LA was amazing though and we went down to Orange County to do the gig. Marci from our US management was upset because someone was taking photos of the show. Back then you were set upon if you photographed or videoed a gig. There was some crowd trouble and Marci thought we were going to get attacked so we had to get out of there quickly. I promptly got lost on the way back, but eventually returned to the hotel. Great times."

Back in the UK, we used the riot thing to get into the papers again although the only potential violence we witnessed was when Crez chatted up another guy's girl. Another story we spun to the press was that we were experimenting with the idea of replacing roadies with robots. Oh, and we were also running for election.

Don't Hesit8, Vote Altern 8!

We will close down Radio 3 and replace it with Radio 303. We will also kick the Royal Family out of Buckingham Palace and rename it Altern Towers, which will stay open to ravers at the weekend... The Hardcore Altern8-ive Party

April 1992. We were well into Altern 8's campaign to get elected to Parliament with Chris standing as a candidate in the 1992 General Election for the seat of Stafford. Phil Collins and Cher had already put their weight behind this campaign by signing our 'Vote Altern 8!' literature at the *Top of the Pops* studios and so momentum was building. I wasn't sure if this was a good idea or not, mainly because I thought we stood a fair chance of winning, and then what?! But I gave way to the General Election campaign concocted by Neil and John. We had a brilliant party manifesto written by journalist Andrew Harrison who liaised with a top political think-tank to laser-target our policies – covering all the hot issues of the day – to the local electorate. *'All police officers to wear bandanas at all times... A 10k sound system to be placed on every street corner...'* Our slogan was simple: *'Don't hesit8 vote Altern 8!'* Westminster was understandably concerned.

We were a victim of our own success in Stafford, though. Our campaign posters were swiped off the walls and lamp-posts as soon as they went up. Our fans were getting some free souvenirs, sure, but the undecideds were not being alerted to our campaign. After all, no one was nicking the Tory posters and placards. How could we compete when we were being destroyed from within?

Joking aside, the Conservative candidate Bill Cash really got the arse with us, because he knew we were taking the piss. When we did a photo with the local press – featuring all the candidates – Mr Cash had Chris cropped out of the picture. We didn't come last, though, and we beat the Natural Law Party; they were spitting feathers. Chris received a handsome 158 votes.

Andrew Harrison *"Chris stood for election and I wrote the party manifesto. The pledges included closing down Radio 3 and replacing it with Radio 303. We also wanted to kick the Royal Family out of Buckingham Palace and rename it Altern Towers and keep it open to ravers at the weekend. I made up a quote, 'Vote Altern 8, you know it makes sense, much more fun than the boring Labour or Tories.' The Sun ran the whole thing, but altered the quotes so it just said, 'boring Labour'. They couldn't even have a pop star in a chemical warfare suit saying daft things if it meant mild criticism of the Tory party. That tells you all you need to know about how mean-spirited people can be. Daft candidates are a part of British folklore; there has always been a man in a silly outfit. Elections are great at getting everyone down to the level of everyone else. We lost of course, but rave was getting politicised with the Criminal Justice Bill gaining a head of steam.*

Still, we beat the Natural Law Party, although we probably split the rave vote as a lot of ambient buffs who smoked spliff probably voted Natural Law. But if you were into hardcore bass, you would have voted for Chris. Hardcore – you know the score!"

***

We were booked to do the *Hitman & Her* at The Eclipse, Coventry. For those younger readers, this was a late-night TV show, on location in a different club each week. It was not the most professional of productions and was hosted by *Springwatch's* Michaela Strachan and record impresario Pete Waterman of PWL. At certain points they would try and interview ravers who were off their nuts. It was a bit of a shambles to be honest, but it featured some great acts and DJs. Imagine a TV show that operated outside the bogs of your local meat market, but with pounding hardcore and amphetamines. That show would be *Hitman & Her*.

It was well hot in The Eclipse that night and Pete Waterman was so sweaty and crumpled he looked like he'd been pulled through a car wash by a shire horse. There is film on YouTube of us on the roof putting our suits on as it was so damn hot in there. The Eclipse had these old narrow stairs we couldn't walk down without treading on people. It was a top show though and it really connected us with an audience even if it was a ramshackle affair. There would be one slot where Michaela would interview female punters who were completely off their noggins, their faces twitching and contorting like billy-o. That said, *Hitman & Her* was a real slice of what was happening back then.

If we weren't doing a PA we'd be on the dancefloor at The Eclipse or Shelley's. We went where our mates went and it was dead friendly at The Eclipse although there were some nasty stories about it. A weird one was this rumour that people with syringes were walking around injecting you with AIDS. Pretty pathetic I know and was probably other clubs spreading lies to ruin a growing reputation.

I never had a bad experience at any clubs. I didn't see any evil things going on. I just danced until it finished and then I was off. Shelley's was always great as well. You had to be tactical where you parked at Shelley's as it got so rammed. So you parked near the exit for a quick getaway. Karen and I got in the car to go home one night and found ourselves blocked in. So I tried to drive between these concrete bollards and got stuck. I got as far as the pavement and the wheels went up and I was stuck on the sill. But then hundreds of people came along and lifted the car up and placed it back down on the road whilst patting the roof of the car. It was all very friendly. I even bought equipment off people in that car park. 'Do you want to buy a drum machine? Roland 727.' Bosh! Don't know how people recognised me. I plugged it in when I got home and all the preset patterns had been used on early Chicago house tracks like *Jack the Groove*. The timbale solo in the middle of *Jack the Groove* is a preset on the 727.

May 1992, we played another Radio 1 do with Mark Goodier in Middlesbrough. We played alongside Utah Saints, SL2 and Frankie Knuckles, which was fun. Playing these gigs was brilliant because I was playing music we'd made. I still had no money and the car was always breaking down, but I always felt that music would bring good luck.

Chris and I got on and did the gigs and whatever, but we were still not clicking. There was something that didn't quite work. There was this underlying tension that just wouldn't go away. But we had recorded albums, remixes and singles together, so it wasn't all bad. The gigs were odd in that Chris and I were working whilst the dancers and MC were obviously more into partying; which was fine. After every gig I'd go straight back to the hotel. I was very innocent about what the others, and indeed the rest of the country, were up to. I was making music and that was enough to get me buzzing.

Tim Garbutt (Utah Saints) *"From day one, I have been a DJ. I started in '84/'85 and in 1988 (aged 19) I got to the semi-finals of the Technics/ DMC UK DJ Championships in London. I got some cheap decks as a kid and just practised and practised. I got my first job as a £30-a-night DJ for a five-hour set in a small club in Harrogate. I then put on and promoted my own house nights in a little basement club under an Italian restaurant, that only held 150 people. Sasha and Graeme Park were among a few who came and played there. I got introduced to the early Sheffield and Leeds sound from that night I was running; Forgemasters, Nightmares On Wax and Unique 3. It was through that club that I met Jez my partner in Utah Saints. He turned up one night with a cassette, which was an early demo of What Can You Do For Me? and we ended up going into the studio together to finish it off. We pressed it up on a white label and it totally blew up. We signed to Pete Tong's FFRR label and three months later it went top 10 and that was it.*

Back then, the cheapest sampler was about a grand to buy and used floppy discs that had a maximum of 15 seconds sampling time, so we would wire our turntable up to a sampler and play a 33rpm record at 45rpm, to get more into the sampler quickly and then pitch it right back down again. As we didn't have much equipment at the time we had to be more creative with our ideas and used the sampler as an instrument in its own right. You had to make good records of a certain quality back then in order to get people to play them as it cost about a thousand pounds to get a record made.

It was a great time back then. Friday night, we would load the car up with keyboards and our equipment and we'd be off. You could be driving to a gig in Braintree off the M25 and then you'd rock up at 3am, play an hour, then back up the M1. Sleep for a few hours, then up to Scotland. This was the same time as the infamous Blackburn raves were going off. It was chaos and loads of fun although many clubs weren't set up for PAs and you would literally have to plug your whole set-up into a left and right channel on the DJ's mixer. There was no sound man and it was a health and safety nightmare in some of these places. No rules, but a totally exciting time we will never forget."

***

Select magazine continued the love-in that spring and did a wicked 'day in the life of…' story with us. The opening spread featured a typical city street with everyone wearing Altern 8 masks. Chris's brother Ade and their nan all appeared as characters in the shoot, as did Crazy Clair the four-year-old MC.

There was MC Crazy Clair sat on the wall in front of the Mini owned by DJ Stan The Devil Tune Man (Network's sales rep). I think Clair's mum was sat on the wall next to her daughter. There were two random lads towards the right looking a bit rocky. Chris's nan was super tiny, pushing her trolley. Having a fracas with the robot was a policeman, played by Ade, which was a joke in itself. Karen's dad was in the background; we just asked him to walk naturally. Bearing in mind he'd been in the RAF he was proper marching, arms outstretched. 'We said normally!' We went back to Chris's mum's house later and he told the journalist that his parrot could say 'Rave on'. Which it couldn't. Ha ha!

We went into Chris's local after. I'd DJed there in '89 when I first knew Chris, Dean and Andy. But it wasn't the kind of pub where I should be playing acid house. I played some stuff that was in the charts, including a version of Lil' Louis' *French Kiss* called *Acid Kiss*. I played the tune at home, but hadn't paid attention to the lyrics. It was a bit rude to say the least. It slowed down for a bit and this girl was going on about sticking it in her arse and stuff. Everyone just looked at me. Oops. We then posed with a fire engine around the back of Lotus Records. As you do.

Andrew Harrison *"Right, go to Stafford and make it look as if the whole town is an Altern 8 theme park, with masks on. Journalist Adam Higginbotham and I sat up all night making masks, painting them yellow with spray paint and black gaffer tape. We made about 70 masks and stuck the As on them with masking tape. We tried a mask on before they'd properly dried and nearly passed out from the fumes and got banging headaches. Took nearly 10 years off our lives, that.*

We went to Stafford on a beautiful, sunny day, grabbed passers-by and rattled off these photos of people going about their everyday lives with these masks on. One of the band's mates had a police uniform and Roboman turned up too. We shot all these pictures next to Stafford train station, presented the entire place as if it was obsessed with techno. It was a little like the Truman Show or something. It looked kinda surreal."

Network wanted to release an Altern 8 album. The time was definitely right. We had released a number of singles and EPs and so we only really needed a few new tracks. The first bit of new material we recorded was *Hypnotic ST-8*, which we laid down at Blue Chip with Mike Bell. The album version was different to the remix for the 12" and in fact when we PA-ed it, everyone preferred the album version. *Hypnotic St-8* was a real mixture of styles. The drums were like Belgian techno, but more breakbeat-y. Music was moving really fast at this point and speeding up a lot. We decided to use a sample from Nexus 21's *Self Hypnosis*, thus the name *Hypnotic ST-8*, which was to be our next single. We added a new riff done on a TB303 and SH101 and panned them either side. We got the vocal from an acapella album and simply found lines in key. I didn't listen to the record itself, just lifted the acapella and then queued and synced it up. It was perfect.

During pre-sales we received a fax from a management company saying, 'You've sampled these vocals. We want this, this and this.' The damage equated to several thousand and they had us over a barrel as we couldn't pull the single and so we had to reach an agreement. I picked up the promo on RCA I sampled it from and it had stiffed; didn't get anywhere near the charts and the label clearly wanted to recoup some of the money. This they did. Thanks to us.

We used footage from a *Mythology* gig in Oxfordshire for the *Hypnotic ST-8* video. We got to the gig really early, but didn't go on until 6am when the sun was up. We were knackered after travelling down in the minibus. Carl Cox appeared in the video and Chris wore a red and white Cat In The Hat-style top hat and no one could remember where he got it from.

We used the same team that shot *Infiltrate 202* who were still quite cheap; which was good after spending so much on the *E-vapor-8* video. Ian had done so much work since *Infiltrate 202* that he had really upped his game.

I hated the sleeve design for the cover of *Hypnotic ST-8*. It featured 'Altern 8' cut out of confetti like a paper chain from a napkin. I didn't get sent the sleeve until it was done and so it was too late to change it. I thought it looked shit, although my anger was quelled a little when I realised that the design was quite clever in one regard. When many copies were displayed in a record shop window, all the confetti chains linked up, thus making an enormous picture. But I still didn't like it. Ha ha.

John McCready told the papers that we had recorded *Hypnotic ST-8* up Ben Nevis to get a certain vibe going. The press duly printed it. The only grain of truth there was that I had guinea pigs as a child called Ben and Nevis.

We did Normski's *Dance Energy* again for *Hypnotic ST-8* when it charted at number 33. Boyz II Men were on too. They had this whole preppy look going on with white jumpers and slacks. It was a mad one because this show had so many different kinds of music on it, so you never knew what kind of crowd would be there. There were a bunch of lads down the front this time, proper going bonkers during the day with all the lights on – it wasn't like a rave where you let yourself go, knowing no one could see you. You're going to be on telly, in someone's kitchen and everyone will see you. But they really went for it.

The *Dance Energy* studio was like a house with different rooms and so we were in the kitchen which had a black and white chequered floor. There was a bunch of Asian lads, all with masks on and hoodies, going absolutely bonkers during *Hypnotic ST-8*. Mark was MCing over the top of it, but we'd got a girl in again who looked the part. She said she could sing, so she mimed to the vocal. We also got her in the recording studio after, but she was awful. So bad. Her vocals were so poor, we all hid. Because the microphone room was made of glass, you could see what was going on in the studio, no matter where you stood. So we all had to hide behind the mixing desk in between the speakers because we couldn't hold back our embarrassment. I don't mean to be cruel, but she was awful. Totally out of key. Terrible singer. We were just laughing out heads off and all we could hear was, 'Is everything alright? Where have you guys gone? I can't see you.' You had to keep pressing a little button on the mixing desk in order to speak, 'Yeah, yeah, everything's OK, keep going.'

So by the time *Top of the Pops* came around again we needed to find someone else to sing live. The writing credits on the promo we sampled named the original singer and so we asked Ghida De Palma to sing live on the show. *Top of the Pops* had clearly forgotten about our ban. I don't know if the producer had changed or if he was on holiday, but either way we slipped back in.

Butler had a headset mic for this performance and mimed to the drums as he'd been a drummer in an indie group called The Seaside. 'Just stand there in front of these electronic drum pads and mime to the breakbeat.' You just you had to add something a little more dynamic for *Top of the Pops*. The record we sampled for *Hypnotic ST-8* was *Takes You Higher* by Energenic and so getting their lead singer was a touch. Ghida was from Portugal and a very nice lady – so enthusiastic and a fantastic singer who wrote the original lyrics for *Takes You Higher*. Ghida also kindly offered to wear an Altern 8 mask, although not on her face. Ghida wanted to attach a mask to each boob. 'Obviously it would be really nice if you, but... we don't think it's strictly necessary.' *Top of the Pops* was great and we had our own banners along the front saying 'Hardcore' and 'You know the score!'

So we had a few tracks already down before we started to think about the album. We knew *Activ 8* would be on there as would *Infiltrate 202* and *E-vapor-8*. We'd also done *Hypnotic ST-8* as well as *Armageddon, Re-Indulge* and *Frequency*, so we didn't have much to do as far as recording the rest of the album. I think one of the first tracks recorded was *First of May* which we did around the time of the *Overload EP* back in 1990. We called it *First of May* because it sounded like a Derrick May track. Derrick often did stuff under the name Mayday, the first of May, so it was a tribute of sorts. *Give it to Baby* was one of the first things I'd done on my own and that made the cut too. I think in total we recorded three tracks to finish the album off. The album version of *Hypnotic ST-8* was very different and so that added something new. Then we recorded *Brutal-8-E* which everyone called *brutalate* although it's meant to be *brutality*. It's got an E on the end, but unless you know what it means, it's a difficult one to get right. What does it mean? We sampled a track called *This Brutal House* and so we so thought, hey, brutality (or *Brutal-8-E*). That track was later remixed for a single release late in '92. There was also *A D8 With Plezure*. It was 'plezure' with a 'z' because we'd sampled a track by Plez.

The track *8's Revenge* is a long story about sampling, which started with Nexus 21 and the Derrick May track *Wiggin* that I took the bass line from for *Real Love*. Then a track came out by Robin Wants Revenge, which used half the bassline and that was a really big underground track. It was an American thing bootlegged onto a Canadian label and it was really big at raves. So when we remixed *Real Love* it started off with half the bassline and then went into the full bassline. So it started like Robin Wants Revenge before going into the whole of *Real Love*. So we sampled the bassline again, sped it up, put breakbeats underneath and called it *8's Revenge*. So, unlike many, we didn't spend four years slaving over our album as we had loads of stuff ready to go.

Around '92 everything sped up so much and you can hear that on the Prodigy's first album. The breakbeats were coming up and it was a lot faster. So the difference between house and hardcore had really widened at this stage. Everything was like 130+bpm, so songs like *Infiltrate 202* and *Move My Body* were quite slow by comparison at 125bpm, although the DJs pitched things up. So whereas Prodigy's album was remixed versions of stuff they had already released, it was specifically pitched at 1992, whereas *First of May* was a 1988 techno track. Indeed, a lot of the older tracks were slower, although the newer ones, such as *A D8 With Plezure* and *8's Revenge*, were a lot more breakbeat-y and significantly faster.

Even though, technically, we'd been in the charts four times, it didn't dawn on us as to how big this band actually was. There was never a stage where we thought, 'Fucking hell, it's massive!' I've always been Mark from Stafford. When you look back there were loads of hit records coming out of that scene from Prodigy, Love Decade and SL2, but we certainly never thought of ourselves as the Kings of Rave; we were just making and putting out music we liked. If someone else liked it, it was a complete bonus. We bumped into fellow 'chart-ravers' Utah Saints around this time, when they booked Altern 8 for The Gallery in Leeds. I said, 'Do you remember us? MADM?' They looked quite embarrassed. 'Oh no, we'd hoped you'd forgotten about that.'

Network went proper with the promotion of *Full On: Mask Hysteria*. I've still got a massive door-sized poster for the album. There were also cut-outs of the mask on the sleeve; my original that got sat on at The Hacienda. If you look closely at the mask you can see a big crack down the left-hand side of the A where the paint is missing, which goes right up to the top of the nose. The masks were quite hard because they were emulsioned twice before we sprayed the A. When the bus driver sat on the mask it was properly bust and you couldn't wear it again. Peter did a brilliant job reshaping that mask when he took the photos for the *E-vapor-8* campaign. That mask had been so important, from giving us a look to gifting me confidence. The mask was Altern 8 and what people instantly thought of when our name was mentioned. Even now, if you look at big EDM (electronic dance music) raves in America, people are wearing masks. They have no idea *why* they're wearing masks and they've probably never heard of Altern 8, but our legacy is there and it continues to get passed on down through the years. There was a little news story – probably fed to the press by us – saying that rave organisers were trying to stop ravers from wearing the masks. *'Altern 8 are at the centre of a controversy over dust masks being made essential rave accessories. Police and council members have banned the masks over allegations that rave attendees have been dousing them with ecstasy.'* That was probably the work of our new press officer Mark Mortimer (John McCready had left by this stage), but there was that whiff of truth behind it again, to make it believable. People really associated us with the whole Vicks thing and we'd do gigs where people would hold tubs of the stuff up wanting us to smear it over their chests. Which was nice. Tommy Lee signed girls' breasts and we got to rub Vicks over sweaty men.

John McCready *"When Network put out that KWS Please Don't Go thing, I couldn't stand it anymore. I found it impossible to see myself trying to create press interest for that. It was time for me to go.*

It had been an unreal situation; having so much fun and getting paid for it. But real PRs routinely deal with things they don't like and so I walked. I never saw myself as a press officer. I drifted into it because Neil asked me and made it clear he didn't know what he wanted – but he didn't want normal. Neil was wild, really. Money came and went. He was infected with that Factory (Records) virus – don't worry about making a million if you can make life exhilarating and intoxicating."

CH. 18

Bombs, Lasers And Voodoo

'These people Altern 8 don't know what they're doing. They're messing with the forces of evil. The occult. Leave the gods be and don't call on the spirits of the dead.' Lord Lichfield, House of Lords, 1992.

We played Northern Ireland during the troubles and flew Aer Lingus to Belfast on an old propeller job. The conditions were dead choppy. The pilot left the door to the cockpit open and, as I was on an aisle seat, I could see straight out of the window, watching the runway lights moving all over the place as the plane shot to the left and then to the right. It was like a ride at Alton Towers. I could see where the pilot was aiming, but the lights kept disappearing. It was horrific.

Some lads picked us up at the airport and as we made our way down the dual carriageway we saw a car that had been split into two across the central reservation. 'That wasn't here when we came to pick you up,' said the driver. I found Northern Ireland quite scary, to be honest.

Then we pulled up alongside a personnel carrier of British squaddies at a checkpoint; they looked so young and nervous and were holding machine guns. One of them asked our driver who we were as we waited to get our papers checked. Then the whole vehicle started rocking. 'Altern 8! Altern 8!' It was a wicked moment. Belfast was a proper reality check for us jokers and did nothing to instil confidence in us.

We couldn't take the keyboard stands to Northern Ireland and so we felt massively exposed on the great expanse of stage that was

Belfast's Royal Ulster Hall. The venue was slow to fill that night. 'Don't worry, lads,' said the promoter, 'it's just a couple of bomb scares.' How could you have 'don't worry' and 'bomb scares' in the same sentence? That properly shitted us up, but I guess it was just a part of everyday life there. Eventually we got the all-clear, however, and we went up on stage as the fans started filing in.

We only had one keyboard, one stand and no drape and it didn't look as if anything was plugged in. I decided I'd twiddle the pitch bend wheel while Chris played the keyboards as that was just about all I could do, bar playing the spoons on my knee. Then halfway through the set, the house lights came on, making everyone look pale. This was a full-blown rave with all the lights on. We looked like a prize pair of dicks standing behind one keyboard, like two saddoes at a carboot sale. If it hadn't been for the masks, I would have died of shame up there, but the audience danced away to their hearts' content.

After the gig, some of the lads went to an after-party in a car park somewhere in the middle of an estate. I went back to the hotel totally oblivious to what was going on. It was quite a hairy situation. A British DJ had recently been kneecapped due to his accent and we were told that if you got into the wrong cab you could end up losing your legs. So I safely tucked myself up in bed while the lads went off into God knows where.

Word had gotten out that some English ravers were hanging around that part of Belfast and so they had to hide under some carpets in the back of a van for fear of losing their knees. Luckily, they got back to the hotel safe, but maybe not that sound. The following day we had a gig in Dublin, which went a whole lot smoother.

Crez *"One of the maddest experiences we had was in Northern Ireland. John and I got invited to a party in a car park in the middle of nowhere and some lads found out we were English and we had to hide under some carpets. This was just outside Belfast, so we were in danger of getting into some serious trouble; there had already been two bomb scares at the venue that night. You had to watch yourself out there."*

***

We challenge the press to a Techno Duel... you are invited to be decim8ed in the labyrinth of The Quasar in Techno City UK. Don't hesit8. Should you survive the wrath of Altern 8 in the maze, you will be granted an interview. But first, prepare to be humilia8ed. You have been warned. ALTERN 8 WILL DOMIN8!

There was only one place that could stage a launch party of the magnitude that *Full On: Mask Hysteria* clearly deserved: Stafford Quasar. I'd been playing a lot of Quasar at the time as Karen and I had no kids and I was often at a loose end during the day. Crez lived nearby and so I'd often meet him at the ten-pin bowling centre. We got really good at this and were rated 'top guns'; based on how many times you fired and how many hits you got. We were shit hot, actually. Believe me, people took Quasar very seriously and there were sometimes fistfights in there. Dads would complain, 'You're killing my son! Leave him alone. It's just a game!' But it wasn't just a game. It was Quasar. I'm not sure if I should be revealing my tips and tricks, but try ducking down by the 'energising point' and as soon as your rivals have lowered their weapons... Bop! Bop! Bop!

We took Inner City and The Reese Project to Quasar in 1991 when we did a track with Kevin Saunderson, who came over to Stafford with Paris Grey to record *Let It Reign* at Blue Chip. Unfortunately, Chris's dad died as we were recording the track and so the main keyboard player had gone. Kevin was pretty much like me, he could get by on the keyboard, but any big chord or piano riff was well beyond him. Well, we were useless I guess. So we recorded *Let It Reign* – which everyone thinks is an Inner City track, although we actually wrote it – so Kevin could take the tapes back to Detroit to mix. His mixes are the bare bones of the track, but you can tell it's the same tune. They used all the riffs, but Kevin's mix was far more Inner City because he had to use it on their album; ours was more hardcore. But we got Paris Grey to sing about ecstasy and while Chris was away Kevin asked me to help him 'do hardcore'. 'I'm trying hard to do hardcore, but I just can't do it,' he said. No way, this is Kevin Saunderson and he wants *my* help! I was in total awe of him. He said he couldn't make his hardcore stuff sound authentic. 'All you have to do is nick this, nick that, nick this, get yourself a good breakbeat and fatten it up with drums. Get a stab noise or a riff of something. Loop it and put it to vocals. Bosh!' I gave him a disc with a load of breakbeat samples on it and he went away and started a project called Tronikhouse. The first Tronikhouse release was a really big hardcore record on KMS. He'd even nicked all the drums off *Move My Body*. Wholesale. He even swiped our drum loop. 'When I said *nick stuff*, I didn't mean all of *our* stuff!'

So Kevin Saunderson had been to Stafford, which was interesting. I took him to Lotus Records to see Pete Bromley and Yvonne who worked there. I phoned them up beforehand and said, 'I'm coming down with Kevin Saunderson.' They were well excited. I was taking my mate Kevin Saunderson into my local record shop. Yvonne went bright red, she was so embarrassed. 'Oh my God, it's Kevin Saunderson!' Pete tried his level best to sell Kevin a crate full of records. Because Kevin had no cash – and the staff were too embarrassed to ask him for an autograph – they photocopied his cheque and framed it. Kevin didn't get to go to Quasar, but Inner City and The Reese Project did and so I thought it would be a top venue for our album launch. The idea: get the London media up to Stafford for some Quasar and booze. We even set the party up as a challenge: 'Altern 8 versus The Press.'

A lot of launch parties have 'questions and answers' sessions with the acts, but as no one could hear us with the masks on, we decided to dodge that. I don't know whether it was our first or second time in America when we found ourselves on an interview panel in the Twin Towers. There we were, sat at a table with all these little mics about – for American college radio – and every question was answered with a 'Mfmmmmfmmf.' They seemed to find it amusing, but it was a waste of everyone's time, really. However, we liked the idea of getting the press to form a Quasar team.

We videoed the Quasar and played the album as we got it on. It was a real laugh and a fun day out for the journalists. So there were people from *Smash Hits*, *Melody Maker* and loads more. Altern 8 prevailed, with Crez and I the top guns. Crez was pretty decent at Quasar after all the practice we'd put in. Because we knew the staff at the ten-pin we asked some of them to join us and they were ace. The only downside to the launch party – we slaughtered the press – was my battle scar. To this day I have a little wound by my eye because I didn't know that cameraman Ian – who did the *Infiltrate 202* and *Hypnotic ST-8* videos – was right behind me filming when I swung around dead quick. His camera lens caught my eye. BANG! I got cut. But hey, that party generated lots of good press for our album.

Paul Lester (*Melody Maker*) "*Imagine a hi-tech war-torn Beirut at night without any real bloodshed, but lots of genuine fear, or a three-*

dimensional "Space Invaders" game with proper human beings instead of computerised cartoon blimps. When one of the thin red beams from the laser guns hits the light-sensitive packs on our backs, a point is scored for the opposition and we edge that little bit closer towards crushing, humili8ing defeat..."

Mark Mortimer (Press Officer, Network) "I came on board after John McCready left. I was joining this crazy party and to be honest I was really ill-prepared for it. In many respects I was the wrong person for the job because when Neil Rushton headhunted me I was a journalist working as a news editor at a local paper in Nuneaton, about to work on Fleet Street. Things were going well for me. But being a musician myself, I was attracted to working in the music industry. My parents were completely mortified. 'You need to work on Fleet Street!' They thought I was nuts basically. I was totally into the idea, though and Neil lured me in with the promise of a trip to Mexico with Altern 8, which of course never happened.

Another reason I was completely unprepared was that I came from a guitar background and so this was not my vibe. My tastes in '92 were not aligned to dance music at all. A couple of years before, I'd been asked to hype up an acid record, and so went to Birmingham, hung out with Neil and managed to create quite a stir actually and it even got to the point where I got questions asked about it in Parliament. I didn't know too much about the scene at the time and a lot of my friends back then were really into traditional guitar-generated music and some were too quick to give blanket criticism to people involved in electronica. You know, like they aren't 'real' musicians if they don't have a guitar hung around their neck. Of course I knew then how stupid that was, so had an affinity with Mark from the start, despising dinosaur attitudes.

Mark was one of those people who always made you feel welcome and was dead friendly from the off; easy to get on with, but didn't suffer fools lightly. I loved Altern 8's punky vibe and so to me it was as much MC5, Sly Stone and Sex Pistols as it was dance, and I was totally into it.

I had to learn on my feet at Network. KWS had a number one the first day I started work there. Altern 8 were flying too. I wasn't that aware of Nexus 21 to be honest and so it was quite a brave decision by Neil. There was real madness dealing with the daily papers who *would ring me up asking, 'What do you want to invent about Altern 8 today?' The John McCready vibe was already there of course and though I was unsure of my ability to follow him, I knew I could bring some extra surreal madness to the party. And I did. Working closely with Neil Rushton, I was inspired. He had a Malcolm McLaren-esque view of the music industry; a brilliant maverick and in some ways had more in common with Alan McGee.*

It was a fairly hedonistic time and all the promotional work for Network was done with a lusty sense of humour. I was pleased with the press launch for the album when we challenged the press to a game of laser warfare at Stafford Quasar. Instead of champagne at a London hotel and all the back-slapping that would involve, we thought it would be much more fun to have a leftfield event where we could manipulate the press, get drunk and play Quasar. I also fixed it so the media team couldn't win.

We went down prior to the party and had a word with the Quasar guys. The average game was 15 minutes, but ours was to be two hours. We fixed it so the packs the press were wearing didn't register most of their hits. Ha ha. It was great fun: Altern 8 V The Press. Sounds, Melody Maker, Music Week and Smash Hits all turned up and we got a lot of coverage. Roboman was there in the arena, gunned up. Some of the journalists took it very seriously and were rock guys who really wanted to beat the electronic musicians."

Network arranged album signing sessions at all the HMVs in the Midlands area, so we hit Birmingham, Derby and Wolverhampton and the queues were LONG! They had to close the shops for a bit because the lines were snaking all the way around and blocking the exits, making it a fire hazard. Whether the fans had already bought it or just scanned it through, we'd sign it for them. A lot of people wanted 'Top one, nice one, get sorted!' written on the front. This young Asian girl – maybe 12 or 13 – slipped me a piece of paper with her phone number on it. On the back it said, 'Mum and Dad are out after 6pm.' We'd often get odd requests like that from time to time. I got a phone call at home once; how on earth they found my phone number, I don't know. I always answered with my phone number and after, this Scottish girl said, 'Hello! Is that Mark from Altern 8?'

- 'Yeah.'
- 'Tee hee.'

Then she put the phone down. If you're going to phone someone at least say something, don't just put the phone down. They must have phoned all the Archers in Stafford.

We were doing all these signing sessions when this new HMV opened in Hanley, Stoke-on-Trent. The shop had not been officially opened as yet and so we were asked by the Mayor of Stoke to do the honours. I think we got asked because Stoke was in Staffordshire and Bizarre Inc were the only other local band, and they didn't have an album out at the time. I think it just coincided nicely. So the Mayor had the scissors on the velvet cushion and he passed it to me, only to get a shaking of the head. I then pulled out these big, green garden shears and everyone laughed. I cut the ribbon and we did another signing session for the album.

They booked a new group to play a PA at the HMV because there was a local lad in their ranks. They were called Take That. Because we had our rave fans and Take That had the screaming little girlies, it made for quite a noisy day. We were interviewed on Signal Radio after, but again, all they got was 'Mfmfmmmm.' A lot of people from Network turned up to that as it was quite a big thing. They even had the HMV dog there and we had our photo taken with it.

Full On: Mask Hysteria did really well. It entered the album charts at number 11 and sold 25,000 copies in just four days. Network did a great job with all the promotional bumf and there were posters all over the UK.

***

'The ancient spirits have to die! This ancestral home to the old gods is to be cleansed!' The witch doctor placed a skull into the air and roared. The crowd raised their fists and yelled as one. This was Judgement Night!

August 1992 we played Stafford Bingley Hall with Prodigy for Starlight's Judgement Night. Bingley Hall was a big, traditional venue and was famous for rock gigs – as well as antique fairs and county shows – and had hosted Led Zeppelin and The Who. Billed as a court-style affair pitching us against Prodigy, Judgement Night was Bingley Hall's first foray into 'rave' and is still talked about in Stafford now.

Stafford Council pretty much tried to close this legal rave down. There was still this whole thing about raves in the press and the media kept on about the supposed violence and drug-taking zombies, but it was all completely ridiculous. Obviously the local paper got on to the fact that there was going to be a rave in Stafford and rather than celebrate that dance culture was coming to this small, provincial town, they concentrated on the thousands of nutters who were to descend upon it, hell-bent on causing merry mayhem. The residents were also worried about the expected noise levels of the event; a quite legitimate concern as it turned out. Ha ha. But the night went ahead.

I stood next to Butler during the soundcheck and we had to shout at each other as you couldn't hear a thing above the din. Your mouth was going and nothing seemed to be coming out. We really felt that this night was going to be amazing. The noise was something else, especially when you added a police helicopter into the mix. Even as the music played out, all you could hear was the whirring of the propellers.

There were loads of undercover police at Bingley Hall, including the police officer at the end of the *Activ 8* video who was in plain clothes. We were backstage, and watching the police briefing before they went in. 'No way, it's you!' we shouted and this copper was like, 'No! Ssshhh! Seriously!'

- 'It's you! From our video!'

The PC got sent home after that because his cover had been compromised. The police looked like a right bunch of Teds. They were steaming up to people asking them if they had any drugs. Everyone knew they were police. It was so obvious. I think they were just there to note things going on rather than to shut it down, but it did spoil the night in a lot of ways. Helicopters whirring around above did nothing for that warm, loved-up vibe we hoped for. That night was the only time we met the Prodigy. I say 'we', as I didn't say anything to them, being far too shy. Butler probably steamed up to them.

We did a voodoo ritual at Stafford Bingley Hall that night to exorcise the rock demons from the venue. Yes, that sounds quite weird written down. Well, it was a publicity stunt really, although who knows for sure, eh? You couldn't just take a photo of a rave and expect a newspaper/ magazine to write about it, because there were loads of raves going on, up and down the country. But we had a distinct angle to this one. We had voodoo. So Network's new press officer Mark Mortimer cooked up this whole scheme where we were to lay to rest the rock demons of Stafford Bingley Hall.

The shaman danced on to the stage with a cow's skull on his head. He wore a grass skirt and everything. Then someone came on and read out this passage detailing the ritual he was about to perform to the thousands of ravers stood there watching. 'Someone says this is an ancient rock venue! But we don't want rock in this building! We're going to exorcise rock from this sacred place!' Then this geezer in a grass skirt did a mad dance. We gave him a guitar and he started smashing it up on stage and everyone was going mad, cheering. It was properly going off. If it wasn't a bona fide voodoo ceremony, then it was dangerously close. The witch doctor told us he knew a couple of words of Swahili, but we never really believed him. He was talking utter nonsense, but no one in the crowd knew what he was saying so he sounded pretty authentic. He was probably ordering chips or something. It was proper daft. Later on, this witch doctor was holding the cow skull by one of its horns when it came off in his hands, releasing loads of maggots. It was proper grim. There's a photo somewhere, with all of us and the witch doctor and it looks as if everyone has face paint on with huge bags under their eyes. I'm not sure why.

Mark Mortimer *"Judgement Night was hilarious. That was really something. I had seen The Jam play Bingley Hall, so I knew it well; it was a rock venue going back to the sixties. We had the idea of flying in a witch doctor to exorcise the spirit of rock and I found just the man to perform that ritual. I also stole my brother's guitar, a cheap rip-off, so the voodoo man could smash it up onstage. The witch doctor was fantastic and the press went mad for it although they didn't suspect that he was actually a photographer from the Nuneaton Gazette. Ha ha.*

The Bishop of Lichfield was really pissed off after and said so in the House of Lords. 'These people Altern 8 don't know what they're doing. They're messing with the forces of evil. The occult. Leave the gods be and don't call on the spirits of the dead.' It became a real hoo-ha, as was intended. As voodoo practitioners were not easy to come by I had to find a man willing to play the part. Matt Page was a photographer at the local paper I used to work for and he was a like-minded rascal. He did a great job playing the African witch doctor. He had a skull and a foot from some animal and a wig on his head. We also blacked him up with shoe polish. I still laugh now when I see the pictures. We got very drunk when it became clear that our scam had got into the House of Lords; that was a real victory and with it I had added a little bit of myself into the Altern 8 story."

CH. 19

Wedding Bells, Ibiza And A Man Called Moby

Quasar and voodoo ceremonies to one side for a moment, I had a pretty normal life really. Karen and I were still at the two-up two-down terrace on Sandon Road and we did all the usual things that any young couple does. Karen and I had been together since we were 17 and been engaged since I was 19, so the next logical thing was to get married. The wedding didn't really have much to do with me at all; maybe Karen was worried that I'd hire a shaman. So, everything got taken over by my mother-in-law and I had absolutely no say in anything, even what we were going to eat. 'This is where you sit… this is the menu.' I didn't want melon balls in port, for example, but melon balls in port it was. 'That's OK, if that's what everyone wants,' I would mumble.

It was a registry office do and I honestly didn't think the papers would turn up, but lo and behold there was *The Mirror*. My wedding was also on the front of the local Stafford paper and mentioned in lots of music pages. My wedding! How on earth was that *news*?!

Now, Karen really wanted Chris to be there, which was a bit odd really. Things were getting a bit frosty between Chris and me by then and to be honest I wasn't mad keen on having him there. We were working hard and spending a lot of time together and I think we may have needed a break. But Karen was insistent. 'You work with him so we can't *not* invite him. It would be dead weird if you didn't.' I just went along with everything she said and nodded my head.

I was very nervous on the day. A lot of Karen's relatives had come up, including her aunties from down south and the only time they'd ever seen us was when we did the Nexus 21 thing on Channel 4's *Dancedaze*. Now because they didn't know which one was me, they obviously thought the most important person was the one right at the front – MC Man Parris – and so they were expecting me to be black. So when they all filed in to the registry office, they completely blanked muggins, sat by the door. I didn't know them and they didn't know me. So we got married and had the reception back at this pub in the village just outside Sandon. Karen's dad paid for the bar to stay open, but they took the money and closed it anyway. Parksy got absolutely shit-faced and kept putting his arm around everyone, telling them how much he loved them.

My dad managed to embarrass someone he didn't know during the meal, which was typical Dad. If something was on his mind Dad would just say it, which meant he could be quite inappropriate at times. So he stood up to read the cards out and spotted this lady in a big crushed velvet hat. Dad waved to her, 'Nice hat, love!' Silence. Apparently this lady was going through chemotherapy at the time and had lost her hair. Nice one Dad!

I had put on quite a bit of weight by then, as well as losing all my hair; it had gradually given up the plot since I was 17. It was soul-destroying. When I met Karen, my long curly hair was my crowning glory and I really thought I was as cool as fuck and that was really important to me after years of abuse. Other than cropping it back, the only option open to me in 1992 was to have a very wide parting and that made me look a lot older, like some dodgy ticket tout. I just didn't feel great about myself at all. I wore a really horrible suit to my wedding that I bought for my brother's big day, the month before. I looked horrendous.

It felt like I was just passing through life at this point. 'This is what I'm supposed to do.' My job was certainly not the norm – although I came within a whisker of being a butcher's assistant – but now life felt as if it was edging towards mundanity and mowing the lawn on a Saturday, even though I had just released a successful album. I don't know why I felt like this, but I did.

We got back from the wedding and went straight to the airport for our honeymoon: two weeks in Ibiza. Just as we were marching down the hall of the house with our suitcases, the phone rang. It was Lee

Fredericks, the MC at Shelley's. 'Hey up mate, how's it going? Are you coming to Shelley's?'
- 'Ermm. I just got married, mate.'
- 'So, is that a no?'
- 'I'm going to be in Ibiza.'
- 'Oh. OK. That's a no, then.' He never lived that one down.

I've never been one for taking holidays when we had work to do, so the honeymoon thing was a real treat as we hadn't even been to Wales for a couple of years. I didn't want to take any time off or miss a single gig.

The honeymoon was fantastic. I hadn't been to Ibiza since that holiday in 1976, although I should have checked it out in the late eighties really. The island had changed a lot since the seventies. We went right at the end of the season and hadn't done any homework regarding which parties were on. We managed to get tickets to Ku for £25 a-piece, which I thought was a tad expensive. Still, I was interested in seeing what they were playing out there.

So we decided to have a drink before we went over to Ku and in trying to order one jug of sangria and two glasses I accidentally bought more than two litres of the stuff. By the time we'd had that, we were going nowhere. 'Fuck this, let's get back to the hotel.' So, who knows, it could have been a great night, but we didn't get to see it.

We managed to catch a Kiss FM party that was going on one night, but the atmosphere was very cold and the sound system screechy. They were playing a lot of hardcore/breakbeat stuff like *The Horn Track* by Egyptian Empire, so we didn't stay long. The truth was, we didn't go out much as a couple as I was always doing gigs and being in Ibiza didn't feel the same as being back home at Shelley's. There didn't seem to be many people about either. Maybe a case of bad timing.

You'd think that I would be sitting on the beach reflecting on how mad my life had become, but I wasn't. The career felt completely normal to me; what else would I be doing? I didn't think for a minute that it would end. I had such a passion for music I couldn't imagine doing anything else. I was very busy and trying to pave my future with side projects and mixing work. I had no real masterplan other than to keep working and learning. If a remix came in, I did it.

I guess Network provided the structure to my career with all the meetings and mixing and I was also gigging a lot too and so had to keep an eye on that. Things were going well and there was talk of signing to a label in the States. Altern 8 had gone over there on imports, but we were not signed to any label, although a bidding war was bubbling up. Neil Rushton always kept us in the loop as to which labels were contacting Network about us. Network were learning too, as it was a large jump from the days of Kool Kat. There was no manual for this type of business and they were experiencing many things for the first time too. So, the holiday wasn't so much a time of reflection, more a case of recuperation before going back to the world of chemical suits and paper masks.

Back in the UK, we hit the road as soon as I got back. I remember we got a flat tyre down in Camber Sands and we had to get the Transit fixed to get up to Scotland afterwards, which took us eight hours. You could fly to LA in that time. We spent ridiculous amounts of time in that van.

We were constantly teasing Crez on the road and would often flick his ears. He'd take so much and then snap and duff someone up. Then we'd all pile on as we screamed down the motorway. The Transit had these big windows down the side and I remember Parksy and Crez fighting in the back once when the window popped. Crez was the only thing keeping Parksy off the motorway. Parksy was screaming as he held on to Crez for dear life. We eventually managed to get him back inside and taped up the window.

A real problem for me in the van was Chris's smoking. It was such a pain in the arse, causing these mega migraines. We all got these cool Network duffle bags and Chris dropped these hot rocks all over mine which burned through the bag. He never apologised. The van was rubbish really; we couldn't even tune in the radio properly and the tape player wasn't loud enough to hear. The driver was this guy some of the others nicknamed Oboe The Troll. He was a nice fella, though. Sometimes I'd take the Cavalier, just so I could listen to some sounds. Our schedule sometimes crossed with other bands such as Shades Of Rhythm, who would leave messages for us on dressing-room walls: 'Hey A8, how are you?'

By this time our stage show was really progressing. We had started taking our own UV tubes because a lot of clubs didn't necessarily have them. We could make the giant A and 8 glow too, which was cool. We used to make sure there was a power socket down by the stage before taping the UV tube to the front, facing the crowd. That was all the UV we needed until Crez danced too close to it one night and kicked the light in. There were lots of these little things we kept adding to the live set and by the time we got to Bingley Hall, we also had an intro routine which included some 8ft x 8ft black sheets. We had fluorescent yellow on the inside of these sheets with long pieces of dowel rod painted black. We drilled in one end and looped some garden twine through it and attached those to the two top corners, so you had the sheet behind you. You stood there with your legs apart and arms folded and if you held the dowel rods up you had your own fluorescent yellow backdrop. But when you pulled the rods in and crossed your arms in front of you it was all black because it wrapped around you like Batman's cape. I'd be one side of the stage, Chris on the other. Butler would come on for this intro thing and Chris and I would walk to the front of the stage and at certain points we'd open our arms out to reveal this massive fluorescent thing behind us, glowing. It would go right off. Then we'd walk to the back, throw off the capes and get behind the keyboards.

We also managed to get what looked like aqualungs that we strapped to our backs. These were massive pump-action water guns fuelled by a tank of water. It was so hot at raves with zero air conditioning and so loads of people would be sweating their tits off. So we'd come on right towards the end of the gig, duck down and pop on the water tanks before walking to the front of the stage where we would spray the crowd. No one was going to say no. People would point at their faces like, 'Splash me! Splash me!' They were really powerful. You could probably have put a fire out with these 'hydr8tors'. One time, mine backfired on me and I ended up soaked at this gig in Leeds at The Gallery. We'd gone to the front and there'd been some kind of airlock when I tried to pull the barrel out – I think a washer had gone the wrong way – and when I pulled it back it just squirted me full in the face.

***

The Sound Factory was a massive club in Manhattan where the famous Studio 54 used to be. We got asked to play the Mask-A-Rave alongside a young Moby, to celebrate Halloween 1992. Moby was making a name for himself at the time and had scored a global hit with *Go*. Moby's promoter was a lovely guy called Scotto and he helped us get out there. Junior Vasquez was the DJ at the Mask-A-Rave which was full of ravers in weird costumes. It was a cool vibe. We didn't see a lot of Moby while we were there, although we shared a dressing room. Our preparations involved pranks and wrestling, whilst Moby wanted us all to vacate the room so he could meditate.

Butler and I got into the DJ booth during the evening and were collared by MTV who wanted to interview us. As we were in the middle of this enormous club, we couldn't hear a word they said. It was very awkward. Neil Rushton arranged for us to meet some people from Virgin Records before the gig and they took us to a well swanky restaurant, complete with belly dancer. I remember we all laughed when Lenny Kravitz turned up and got refused entry.

I got quite drunk that night and when someone asked me to play *Strings of Life* on the restaurant's piano, I did. Very badly. Although we had done so many things over the last few years, I still found it odd meeting record executives. 'Why do they want to meet us?' I was still very shy and just sat there trying to answer their questions. It felt like I was back at school, I guess.

The gig was odd, but in a good way, with lots of people dressed up in all sorts of bizarre stuff. It was a huge gig; and way bigger than the Limelight. I really liked Moby's stuff around that time, tracks like *Go* and his earlier stuff under different names. The New York stuff was much harsher than the Detroit techno. Some tracks were being sped up to 1,000 bpm, which was not my thing at all. Moby was going absolutely bonkers on stage, throwing his keyboard about. The place was going right off and it was a proper show.

Scotto *"Mask-A-Rave was an incredible story really. My memory is a little fuzzy going back there to be honest. I was technical director at Limelight and left there, late '91. The Limelight was hectic and I was working 100 hours a week there. The place was full of ecstasy and gay kids, sex and debauchery. It was a surreal place. When techno got commercial appeal, New York needed a licensed venue and the Limelight was it. I first met Altern 8 at Limelight and Prodigy played there too.*

I started NASA in July '92 which was the Summer of Love for America. I had been working at the Ritz for a bit and that was how I met Moby and we started working together quite frequently. We did an AIDS benefit gig at Webster Hall and worked with Frankie Knuckles and Dave Morales. We then managed to convince the Sound Factory to do Mask-A-Rave at Halloween on the Friday. Junior Vasquez and Moby's manager Marci Webber put it all together under the NASA umbrella.

Altern 8 were to perform their hot hits at a sold-out venue, so it was pretty epic. That was my first big encounter with Altern 8."

Crez *"Mask-A-Rave in New York was a Halloween fancy dress thing and I remember this fella covered in blue paint with white shorts who said, 'Hi I'm a Smurf!' I just laughed.*

   -    *'Hope your mother's proud.'*

That place was full of weirdos, but they were great kids. Moby and his missus had these dark glasses, bald heads and black polo necks and they were meditating or something which wasn't something we were into.

I guess we were considered the 'Slade of rave' at the time, which was a bit harsh I guess. We didn't take ourselves too seriously, though, and had a bit of a comedy to the stage act. But the music really was blinding. It had to be."

That trip to New York got us signed to Virgin in the US and Neil Rushton got a substantial advance payment from the label with 25% split between Chris and me. It was a successful trip all round and it was great to be back in the Big Apple. As for the man known as Moby, I don't know what became of him.

CH. 20

Aggro, Detroit And The Xen Mantra

Chris and I were really not getting on. I found Chris quite aggro, always pushing things between us. Sometimes he'd phone up and be really shitty and I could never quite comprehend why. But the minute I was shitty back, he'd spark up: 'Why the fuck are you being like this?' It was a total headfuck. In those days I couldn't be arsed with it all and I'd put the phone down. Our house on the Sandon Road was a short walk from his and sometimes he'd come round and start kicking the front door in, proper booting it. I would try and ignore it. Then I'd pick him up to go and have a meeting at Network later that day and he'd act as if nothing had happened.

There were occasions where he'd lose it in meetings at Network and start having a go at me in front of everyone. He did this once in a pub because I'd not liked one of his ideas. Everyone would be into the whole brainstorming thing, coming out with ideas and Chris once suggested a box set full of Nexus 21 and Altern 8. I just couldn't see how it would work, as we had released everything fairly recently and there wasn't an awful lot of material; it wasn't as if it was a 25-year-anniversary type or anything. I said, 'No one's going to buy that because it's going to be so expensive and all the tracks are already available. We're not far enough down the line to do a commemorative box set.'

-    'Fucking typical! You shit on all my ideas!'

He had a full-on bawl in front of everyone. He couldn't take that kind of criticism. Working together in the studio was becoming rarer and rarer and when we did, it was fractious. I knew how I wanted the music to be and some of the arguments were totally needless. I've worked with many people since then and a difference of opinion has often produced a better solution, but with Chris it was personal. Chris wasn't into the music at all, so if he tried to steer the direction it would often take us down a blind alley. So I was recording a hell of a lot more at home as a result. Chris was definitely pushing to do more of his own work though. Chris did a track called *Life is a Never Ending Sound* which was basically a track that Nexus 21 played live. He decided he wanted to do it as an Altern 8 track and brought it to my house and we added drums and a sample to it. It was something we both worked on, but it was a Nexus 21 thing and had a weird tone. It wasn't Altern 8 at all. It came out as a B-side on an *Infiltrate 202* remix. Chris did that one track completely on his own, but that was the one and only time really. The only reason that track came out was that it had got to the point of 'If you're having this track, I'm having that.' He didn't do anything on his own and to be honest I don't know what he did with his time. I was often at home, making tracks like *Re-Indulge*, *Armageddon* and demos of *Activ 8*, *E-vapor-8* and *Frequency*, completely on my tod, but we always split the money 50/50. I've got no beef about splitting the money because it was Altern 8. As an example, I did the *Frequency* track as well as *Give it to Baby* on the other side. I then did a remix of each, on my own. The 12" had absolutely nothing to do with Chris, but 50 per cent of the royalties went to him. I've got no problem with that at all. That's how we did things. But he'd got a real issue with me never liking his ideas.

In '92 we decided to start the Stafford South label. We thought it would be cool as Network would do all the business side of it and we'd make songs to go out on it that were a little more low-key than the Altern 8 stuff. I'd been given the name DJ Nex by our original dancer Jon McDonald, who had kept a load of mixtapes I'd done in '88/'89; each copy of these cassettes had 'DJ Nex' written on them, because I was in Nexus 21. I thought, 'No way, that's not a bad name.' I ended up using DJ Nex for all my non-Altern8/Nexus 21 work, the name also credited to the *DJ Nex EP*. Geoff from Leicester who'd done the *Cyclone* release had done some track under the names Rhythm On The Loose and Organ, Musical And Boxes and I asked him if he had any other any tracks for Stafford South. I enjoyed working with Geoff. I was also doing DJ Nex remixes on my own and recording a second DJ Nex EP which was eight tracks recorded for next to no money: *The Poundstretcher EP*.

My friend Lee Fredericks, the MC at Shelley's, was performing under the name 'MC Lethal'. Lee had MCed a lot at Amnesia raves and stuff like that and was mates with Daz Willot, Stoke-on-Trent's 'homeboy' and resident DJ at Shelley's. Lee was often Daz's MC and had recently recorded a track completely off his own bat with a group from Stoke called the Rhythm System (who later changed their name to The System). We'd done a PA with Rhythm System in Stoke once. Lee did this track called *Rave Digger* and he gave me a white label of it. It was a blinding tune. I said to Lee, 'This record is too good to be on white label,' so I took it to Network. I said to Neil Rushton, 'This is big and it's only on white label at the moment – and it's selling!' Neil could see that it could do well. So they signed Lee up and *Rave Digger* came out on Network.

I did a DJ Nex remix of one of the B-sides on *Rave Digger* and Lee did a follow up called *Phantom*, which I also remixed. I was doing a lot of DJ Nex bits and bobs, which Neil Rushton thought was a great idea. I was constantly phoning them up with ideas for remixes. I don't know if there was a bit of jealousy because I had never sat down with Chris and asked him about why things went the way they did. I don't know whether he got jealous of the relationship between me and the record label or that my ideas were getting picked, but this was quite a dark time really, whatever the problem was.

Lee 'MC Lethal' Fredericks *"In the eighties, Shelley's was a 'Sharon and Tracy' club, which wasn't even in the main city centre of Stoke. If you went out in Stoke in the eighties you'd have probably headed for Hanley, not Longton. Shelley's was the sort of place that did wet T-shirt competitions whilst someone got the living daylights beaten out of them in the toilets. It wasn't nice.*

Then in the late eighties, as dance music exploded, a couple of people approached Shelley's with a view to holding events there, but the owner at the time was having none of it. There was no way they were having the devil's music – and all the associated trouble – in Longton. A friend of mine tried to put a night on there and Shelley's agreed until they found out it was 'acid house'. My mate put the night on at the nearby Leisurebowl around the corner instead, though, and it was really successful. The first weekly rave night in Stoke, that was, called Introspective. When Shelley's saw the success they gave up the ghost and got promoters to put house nights on. Friday night eventually became known as Delight and was run and promoted by Mixmag photographer Gary McClarnon and Sasha was installed as resident DJ. Before that, some Liverpool lads had a go I think with Richie Aspinall as resident, but it exploded with Sasha.

Then some lads from Birmingham tried to get something going on a Saturday night with some darker, harder sounds compared to the housier Friday. Daz Willot was a popular local DJ and he was involved in every dance night in Stoke. He was the local Stoke DJ and all promoters dealt with him. Daz had a go at promoting at Shelley's after the Birmingham promoters finished. Daz started working with some guys in Coventry who ran Amnesia House, and they installed him as resident DJ at Shelley's when they eventually took over. Amnesia House became the longest-running night at Shelley's.

The first Amnesia night there featured a live PA from N-Joi and DJs included Grooverider, Doc Scott and Daz Willot. There was a clip on Dance Energy showing the queue at Shelley's on the Saturday night and it was ridiculous; it took an hour to get in. The success of Shelley's was down to great timing and the success of Amnesia House.

Mark was at Shelley's every week, on the dancefloor all night if he had no gigs. I remember seeing a Nexus 21 PA and thinking, 'That's Mark from Stafford!' I was getting quite a rep at the time as Daz Willot's MC and did a lot of local gigs at Shelley's and Entropy and used to see Mark every Saturday. We struck up a good friendship on the dancefloor.

I recall the video shoot for Activ 8 at Shelley's. I was MC for Daz Willot that night and our performance was quite late on and consequently I was one of the last ones out of the club. Sad to admit it, but I missed the start of their performance. That video has gone down in rave history, really. It was phenomenal!

I had an idea of making a record myself for a while, but the difference was that I was a rave MC and not a DJ or a rapper. I just had a love for music and a burning desire to release the first single by a rave MC. I was quite forward-thinking I guess as I didn't want to get left behind. I wanted to get into the studio to show what I thought I was capable of. There was a feature in Mixmag called 'How to press your own white label' and I used that as a guide. It told you how to go about distribution and saving money etc. So I took out a loan and went off to make a record. Comical, thinking about it now! Mark was a great help in this and he advised me really well.

I eventually booked some studio time, but I had to cancel the first date because my mother was ill. Then word got out and I heard that local band Rhythm System were interested in helping me. I didn't fully appreciate the work and skills involved when I went to the studio, but within two hours the guts of the record were done. I went back into the main studio a couple of times to polish it and then got it pressed.

I remember taking the white labels home and stamped my phone number on every copy of those 1000 records. It was a much bigger job than I first thought. Now I had to shift them. Eastern Bloc in Manchester was an influential store – owned by 808 State's Martin Price – and so I went there, armed with my white labels. 'It's really good, this. We'll have 10,' they said.

'10? I've got a thousand of these.' I was a bit disappointed to be honest.

I was getting rid of the track in tens and twenties and soon realised I'd bitten off more than I could chew. I needed a distributor. So I got Extreme Noise to do the north and Great Asset to do the south. They took just under 500 each and it sold out within a week. The phone started going mad. Mark then stepped in. 'You need to take this to Network.' He was right and this was integral to me and Mark becoming friends. I got interest from Perfecto, Production House, Arista and a few others, but Mark really pushed for Network. That was a massive help to me. The reaction to Rave Digger was incredible and the first DJ to contact me about it was Easygroove.

Mark was very different to a lot of the ravers at that time. He was there for the music and just the music. Even when success came along he never really changed, although he got a little spikier maybe. I guess it's hard to have the same conversation 20 times a night with different people. I was really lucky to have him in my friendship circle and he was one of the nicest people from that era. I have seen very few people who are as dedicated to music as he is.

I remember Mark taking me to an Altern 8 PA in Leeds at a venue co-owned by Utah Saints and I was blown away by the hospitality. Because they had chart success, they had a hotel and a nice meal and all the trappings. They were treated like proper stars. DJs back then never got hotels and meals. Their soundcheck was an eye opener for me, too. A soundcheck!?

Mark's ear for music was incredible. When you start to produce music you never listen to it in the same way again; you lose that carefree *innocence. Mark was constantly dissecting tracks. 'That drum pattern is not right... there's too much bottom end in that kick drum... this was sampled off such and such keyboard and not very well timed.' This is what Mark would do. He would break it all down. He had that special mindset that professional entertainers have. Music was his life."*

Whether Network liked me better than Chris, I have no idea, but after the album through to '93, even though the gigs were OK, the working relationship had gone completely sour. Up until this point it wasn't that I couldn't stand Chris, it was just that we seemed to grate against each other. The thing is, we were never that close in the first place, so we had nothing to fall back on. A lot of groups have members who met at school or university with a common interest whereas we were put together by the studio because Chris could play keyboards and I couldn't. There was never that bond at all. That said, without Chris, we wouldn't have sounded the way we did. He was great at the tricky stuff.

***

Brutal-8-E was to be the next single before Christmas and we remixed it up so it was different to the album version. Music really sped up through '92, so the album version was vastly different to the single. 1992 saw a massive split in the scene between house and hardcore and late '92 saw the word 'jungle' being bandied about. Progressive house was getting popular with tracks like *Talking to Myself* from Electribe 101 (from 1988, featuring Billy Ray Martin) charting. Electribe now went under the name Groove Corporation and they did some progressive house mixes of *Brutal-8-E* as well as a *Jungle Brutalism Mix* which featured Man Parris chanting over the top. We called Letrice from Detroit and got Jeff (Man Parris) and her into the studio to record the vocals.

Brutal-8-E charted at number 43 and got us back on Normski's *Dance Energy* and we shot our own video from the recording with some new bits thrown in. It was around this time that we heard rumours that Prodigy had been taking the piss out of us and still to this day I'm unsure as to the truth. The *Out of Space* video was the centre of a few stories as it featured someone wearing a white suit and a mask dancing like the clappers. So many people would come up to tell us that the Prodigy were taking the mick. We don't know if it was a nod to the fact that people were wearing paper suits at raves or whether they were indeed taking the piss, although the rumours were getting louder and louder.

We all went round to Ian the cameraman's house – who did *Infiltrate 202* and *Hypnotic ST-8* videos – to record some funny little scenes for the *Brutal-8-E* video. As a tongue-in-cheek reference to Prodigy we designed a T-shirt called 'The Dodgy Experience' and used a cat to represent Charley who sat on these little fence posts. We had a long blond wig for 'Keith' (played by Parksy) who did a silly dance in a beanie hat and placed a ginger mop wig on a broom pole to represent Liam. The single just missed the Top 40, marking a bit of a decline for Altern 8 – we had gone 28… 3… 6… 16… 33… and now 40-something. It was a bit disappointing to be honest. There was a big backlash against rave at this time with the whole 'repetitive beats bill' and the government was tightening the screws on illegal outdoor raves. We received a lot of love on the way up, but now there were sneery articles in magazines that blamed us and Prodigy for the 'death of rave'. Much of the music press was devoted to house, which was much sexier and less grimy and dark than hardcore and jungle.

Nexus 21 had always owned my heart, although I loved the work I'd done as Altern 8, and when a meeting with Network ended with the decision to terminate Altern 8, I actually felt quite optimistic about the future. Ending on a high seemed to be a great idea. I didn't want to flog a dead horse and run it into the ground. Altern was about the sound of 1992 as the scene was changing. We weren't a jungle group and didn't feel that was something we should do. Looking back, I still think we did the right thing to end Altern 8 and revert back to Nexus 21. Work was to start straight away on a new Nexus 21 album and we would continue gigging even after a final Altern 8 single. Then at some point in 1993 we would cease communications as Altern 8. The masks would be worn for the final time.

I did a remix for Parksy: a funky footwork tune called the *One For John Strangul-8 The Chicken Mix* just as the tracks were really speeding up. I really wasn't feeling that fast stuff. During that year technology was more readily available for people to record at home – not necessarily musicians – and a lot of tracks had the chipmunk vocals and things out of key. Meanwhile Pete Bromley at Golden in Stoke was playing a lot of US house and garage. I went there one night with Lethal Lee and we heard this Masters At Work remix of a Trey Lorenz track and I thought, 'This is decent. This is where I'm at.' I started buying a lot of American house from the Cutting label, as I slowly pulled myself out of the whole hardcore thing as Xen Mantra. I was also continuing to work as DJ Nex as the progressive house of Xen Mantra (Xen being Nex backwards) kicked off. I was a bit disillusioned with hardcore, although we were still doing Altern 8 gigs and mixes.

Altern 8 had started as a side project, a name to put to some tracks, but in the space of two years we'd come so far, and I wasn't sure how long the public would continue buying into it and so it felt fitting that the band should have a dignified end.

***

1993 started pretty well. I was bowled over when we got asked to play Kevin Saunderson's birthday in Detroit. As we had no visas or anything we had to tell the US customs that we were doing promotional work and playing someone's birthday for free. As we flew back the same day, and it was the same cabin crew from the way out, they were understandably suspicious. 'Weren't you on the plane yesterday?'

Reese Project and Richie Hawtin were on the bill and this was the first time I met Richie, one of the leading figures behind Detroit's second wave of techno (circa 1990). We also bumped into Letrice who did the vocals for *Brutal-8 E*. The gig was a bit of a culture shock, to be honest. Parksy always sprayed the crowd with water, but the homeboys of Detroit really didn't get it and just stared at him. 'What the fuck have you just done?' This wasn't a tops-off-chewing-your-face British crowd.

We were interviewed by MTV in the dressing room with us on one side and all the Detroit legends on the other. MTV kept calling our music *hardcore techno* when it was just hardcore – this was largely a US thing. The Detroit legends weren't happy with that. 'This ain't techno! Don't be calling this techno.' I guess what we were doing was the bastard son of techno that was definitely influenced by, but not actually, *It*. The Detroit crew were really distancing themselves from hardcore, although Kevin (Saunderson) had taken it on board.

At the time we were licensing tracks to Kevin Saunderson's KMS, which was a proper Detroit label. The Nexus 21 remix of *(Still) Life...* came out on KMS, a credible Detroit techno name. They licensed the

C+M Connection release too, which was a major deal for me. R&S put out *Logical Progression/Techno City* around the same time, all thanks to Network, who really upped our profile.

It was a wicked gig and I loved visiting Detroit again and meeting all those musical heroes. It was a great honour to be invited to play Kevin's birthday party and was a massive deal for me, personally. It wasn't long before that Chris and I had turned up to the US to learn from the greats. Sadly, the MC introduced us as The London Boys, which was unfortunate, considering the band of the same name.

Network continued to enjoy close connections with Detroit and New York. We did a lot of mixing for Andrew Komis too, on his projects with Pandella. Andrew would act as the New York base for Network and was very innovative with his own label and used to produce a great little magazine to accompany his press releases. Years later we would link up again.

We did the gig and came straight back to the UK where Crez announced that he could no longer dance with us as he had taken far too much time off work and couldn't keep the two plates spinning anymore. So off Crez went to concentrate on ladies' fashion. I have always remained good friends with Crez and he was an ace addition to Altern 8. It was sad to see him go.

Crez *"When the gigs started to become less frequent I needed to earn some money from somewhere and had to leave the band. I flew out with the lads to Detroit to play at Kevin Saunderson's birthday party, but that was the final straw. It was a great night, but I was knackered. We flew out, did the gig and then came straight back, jetlagged, nervy and grumpy. I'd had enough and they were nearing the end of the road anyway. It seemed like the touring was never going to end. It was pretty intense, every single weekend. 'Where is it tonight?' But it was a truly memorable time, gigging, clubbing and partying and I wouldn't have changed a thing."*

So, the landscape was changing. Altern 8 was being laid to rest, new projects were waiting and my home life with Karen was about to undergo a massive change.

Impregn8, Brand New House And A Bag Of Brazil Nuts

Karen had polycystic kidneys and part of the condition – which can't be cured – is that it slowly gets worse and worse as cysts start to form on your kidneys. If you're pregnant, the baby uses your organs and so sufferers endure some pretty painful pressure upon their kidneys. Therefore, it was always made clear to Karen to have kids as soon as she possibly could. Leave it too late and you won't be able to. So as soon as we got married in 1992, Karen and I started trying for kids. By Christmas, Karen was pregnant.

Our place on Sandon Road was too small for a family and so we started looking for somewhere bigger. We went all around Stafford at the start of '93, which wasn't easy as I had to constantly pull over so Karen could be sick. She had really bad morning sickness.

Selling our house had its tribulations too. I remember Karen getting the hump one Sunday – 'Who the fuck is this?' – when there was a knock at the door. 'On a fucking Sunday as well!' The couple on the doorstep had come to look at the house and seemed a little shell-shocked. That was when I realised that the little fan in the window above the front door had filtered the swearing straight out into the open air. The man looked at his feet. 'We can come back another time if it's not convenient.' To be fair we'd not been told that anyone was coming.

We needed to move quickly and so we sold our terrace for £29,000 (we bought it for £35,000) and put in an offer on a big new four-bedroom house on an estate just outside Stafford for £65,000, which was a real snip considering the size of it. Karen moved the mortgage to the new property and I paid the deposit and solicitors' fees from the rest of the Network advance (for US licensing). I handed the solicitors a cheque for £44,000 or something and was also able to buy a new car around the same time. I gave the Cavalier to Blue Chip studio engineer Mike Bell and replaced it with a Honda Civic. The car salesman definitely thought I was 'looking and not buying' and so it was with some satisfaction that I handed over a cheque for the entire cost of the car.

This Honda Civic did wonders for my self-esteem. I was losing my hair, putting on weight and looked like a right old duffer, but this sporty little car made me feel young again. New house, new car and a baby on the way. Life was changing fast.

***

Needing a new dancer, post-Crez, we recruited Julie Ann from Amnesia House. She was a great dancer but, as we soon found out during her first Altern 8 gig in Athens, she was prone to accidents. Parksy always sprinkled water on the stage and when Julie Ann trotted out on stage, doing these kicks and skips in her skimpy clothes and big boots, she slipped in this puddle. Woof! She went straight up and over a wedge speaker. She was dangling over the edge with her back to the crowd who were holding her there, but didn't quite have the strength to push her back up. All you could see were her legs all over the place. Parksy and Butler were laughing their heads off. In the end one of them grabbed Julie Ann and pulled her back on stage. The gig went brilliantly and we had a wicked time out in the sun. A young fella called Solomon had been sorting some gigs for us back home, and he had managed to blag his way onto that jolly in Greece. Solomon was a proper ladies' man and as soon as Julie Ann clapped eyes on him, that was it.

Solomon was DJing at a private party that first night, with some housey stuff. I was so drunk. I hated it when people did this to me, but I started pissing about with the controls on the decks. I pressed the stop button on one deck while Solomon was in the mix. I was being a proper dick. Then Butler and I came on after. We did a load of '93 dark hardcore and just didn't care. We loved DJing. We didn't go down too well, though. Although the crowd didn't get our stuff, a small percentage did and people still go on about that set, so it wasn't a total disaster.

So we bundled into the van after and went back to the hotel. I was that pissed when I got into the lift, I knew I was going to chuck. It was so fusty in that elevator with carpet on the walls and the ceiling and it certainly wasn't helping my heaving. It was like being trapped inside a shagpile rug. Ping! I stumbled out of the lift, but there was no way I could get my key into the door in time and started sicking up.

The next morning, my mouth was so dry. I had the worst hangover ever. Then out of the blue, someone offered me some fresh water. It was Chris and it was possibly one of the nicest things he had ever done. It was a godsend. What a star! Then someone suggested getting some food and so we walked along the sea front. There were all these little cafes and eateries and Butler started hitting the fruit machines. I bought a Coca Cola, which I thought would sort me out and instantly I realised it was a mistake and the whole lot came back out through my mouth and nose in front of all these holidaymakers. It looked like I was leaking. One can went in, ten cans came out. But then I was sorted. 'Let's go get a kebab!' Greece was a lovely carefree time even if we were your typical Brits abroad.

Just before the second gig Julie Ann and her friend Louise were mucking about in the dressing room when they sat on the sink and managed to pull the entire unit off the wall. This dressing room was trashed, bits of masonry everywhere.

Solomon was DJing again after the second gig and dying on his arse and someone asked me and Butler to save the evening. It was lovely being able to play some tunes following a successful gig.

***

The split between being a husband/father-to-be with life as a professional raver, was often hard to balance. I got the news that we would be joining Moby on a tour of Brazil whilst getting the nursery ready for our new arrival. As visiting Brazil required inoculations against tropical diseases, I hadn't fully considered the pain of the jabs when I promised Karen that I would finish painting the nursery. There I was trying to hold my arm up, in absolute agony from these jabs, trying to finish the decorating. The pain was bringing proper tears to my eyes.

The three gigs in Brazil were to be Sao Paulo, Curitiba and Porto Alegre and Altern 8 were to zip cross country by coach with Moby's people and a bunch of DJs, technicians and musicians. We had the full

Altern 8 crew out in South America and I have to say I'd wondered how we'd all get on over there, especially as no one knew anything about Brazil and Moby had a reputation for being a little shy. But setting off on that trip was one of the most amazing feelings I have ever experienced. There are some moments that live with you forever and you're even aware of them as they're happening.

We touched down in Rio and I remember two guys coming straight up to me and Chris to present us with long sleeved T-shirts with Altern 8 on one arm and Moby on the other, complete with the tour dates on the back. Altern 8 had a tour shirt! That was a first. The mini tour was sponsored by the cigarette company L&M and there were hundreds of girls going around these raves with trays of fags. This was quite a common thing back then, even in the UK, and I can definitely recall parties hosted by brands like Marlboro Medium and Camel Lights who were trying to recruit new smokers. The gist of it was that you gave the girls what was left of your usual brand to receive a brand new pack of their ciggies in return. Butler was up for this, but he hadn't realised that you could pocket a few of your current brand and simply hand them back a solitary cigarette for a full pack, but hey ho. I don't smoke, but I was told that they tasted like camel shit. Many of the ravers were wearing these free 'sock hats', which were a little bit like a beanie but made from a tube of material that tied up at the top. They were white with the cigarette logo on them and everyone had them. They made the wearer look like a human condom. I got the impression that Moby wasn't too happy being associated with the tobacco industry; he was a vegan and, unlike us lot, had proper principles, although I truly hated cigarette smoke.

The gigs were in these enormous aircraft hangers in the middle of nowhere, with cordoned-off sections. As more and more people entered the venues, the cordons were then lifted until virtually the entire hanger was full. These are now seen as iconic gigs in Brazilian dance music history as the country was still quite new to all of this. Things had only really kicked off there a couple of years before, when they received all the genres all at the same time: acid house, UK hardcore and techno. It wasn't easy for Brazilians to get hold of the records either.

The crowds seemed to take a while to warm up and although they were hyper-enthusiastic, a large portion didn't seem to know what to do. Moby's stage show back then was quite punky and dynamic and I enjoyed sitting backstage watching him leaping about and going ape.

It felt like we went down very well and it was a rush playing to such an unfamiliar culture. Europe and the States we knew about, but Brazil was an unknown quantity to us.

The full line-up included local DJ Soulslinger and Mark Kamins from New York, who discovered Madonna. Sadly, Mark is no longer with us. Mark was larger than life and he regaled us with stories about Madonna, including her 'dead straight pubes'. I guess if you've seen Madonna's pubes you're going to brag about them.

Scotto *"As NASA became big we had the opportunity in '93 to play the first EDM tour of Brazil for Sunshine Events who sorted Madonna's tours. There was Soulslinger, Moby, Altern 8 and Mark Kamins from Danceteria. Brazilian DJ Mau Mau played too and he is the godfather of EDM down there."*

There were long coach journeys between the gigs and Moby's promoter Scotto was constantly filming life on the road. It was a strange atmosphere on the coach. We were all travelling together, whereas Moby was often sitting on his own at the front. I was desperate to go and talk to him, but being shy I just sat back and stared out of the window at the towns and villages that sped past. We had some laughs, though, and I remember the whole coach singing the Jungle Brothers' *I'll House You* as this Brazilian lad acted as a human beatbox. It was great fun.

Rumour had it that Moby could come across as a bit brattish, but we didn't see any of that whilst travelling across Brazil with him. Moby looked young, although he was older than me. He was quite demanding I guess, but then he was signed to a major label in the States. Moby wouldn't let anyone fuck him around and why should he? Moby's promoter Scotto threw a right paddy over the lights at one gig. Scotto looked after Moby's lighting and sound and had brought these huge lighting rigs with them from the US and one of them wouldn't work. Scotto broke his toe booting this rig. I'd never really seen anyone have a proper flip-out before. 'Woah! What's going on here?!'

The Altern 8 boys were still suitably 'Brits abroad' and Yorkshireman Butler wasn't touching any 'foreign muck'. I tried everything I was offered, as I could see that this was the experience of a lifetime – although we were told not to drink the local water. Brazilians love their meat, which meant that you could get a little 'backed-up' if you ate too much. On our first night Chris went straight to the hotel toilet and blocked it up. We had to get a porter to come and chop this turd with a stick. You can't beat British bogs!

We knew that Altern 8 was drawing to a close at this point and so I'm not sure if I viewed this trip as one of the last hurrahs or whether I was looking forward to touring the world with Nexus 21, but either way – and it seems odd saying it now – I did get to tour Brazil with Moby.

CH. 22

"We Were Like 19th Century Colonial Explorers..."

An Interview With Moby

"I remember Mask-A-Rave really well; it features very heavily in my memoir (Porcelain). Halloween '92, I was living in New York, going back and forth to the UK, playing in raves, touring as much as I could and releasing 12"s and remixing. The Mask-A-Rave event was my first attempt at being a club promoter.

My managers, a couple of friends from New York and I – and I don't know how exactly – managed to rent the Sound Factory in Manhattan; one of the most hallowed and esteemed venues in the world. They rented the former Studio 54 to us on a Friday night, which was very confusing to me. Why were they willing to do that? These were very early days in the American rave scene; practically speaking it had only existed for about a year prior to this, and so we had no idea, really. But we now had this 2,000-capacity venue to fill and no idea if anyone was going to come.

I remember I turned the corner on to Tenth Avenue and there it was: this huge line of ravers snaking down the street and around the corner. That night was a really joyful experience. It was also that time in rave when the music was so unapologetically happy; only a year later it started to get a lot darker and a lot less celebratory.

1991-92, people were still going out and taking ecstasy and dancing to pianos and breakbeats and Altern 8 were one of the kings of that scene, that very sample-driven celebratory genre. I very much wanted them to be at this event, but I thought they were out of our league. Somehow, one of my managers was friends with one of their people and this association made it happen. This guy had the biggest loft I had ever seen, in Tribeca, which now would be worth about $30million. I was living in an abandoned factory at the time and I remember going to his loft to talk about Altern 8 playing this rave and I couldn't believe he had 5,000 sq. ft. of space. He seemed so much more professional to me because he had a legitimate place to live.

In addition to making records I was DJing a lot and playing lots of Altern 8 and Nexus 21; their more Detroit techno, less-sample-driven side project. Nexus 21 were more synthy. I heard Altern 8's Activ 8 – top one, nice one, get sorted – at a rave up north (in the UK) and nothing sounded better than that. Activ 8 represented that cut-and-paste approach to rave tracks, indicative of a lot of things on XL. Hearing that tune at the rave was one of those moments when a piece of music perfectly encapsulated an era. There were 10,000 people there when the breakdown happened and when 10,000 kids, all on ecstasy, screamed at the top of their lungs, it felt like such a moment. Activ 8 was not just a great song, but a track that represented the joy and innocence of that scene.

The UK was a unique crucible for this music and culture because they embraced it so quickly and so wholeheartedly and that didn't really happen anywhere else. Ever. Almost overnight I was hearing about Kevin Saunderson going to the UK where he was a household name and playing Top of the Pops and yet he was a DJ from Detroit. How was this even possible? Overnight, dance music was the music of the UK and it started influencing rock bands too. Suddenly U2 wanted to make dance music and so I can see that if you grew up with that, it would seem like this normal, musical paradigm, but it is worth remembering that six months earlier, it hadn't existed. I had seen them (Altern 8) in the UK once before and they were incredibly visible because of the suits and dust masks. They had such an iconic visual attached to what they did that every music magazine and ravezine wanted that really graphic image.

The way most of us performed back then was to play a digital audio tape (DAT) as well as keyboards and samples to trigger drum loops on top, but a lot of the show came from the digital audio tape. I remember that Altern 8 only brought one tape with them to the Sound Factory and that truly scared me. I brought four back-ups of *everything I did, to every gig, just in case anything went wrong and yet they had flown across the Atlantic with just one DAT. The success of their entire show was dependent on this one tape; if it broke they wouldn't be able to perform.*

Before the dawn of DAT, we were doing a lot of the shows live and I would bring all my equipment with me. I would set it all up onstage, but then you realise... 1. You can't control the sound that well and... 2. Sometimes you'd be playing two or three shows in one night, which was hard enough, without all that equipment to transport. There was a club in Coventry called The Eclipse and it was so small, sweaty and chaotic and insane and it was hard enough plugging in a keyboard and getting them to play a tape, never mind getting them to try and support an actual live show with real equipment, so there was no way that was going to happen. DAT was used simply to expedite performing, as the rave scene had no technical support. Raves were often organised by kids who had rented the cheapest sound system they could.

The DJ who went on before Altern 8 at Mask-A-Rave was a British guy called DB and for us it seemed that the scene was suddenly so legitimate. The rave scene before this date seemed so small by comparison. The first rave I went to in New York featured some DJs from a London club called The Brain who came over and DJed at a bar on Third Avenue and just 30 people turned up. It was fun, but there were only 30 people there. Fast forward 18 months and here was Altern 8, ostensibly one of the biggest rave acts on the planet, playing to 2,000 people in a sold-out venue in New York. It was a big moment for the New York rave scene, having them there. I remember them so distinctly on stage with the dust masks and the 18/19-year-old kids all throwing their hands in the air and dancing, blowing whistles and the foghorns. It was really remarkable.

I came from the punk rock world and grew up playing in punk rock bands and that element of performance was integral. So when I started performing as an electronic musician I found myself on stage and I didn't know what else to do and so I started jumping around hitting things. I think a lot of people in the rave world came from the rave world and were 18-year-old kids who had always been electronic musicians and DJs. When a lot of electronic musicians perform, they are very shy and just stare at their keyboards and wait for the show to end and that's one of the reasons Altern 8 did so well. In addition to the fact that they made these celebratory tunes, they also had a performance ethos. It wasn't just a couple of scared kids scaring at synthesizers. There was an iconic visual element and it made perfect sense in that world. The funny thing about the rave scene was this celebratory thing and this dystopian, apocalyptic aesthetic going on and that was the paradox of Altern 8. Altern 8 looked apocalyptic and dystopian and yet they made really happy records.

Brazil was an odd, fun tour. Interesting. Most of us had not been to South America before, although I have since been back many times and had such wonderful experiences there. The surprising aspect to that trip to Brazil was that I thought electronic dance music would make perfect sense to Brazil, the land of carnival. Everyone liked to dance in Brazil of course, but the shows were remarkably restrained. Normally, Altern 8 and I would be performing and the crowd would be going crazy, but in reality the audiences in Brazil were remarkably quiet, almost as if they were at a shoegaze concert. I thought it was going to be more like the States, Germany, France and the UK, where there would be this almost bacchanalian and chaotically joyful celebration, as Brazil was the land of bacchanalian, chaotically joyful celebration, but for some reason it was very polite. We were a little confused by that.

This was before the internet revolution, of course, and the only way to listen to music was through buying records or listening to the radio and so I think a lot of people in Brazil had maybe read an article about rave, but hadn't actually heard the music. So for many people attending the shows, this was their first experience of rave music and culture. It was like that 19th-century tradition of British people going to the Crystal Palace to see an exhibition. Curiosity.

So it was an interesting and fun tour, albeit a little tricky for me because I was a vegan, and being a vegan in South America in 1993 was kind of challenging. I ate a lot of oatmeal and raisins, which you could get kinda anywhere.

The trip to Brazil was also tricky in that there was a lot of us: about 25 people. I don't know how they afforded to do this. There were DJs, girlfriends, lighting people, random people who didn't seem to know what they were doing there. There were so many people, we didn't get the chance to know them all that well.

The rave scene was so new then and we forget about that. Everything was new. The music was new, the clothes were new, the equipment was new, the drugs were new, the aesthetics were new and the distribution channels were new. Everything about it had been invented in the previous two to three years and with hindsight you realise just how unique that was. You talk to any DJ or performer from that time about the occasions when you would turn up to a place and no one had an idea as to what you were doing. We were almost like 19ᵗʰ-century colonial explorers in Brazil, visiting parts of the world we had never been to before and we didn't know what to expect. Sometimes it worked and sometimes it didn't.

A friend of mine was the first DJ to go to a rave in Russia and they had to import the turntables, although they forgot to get needles. So before going on, a local engineering student had to make needles for the turntables. Prodigy and I once played a rave in Oklahoma – the first rave there – and they had forgotten to get power. They found a street lamp and jerry-rigged a cord off it, straight into this warehouse in order to power the lights and sound. The rave was powered by an extension cord coming off a street lamp. So going to Brazil and being the first to bring this music to them was like that.

Altern 8 occupy a truly unique place in the history of electronic dance music. Altern 8 were hugely successful and yet their alter-egos Nexus 21 were very credible. They were the only people who lived in both worlds. There was Prodigy who were hugely successful and then there were people like Derrick May who were very credible, but a lot of the journalists back then didn't like the popular stuff. There was an antipathy on behalf of journalists back then, to the hands-in-the-air rave stuff. Journalists championed the much more obscure, minimalist techno, and so a lot of musicians couldn't go between those two worlds. Richie Hawtin didn't make hands-in-the-air piano based music and underground, minimal techno. Mark was the only person who could go between these two worlds and so as a 25-year-old kid from Connecticut suddenly in Brazil with this British electronic music legend, I was a little too intimidated to get to know him... I mean I didn't think he or I were in the same league. A. He was British which gave him instant credibility. B. They were hugely successful and had sold a ton of records. C. They had this strange credibility of being in this incredible underground techno act and so it was kind of intimidating meeting them. That's what happens when shy people meet shy people: there's an awful lot of shyness. On the other hand, he might say, 'There's this guy from New York, the land of dance music and he's had some Top 10 records and has some credibility in making electronic dance music...' That's not how I would describe myself, but it is definitely how I would describe them."

CH. 23

Altern 8 Have Left The Building, A Pair Of Smelly Feet And Che Guevara

Altern 8's swan song, scheduled for the summer of 1993, was *Everybody*. This was us signing off and a massive thank you to everybody who helped us (apologies if we left you off). *Everybody* was originally a DJ Nex track and when I played it to Butler he said, 'This is far too good to be a Nex tune. This should be the next Altern 8 single!' The reaction to *Everybody* annoyed Chris a bit as it was another track I'd done on my own, but we agreed to re-record it and used the DJ Nex track as a remix. Chris recorded the piano and pads I'd done with a new bassline and drums and there it was: Altern 8's farewell.

We got some wicked remixes for *Everybody* from Two Bad Mice and Phuture Assassins, who were on Suburban Base. Moving Shadow, Reinforce and Suburban Base were the three biggest breakbeat labels at the time, so it was a smart move. We agreed to do a remix swap with Suburban Base and went to meet Danny Donnelly who ran the label. We did a remix of Phuture Assassins' *Roots N' Future* and I think they were an expecting an uplifting, more commercial mix, in stark contrast to their darker proto-jungle tunes. But by the time I was done working their samples, it was a very dark, breakbeat thing. This was a moody tune that made you want to sit in the corner and suck your thumb. Mike Bell engineered it and it has this acidy pattern on it by Chris; everything was done at home. Suburban Base weren't expecting this. Maybe we were trying to leave the world of hardcore behind with mixes like this.

Neil Rushton *"The album had sold well, not overseas particularly, but did well here. The problem was that Mark and Chris weren't getting on that well and they couldn't see the bigger picture. I remember going for lunch with my partner Dave Barker and both Mark and Chris. We all agreed: 'Let's concentrate on Nexus 21.' But what soon became clear was that they'd lost that spark, which was a real shame."*

'This is it for Altern 8, we're coming back as Nexus 21!' The picture on the back of *Everybody* was of a chest stuffed full of Altern 8 merchandise: jackets, T-shirts, slipmats, pin badges and the masks. We were closing the lid on Altern 8. The picture featured the top of Chris's face and the bottom of mine, with no suits or masks. The 12" and the remix 12" featured lots of mixes including DJ Nex's original, renamed *Mackerel Is A Damn Wide Fish Mix*. The title was inspired by comedians Vic Reeves and Bob Mortimer who had this jokey range of 'Reeves and Mortimer' products. One of their inventions was a pipe that went directly from the North Sea straight up into your freezer. The fish would then swim up the pipe and into the freezer drawer, but there was only one problem: 'The mackerel is a damn wide fish' and so it was prone to getting stuck in the tube. Another tune on the 12" was my tune *Hole in the Speaker* named after an incident where Karen kicked a bloody big crater into a woofer, whilst putting the washing away.

Chris wasn't happy. 'You've got your tunes on this release, so I'm having one!' Chris had produced this tune called *Dubpl8* and it was a slow Italian piano tune that had nothing to do with the scene at the time, but I wasn't going to fight it. Anything for an easy life. 'OK cool! If you're insisting that this goes on there, fine.' *Dubpl8* caused some problems with the label who couldn't understand what we were doing. 'What's going on with this track?' Another extra tune on that final release was *Domin8* which was aimed at America more than anywhere else. There you had it. Altern 8's very last single. *Everybody* charted at 58.

Altern 8 would continue gigging, especially as the US had licensed some tracks, but things were definitely slowing down. We were meant to play a gig in Turkey called Head, but that was cancelled. Head had a brilliant line-up. I don't know whether the promoters put you on the flyer to sell tickets only to then drop you, as that happened quite a bit back then. Sometimes they'd actually tell you, 'We've gone over budget, we can't do it.' Sometimes they'd tell you it was cancelled and it was up to you to find out if they were telling lies or not. You had to take someone's word for it.

The plan now, musically speaking, was to go into the studio and record as Nexus 21 again. I was feeling optimistic at this point. I had set up the Stafford North label for breakbeat material and Stafford South for the housier tunes and had two DJ Nex EPs under my belt. I was also putting together the first Xen Mantra EP aimed squarely at the Stoke club night, Golden. Because Golden featured Che Guevara in its logo, on a red and black poster, I pressed the first EP on red vinyl with a picture of Che on it and called it the *Midas EP* as everything the king touched turned to *gold*. I targeted Golden in order to get some buy-in from the Stoke scene. So I pressed it onto acetate and gave it to Pete Bromley to play out. It went down brilliantly. Pete asked if the intro could be a little longer to aid mixing, though, and with a few tweaks, we were there. Getting support from a local scene can be vital to getting momentum going and one route is to get a popular DJ to mix your tune and that's what Pete Bromley did; with a mate of his from Stoke called Danny Weaver, who was a real whizz in the studio.

Danny had various bits of gear at his house and could play keyboards and together with Pete – who wasn't a studio person at all – they put together a wicked remix of *Golden Delicious*. I oversaw the mix and piped in now and again with some thoughts: 'I like this noise… and I like that bit.' Pete scratched a little over the top. I also did another tune called *Goowon!* named after the Stokey phrase and it had handclapping during the breakbeats. Geoff Hibbert did a progressive trancey mix of that record, which was to cause massive problems between Chris and me.

Because Pete played the track as the last tune of the night, every single week, *Golden Delicious* became an anthem at Golden and people would hassle him to find out what it was. This little release on a tiny label was destroying Golden every week and it sold a lot, although no one knew who was behind it. Most people thought it was Sure Is Pure, Stoke's big producers (formerly Candy Flip) at the time. No one knew it was me.

***

We didn't know it at the time, but a festival gig in Orlando, Florida in October 1993, was to be our last. The final Altern 8 single *Everybody* had been and gone and I was working on all these side projects. I was still recording as DJ Nex for Network and had the follow-up to the *Xen Mantra EP* done. I now had a family, too. My daughter Emma was born six weeks before the Florida festival, which caused a few rows with Karen. I didn't necessarily *want* to leave my daughter, at just six weeks old, – she was still so very new – but there were to be no more UK gigs and the bookings abroad were still quite good as hardcore spread around the globe. The photo on the Stafford South's *Xen Mantra EP* was of Emma at two weeks old.

One of the tunes on this six-track EP needed a name and so I did a phone-in on a local radio station where the best suggestion for a title, got a free copy. We had some poor suggestions such as *Bizarre* and *Licergic Positive*, but in the end we settled with *Hollow Vibe* and got MC Lethal to do a remix of it. Danny Weaver had done a radio advert for the Global Groove record shop in Hanley and needed a tune and so we cut up an old Bob James track and Danny did the voiceover, but as we didn't have clearance for the sample, it was scrapped. But all this work was really starting to piss Chris off.

The Orlando show was called Tranceatlantic and the line-up included Carl Cox, Digital Orgasm, Dream Frequency and Guru Josh. The organisers were using Peter Gabriel's festival set-up at this massive outdoor rave and it was certainly one of the biggest gigs we'd done.

Guru Josh caused a stir when he came on. Josh seemed to be quite the artist and when his music went weird mid-set, the audience got peed off. His set sounded really disjointed with some jungly bits mixed with some old 1990 stuff and new versions of old tunes. Josh threw a bit of a wobbly to be honest, but luckily he was one of the last on. Josh kept stopping the set in order to shout at the audience. 'If you're not going to dance then you can all fuck off!' And they did. He absolutely killed it.

Orlando was so hot it was perhaps no surprise that their Big Gulp containers were the size of beach buckets. I was drinking that much fizzy orange I could hear it sloshing about inside me as I walked. Then five minutes later I was thirsty again. Everyone was fat there. Even the grass was fat; it was sharp and totally different to British grass and wouldn't have been nice to walk on. I had put some weight on too, but didn't feel that porky out there. Butler and Parksy took a fancy to Dream Frequency's dancers and were following them around all the time.

I was playing my Xen Mantra stuff while we were out there in the cabs and clubs and our dancer Julie Ann loved it, as did Ian from Dream Frequency. The positive feedback was definitely annoying Chris. Then someone else mentioned that they liked Xen Mantra and Chris didn't like that at all. I had done something on my own and it was getting somewhere and Chris seemed to be getting very jealous. We were all in the same hotel room one afternoon, while Chris was on his own in another and so Julie Ann went to see if he was OK. Chris was being particularly moody at the time. The relationship between us was going downhill fast.

Eventually, Chris walked into the room, sat on the bed and kicked his shoes off. He had the most evil feet. Somebody shouted, 'Fwoar! What's that stink?' Chris bristled.

- 'I've got a problem with my feet, OK, and I don't want anyone to mention it!'
- 'Woah! OK there!'

Then Butler walked in. 'Someone break my fucking nose! Has someone died?'

I guess I knew a lot of the fellas outside of the band and Chris must have felt on the periphery of all of that. I went up to Sheffield with Butler and had played Quasar with Crez. I had known Parksy since I was 15. They were my mates, as well as being part of the group, although Crez had just departed. It must have been hard on Chris and he possibly felt pushed out. That said, Chris was often aggressive and difficult to be around, which didn't help.

Chris was getting well into computers at this point and was in constant dialogue with *Amiga Magazine* to develop an Altern 8 game where the characters went around throwing Christmas puddings at promoters or something. He did an interview with the magazine and invited them to his house and this wasn't done through the record label or anything. These negotiations rumbled on for quite some time, but nothing ever happened as far as I know although I heard that Amiga had developed some Altern 8 characters which went on the cover of a magazine.

I got to hear *Live the Dream* live (by Dream Frequency) in Orlando and loved it. 'Oh my God!' I had first heard that track back at No.7s in 1990 and so hearing it live was fantastic. I met Ian Bland, the man behind the track, and told him how good it was. Ian is a really close friend now and we had a great time out there although I was missing Emma back home.

Ian Bland (Dream Frequency) *"In 1993, Dream Frequency travelled to the US with Altern 8. That was the first time I really started chatting to Mark. We got on very well and struck up a friendship. We were lucky enough to be invited to play this massive rave in Orlando looked after by an English promoter. I'm not sure they knew what they were doing as only a thousand people turned up and yet they were expecting 50,000! This was Billy Ray Cyrus territory.*

Before we went on I was chatting to Mark and Felix who were also playing and I remember this guy (Felix) being a right little arsehole; just demanding loads of things. 'I want this before I go on stage. I want a bigger dressing room,' and all this. He was really upsetting everyone and so this promoter went up to him and said, 'If you don't go on, I'll break your legs!' They were that pissed off that no one had turned up, and then this little diva started kicking off and Mark and I just stood there laughing.

I did my act and then watched Mark do Altern 8 and was amazed at what they'd done, especially when you heard it all in one set. 'They did that. Oh my God! They did this…' Smash after smash after smash. I said to Mark after, 'That was an ace PA! Really was. Pity there weren't more people there.'

On the way back we were spread all over the aeroplane, and Mark ended up sitting with this really fat couple, crushed up against the window. He just kept looking back at me trying to catch my gaze. He ended up standing by the toilet for an hour to get some space. That was a fun trip.

Mark is really understated and I really like that about him. He's not a chest-beater. Mark's contribution to music is massively underrated. He has done some seminal rave and house tracks. He's very talented, but he just won't have it."

It was weird playing these massive raves in the heat when you consider that we'd been playing Doncaster Warehouse not long before. The stage at Tranceatlantic was massive and had these massive speakers hung up either side. The ravers wore little backpacks and bell-bottom trousers, which was quite strange. It was a very chilled vibe.

When we landed in the UK, we all got on the bus at the airport to the car park to say our goodbyes. Julie Ann had not experienced any accidents on this trip, which was unusual for her, but as we turned to go our separate ways, she tripped over her suitcase and went arse over tit. With that stumble on the pavement, Altern 8 was over. We just didn't know it at the time.

8 Of The Best: US House & Garage

1. Louie Balo – *Don't Shut Me Out*
2. Masters At Work – *I Can't Get No Sleep (MK Mix)*
3. Happy Trax Vol.III – *Cha Cha*
4. Crustation – *Flame (Mood II Swing Vocal Mix)*
5. Michael Watford – *Michael's Prayer*
6. Voices – *Voices In My Mind*
7. Aaron Smith – *U Got Me Going Around (UBQ Make U Dizzy Mix)*
8. Sound Of One – *As I Am (Todd Edwards Mix)*

Solicitors, Bells And A Life In Slo Moshun

"...barrier-burning bliss..." Review of *Bells of N.Y.* (Slo Moshun)

Chris was spitting feathers. He was having an absolute wobbler. 'I want what's mine!' he kept spitting down the phone. Altern 8 had gone and now Nexus 21 were in a state of emergency. Chris had snapped and I was getting both barrels.

I was doing loads of work on my own in 1993, as I had been for quite some time. I loved making music and couldn't turn it off. I was DJ Nex, Xen Mantra and had also started working more with Danny Weaver, who had helped out on the *Midas EP* for Golden. I was also a former member of Altern 8 and one half of Nexus 21. I was always putting tracks together whether I was at home or in the studio. That's what I loved doing more than anything else and I didn't consider it to be anyone's business but my own.

Dan Weaver was sound and we worked well together and I helped him finish off an EP he was putting together at my home studio. Danny and I also mixed *Definition of Love* by Kaos. The working relationship was different to that with Chris in that we had lots of fun experimenting with sounds.

There was a short-lived character in *EastEnders* at the time, an Elvis impersonator called Danny Taurus who really fancied Pauline Fowler. Danny wanted a new name, as he thought Weaver was a little lame, so he stole the surname from this soap character. For the sleeve of the EP we photocopied a Colman's Mustard jar and took the cow off it for his logo and with that, Danny Taurus was born.

Both Stafford South and North had been busy. We put out an Organ, Musical Clocks & Boxes remix, *The DJ Nex EP* and *Xen Mantra EP* and Danny Taurus's tunes. All this work was being done by me. Or to put it another way, it had nothing to do with Chris.

Late '93, some money came through from Stafford North and South, mainly from DJ Nex and the first Xen Mantra EP and I don't know how, but Chris found out I'd been paid. He rang me up one evening wanting half the money. 'This money you've got from Network... well I want half of it. That's mine!' We made an agreement that anything we did as Nexus 21 and Altern 8 was half and half, but this had nothing to do with Chris. This was my work. 'If you don't give me half the money, I'm going to sue you!' Chris went on and on, getting more and more angry. Eventually he put the phone down and cut the 'conversation' dead.

A little later I received a solicitor's letter telling me that I was in breach of a verbal agreement and that I owed 'X amount' to Chris. I rang the solicitor straight away and he was really quite short with me; I thought they weren't supposed to be arsey. 'Hold on a second, you've had someone come into your office and tell you something and you've taken it as gospel. But this is the truth... anything we did as Altern 8 or Nexus 21 was split down the middle to avoid arguments, but this is something completely different. This has nothing to do with Chris.' The solicitor went quiet.

- 'Ah, I see.'

If anyone tries to sue you that's pretty much your working relationship over isn't it? The relationship had now completely disintegrated. Altern 8 was dead and the only thing bonding me to Chris was Nexus 21. Now Nexus 21 was attached to a drip, too.

So, wanting to keep things amicable I went into the Bassrooms Studios in Stoke to make some music with the guy who was trying to sue me. I was getting more and more into the garage side of things around then, which wasn't really Nexus 21 and so I had left the whole Detroit techno thing behind. Whenever I went into the studio, I was gearing towards that American house sound and Chris just didn't buy into it at all. Financial disputes to one side, musically we were trying to push gravy up a hill. Chris was spending a lot of time upstairs on the phone to these people at Amiga talking about computer games and I was left on my own, scratching my head. It was a frustrating dynamic and proving completely fruitless.

We spent two weeks in the studio and came out of it with zip. Not a sausage. The engineer Mike Bell might recall if there were any rows as my memory's not that clear, but we definitely couldn't work together any more. So that was when we stopped. Not the greatest of splits, but then they never are. So Altern 8 and now Nexus 21 were dead and buried. This outcome made me sad, as Chris and I had taken these two bands all over the world in such a short space of time, but I was also relieved. I just needed to get working again and all this bickering was getting in the way.

I was still working with Danny Taurus around this time and we'd been asked to knock up a hip hop beat for a new lad at Network called David Lewis. Someone sent David Lewis a DAT and he wanted a hip hop beat for it. I played Danny T the hip hop beat I'd been working on and he decided it was too good to give away. 'But neither of us does hip hop, Danny!'

Danny had a brilliant idea. 'Why don't we do a track that starts off with house and then slows down to a hip hop bit, before speeding back up again?'

-    'How the hell are we going to do this?'

Each time we did a track using Cubase on the Atari, we set the tempo and that was it, all the way through the track, so we needed to change our method. So, we loaded the hip hop bit, started working on some housey drums and put together *Piano Groove* – and it was terrible. So we decided to alter the tempo of the track to give it distinct sections. Danny did a few piano lines and when it got to the point where the track changed, we had to go into Master Tempo, bar by bar, to slow it down and alter the tempo of each bar, further down. We made the tune slow down from a 127bpm house tune into hip hop for a minute, before speeding back up again. I had another Xen Mantra track, which Danny wanted as the A-side, and we ear-marked the new tune for the B. It sounded great.

The new tunes sounded really American. There was a lot of snobbishness in the dance scene at the time – if it wasn't Chicago, it was no good – and so we decided to pretend that we were Yanks. Although UK tracks like *House Arrest* by Krush were really on point, many thought the Brits just couldn't do it as well as the originators and so we decided to make our tune look like an American release. The band were Slo Moshun and we both felt that our debut single *Bells of N.Y.* was going to be pretty big.

We took the track to the Network offices and popped the DAT into their system and waited. But everyone just kept on working. Not a flicker of excitement. Shit! We were convinced that we had a big tune. Anyway, we had a sit-down with Network and asked if we could promote it ourselves to make it look like an American import; I think we feared that Network didn't like it and weren't about to push it sufficiently. They agreed with our idea and so we set up a fake promotions company called DX which operated out of my house. We designed a template for press releases, which had one of those sentences along the bottom saying, 'Now don't forget: Potato Waffles are waffly versatile!'

I remember getting the DJ reaction sheets back from the promos and the only guy who didn't like it was Dave Seaman who said it was 'terribly produced'. Although the tracks had been made in the bedroom studio, I had more equipment at that point. I had a 909, 808 and the 727 I bought from a guy in Shelley's car park. Then Network suddenly got excited by the potential of this tune and went full in with the scam, which was something they were great at.

To create a believable false persona for the Slo Moshun act we got a bunch of American records from similar labels and pinched their names; the first name of one, the middle name of another and the last name of a producer or whatever. Then we mixed all the names together. The track was credited to Ed 'Chunk' Rodriguez (me) and Anthony 'Monty' Montana (Danny) who operated out of Brooklyn, New York City. We wanted the phone number to look American too, so we nicked sections of landline numbers from these records too, just as we did with the names. Only, the records were all from the same label and we ended up printing a full phone number. We then shrink-wrapped the sleeve and gave it a sticker saying: 'Contains the House 2 House Mix' on it. Some record store staff claimed they knew it wasn't American, but most people fell for it. They said the shrink wrap wasn't right and the inner sleeve was wrong or something, but everyone else was hoodwinked.

Because the phone number we used was real, this label boss in New York started getting loads of calls about this track *Bells of N.Y.* and got quite angry. 'I don't know anything about this record!'

- 'But it's got your number on it.'

In the end this label boss made another record by Ko-Moshun called *New York Bells*.

So we had this tune out coming up to Christmas and the reviews were fantastic. *Bells of N.Y.* was in all the buzz charts and many magazines had it at number one. The house scene had a lot of charts and Slo Moshun hit those hard and featured in every one. Network got Andrew Komis to pretend he was Ed Rodriguez to make it sound more authentic should anyone ring our promotions company; that way journalists and label bosses got an American on the other end of the phone rather than a geezer from Stafford.

When the truth finally broke it was like, 'Did Altern 8 have the last laugh?' It was a good scam and it got people talking at a time when – post Altern 8 – I could have faded into the background a bit. It was important that the first release I did was a good one and people seemed to love it. Network went overboard with the promotion and put it out on a new label of theirs called 6X6 and gave it a proper release in 1994 and also licensed it to Columbia in the States. Suddenly we were on the same label as Mariah Carey!

At the time it didn't feel as though music was ever going to end. I'd gone straight from Altern 8 into this. We had a spot of bad luck, in that the week *Bells...* came out, the charts were being compiled by a different company and they had changed all the machines. The only shops that had the new machines were the big stores and so the independents weren't registering sales. We sold shitloads that weren't getting swiped. Network reckoned we had sold as many as *Activ 8* (number three) and yet only entered the charts at 25.

Like *Infiltrate 202* the new track got played on the chart rundown on *Top of the Pops*, but that was it. It was a massive stroke of bad luck. I did a remix of *Bells...* and got Manchester guys Luv'dup to do the *Luv'dup Mix.* David Morales put the Xen Mantra mix on his Cream compilation which annoyed Danny a bit, but he was dead happy that we were featured. Jon Carter featured the Ko-Moshun track on his *Live From The Social CD*, but credited it to Slo Moshun and so we got the royalties! The 12" of *Bells...* had a *Big House* version and the *Hip-Hop Mix* that you could play at a BBQ.

Bells... was something a bit different at the time and the clubs loved it once they got used to it. Danny and I took an acetate to Golden one night and gave it to Pete Bromley and when it got to the piano bit, before slowing right down, no one on the dancefloor knew what they were supposed to do. Then a few weeks later, people got it, but it was worrying at first. That tracked was bootlegged so many times and some people scratched Public Enemy over the hip hop bit. I was really proud of what we had achieved.

Pete Bromley (DJ, Record Shop Owner) *"I met Mark at a club night I used to do at Central Park in '89. It was a night called Adrenaline. He came to the DJ box to introduce himself one evening. He was very humble. 'Hey, I'm Mark! I've made some records. You might want to listen to them.' Mark was a little bit shy to be honest. That was how he was at the time; he hadn't had any success as yet and they were still with Blue Chip.*

Mark couldn't believe that I took time out to listen to, and appreciate, his music. There wasn't a lot of people really into house music at the time. I mean people would go and dance to it – and a handful of people locally were properly into it – but few had the effort required to actually make records.

One of the records was the Nexus 21 album and the other was the (Still) Life... 12". I was at that age when I wasn't used to getting free records and promos and so I was quite chuffed to be honest. I didn't have a clue as to what they were like, but I played them. And loved them. I used to play (Still) Life quite regularly as well as the Real Love track off the album.

I worked at Lotus Records in Stoke and Mark was a regular at the other branch in Stafford. We used to pass messages to each other about records we liked, through a mutual friend at the Stafford store. This went on for a while until we met up again.

I played quite an important role in the making of Activ 8 because Mark wanted the strings from a Kid 'N Play remix – popular in Stoke and Manchester at the time – and I was the only person he knew who had it. You have to remember that there was no internet then. You had to hunt down your samples. Many people had the bootleg of the track 2 Hype, but I had a proper promo. So I sent the record over to Lotus in Stafford and Mark picked it up and sampled it. I didn't see Mark until the record came out, but I eventually got the record back, which was good, or I would have sent the boys round. That promo was the Holy Grail at the time. Mark has always been ultra-respectful of records, though. He had been a keen collector from way back in the electro days.

I used to go to Shelley's on a Friday when it was Sasha and Dave Seaman and became a resident DJ there for a while prior to Amnesia

House taking over. Shelley's was big for the area and when there was trouble in Manchester, with gun and gang problems, they would come down to Stoke, which was neutral ground within an hour's drive. There was never any trouble in Stoke as it was properly loved-up back then. I wasn't there the night they filmed the Activ 8 video, but it was a great idea; really playing the game. Network were great at getting Altern 8 into the press. There was a lot of good music around at the time, but precious few memorable images. Many acts just disappeared, whereas Altern 8 hung about.

Mark started to come to a night I was putting on called Juice at the Freetown and named the track Re-Indulge (Freetown Mix) in honour of it. It featured a sample from the Neal Howard track Indulge that I played quite a bit at Introspective in 1990.

We met quite a bit over the next few years and chatted a lot about hardcore, hip hop and electro. I guess I acted as Mark's direct link to Stoke. The 'Stoke connection'. Mark would often come and visit me at the record store in Hanley (I still manage it to this day). Then I became the weekly resident at the "superclub" Golden that ran for the next 11 years.

After Altern 8, rave was almost a dirty word for a bit and I knew Mark had been working on some new projects. 'Hey Pete, this is a side project on I've been working on,' he said, handing me a Xen Mantra cassette. 'It's more on a house tip.' I loved it. It was similar to some of the stuff I was playing out and Mark thought it would be a good idea if I remixed the track. Wow! The only issue was that I'd never been in a studio before. Mark wasn't fussed though. 'Don't worry, just come round and throw your ideas about.'

I worked with a guy in the record shop called Danny Weaver and he was always doing loads of demos and stuff. Danny was quite geeky and very talented and knew how to use all the equipment. Danny was well up for it and so we took a trip to Mark's studio which was in a spare bedroom at his house. 'Yeah, this is where I keep all my stuff,' he said, closing the curtains.

Mark had these two really-muffled-sounding speakers and he assured me that it would give the mix a 'club sound'. It sounded to me like the tweeters had blown. I took a lot of US-inspired records with me for samples and ideas and we eventually came up with this remix. It sounded great and so all we needed was a name. As I was holding a bottle of dandelion and burdock we called it the 'Dandy Lion & Burdock Mix.' Network then put it out on Mark's own Stafford South offshoot.

The Hacienda was the Mecca for all the house heads up north, even in Stoke. Lots of Stokies went to The Hacienda. I was a massive Graeme Park fan at the time. If you went to the DJ box, you could buy these tapes from previous nights. As I was DJing every Saturday, I only got to The Hacienda every now and again, but people used to bring these tapes back and I would analyse them to death. Xen Mantra was on one of these Hacienda tapes as Park was playing it out there. That was a big acknowledgement that you were doing something right.

I was never that into remixing, to be honest, I preferred playing other people's stuff – but Danny and Mark really clicked at that point and not long after Slo Moshun was born. I sometimes took Danny to Stafford to meet as he couldn't drive at the time. So they would twiddle knobs and that sort of thing and then Danny ran the demos by me back in the shop. I remember him playing me a house track with a piano riff and another sample of some hip hop and I don't if it was me who suggested it, but they eventually decided to fuse the two together. I think the K-Klass mix of Bobby Brown slowed right down in the middle and this came after, and was inspired by, Bells of N.Y. The only other house track I can remember doing this was Lil' Louis's French Kiss.

Danny came to Golden most weeks and gave me one of the first test pressings of Bells and I played it at the club, peak time, for weeks! Mark always made sure I had an acetate of his Xen Mantra tracks to make sure he could hear it premiered on the Golden sound system. Mark liked to witness the crowd reaction and to hear if the EQ levels were OK.

Acetate was a major deal back then and really expensive to produce. I would play a lot of Mark's acetates. I was more of a house DJ really and the rave stuff ended for me around '91/'92 when I went on more of a US house tip. The stuff Mark ended up doing on the Dansa label – with all the filtered and compressed house they did – worked really well at Golden.

I will always have a lot of affection for Mark and I can still remember this shy guy coming up to the DJ booth in '89 to give me some records, really pleased that someone was actually going to listen to them."

***

Early '94 Chris and I had a meeting to dissolve our business partnership. We had a joint account and any money that went into it was scrutinised.

As we had to dissolve the whole partnership, the meeting was quite intense. Network's lawyers oversaw it and I was visibly shaking while we were there. I hated confrontation like this. These nerves were not helped when Chris had a proper go and slated me in front of everyone. But after a while, that was that. We were dissolved. Chris clearly had a very different view of the working relationship to me, but I couldn't change his mind. I don't really know why it went the way it did, but it was over. I think the phone call from the solicitor had ended it for me. That, as they say, was that. Nexus 21 were dead and buried too.

I was working in the studios with Terence Parker for the UK division of the Detroit label Serious Grooves one day, when Chris phoned through. 'What the fuck are you doing there?!'

- 'I'm working. I'm not allowed to work with other people?'

Chris just couldn't seem to move on, as long as I was still working. It was very odd.

The only music I heard Chris do after the split was for a group called Banging From The Bedroom on a label called Gash records with a song called *Let Me In*. It was double entendre heaven. I don't know if that was the plan or not. According to Mark Gamble from Rhythmatic, Chris had gained the nickname Dr Doom and I don't know if he was aware that this was a piss-take, but he used it on this track. Chris had bought this mad system which was a second-hand control panel that moved the sound around 'as 3D', but unless you had the correct speaker set-up you couldn't actually hear the three dimensions, so it was pointless really. Dr Doom's *Move Your Sound Around Boy Mix* spun the sound around left and right and I believe it was the last bit of music he ever released.

The next time I saw Chris was in Stafford about seven or eight years later. I went right past a River Island and saw him inside. I didn't want a confrontation and so walked straight past. He contacted me on various occasions, later on, but we never met face to face. Oh, and the verruca I had suffered with ever since we started recording together (a gift from Tina) disappeared too. I had constant shooting pains in my foot and had to walk on one side of it when it was really painful. If I placed my foot down wrongly, it hurt like a bastard. I tried everything to get rid of that from my foot, even sanding it off, but as soon as the partnership dissolved, it went. Every cloud and all that...

CH. 25

Curtain Twitching, Cheese Burgers And Please Don't Go

The neighbour walked right up to me as I was mowing the front lawn and stopped in thought before piping up. 'Hiya.'

- 'Morning.'
- 'Yeah, lovely day.' After a bit of small talk this neighbour went in for the kill. 'So… what exactly is it you do for a living?'
- 'I'm a musician. I was in a group that were quite successful a few years back.' The guy was visibly relieved.
- 'Ah, we all thought you were a drug dealer!'

It transpired that the neighbours had been having meetings around the estate, wondering who the weirdo was and how he'd made his money. Maybe that fella had wanted to score?

Life on the estate and in the bedroom studio was hard. In 1995, Emma was coming up to two and life was so different to my existence at the two-up two-down. I couldn't go into town looking for records or fiddle about in the studio any more. Once Karen left for work I was with a two-year-old child. Then when Karen got home in the evening, I would have to saunter off to make music, which Karen often took as an insult. This made life quite hard for a working musician. At the end of my first day of 'daddy day-care' I thought, 'How am I ever going to cope with this for the rest of my life? Will I ever make music again?' I was shattered.

I had to take it one day at a time and try to avoid thinking too long term. I spent days making sandwiches and preparing the tea for when Karen came in and apart from making music, my existence was mowing the lawn and washing the car, which was now a larger and more practical Vauxhall Frontera – a four-wheel drive thing as we couldn't get the buggy into the Honda. I was a very big lad at this point. I was only 25, but had lost my hair, had no dress sense and was a proper square. Apart from making house tunes, I was a chubby househusband.

I started to put on a bit of timber back in '93. I had never really drunk much, but I had a vice: Wimpy. Stafford was in a wonderful situation in that it had three Wimpys at the time and my favourite food ever is their quarter pounder with cheese. I had always liked Wimpy. Way back in Bishopswood, Andrew Bugey's parents took us swimming in Stafford and we would always visit Wimpy after. When we moved to Gnosall there was no McDonalds or anything and Wimpy was the place for a sit-down burger. There was a Wimpy out the back of Woolworth's and a prefab chalet affair near the cinema and another at Milford. A fourth came much later at Stafford Services. My love for Wimpy increased as I stopped clubbing so much, because of all the gigs I was playing. Saturdays were often spent shopping in Stafford with Karen and we'd always go for a Wimpy after. I had gone from nine stone to about 16 at this point and wasn't undertaking any exercise. I was just sat in the studio or slumped in front of kids' TV. I was becoming a big lad.

Workwise, Slo Moshun were getting a lot of remix gigs in 1994, which was well handy. We did a tribal house remix for Talisman called *Only You* and hardly used any of the original. We sent it off to them and they really didn't like it. Oops!

Danny and I started Dansa records as a label through Network and ceased with Stafford North and South. It was a chance to collaborate on making and mixing music. Danny drew a freehand logo for this new record label whilst riding the bus one afternoon. We kicked things off with a 12" called *Ropey Trax Volume 1* under the name Ramone "LL" Ropiak. Some mixes were by Xen Mantra, others by Danny Taurus and we also started working with two guys from Nantwich, Crewe called Scott and Ken – or Madagascar – who did US house. We were also DJing as Slo Moshun too.

The 1994 follow-up to *Bells of N.Y.* saw us disappear right up our own arses. We were trying to make new music rather than following the latest trends and with that in mind we had this idea for an epic

16-minute David Morales-style classic house anthem. Danny did a lot of work on this tune and we thought it was brilliant. We even fell asleep in the recording studio getting it right. Dan was a proper workhorse and ideas were firing off left, right and centre. Dan was also a great keyboard player.

This track had a slow portion like *Bells* that slowed down to almost nothing, before building up. There were three different distinct parts to this 'epic'. Ann Saunderson from Kaos wrote some lyrics for it and recorded lead vocals. We then got singers Tracey Bilston and Andrew Peake in and multi-tracked and multi-tracked until it sounded like a gospel choir by the end. It went out on Columbia in the States and 6X6 over here and the promotion was fantastic. It just didn't chart so well.

Radio wanted to cut *Help My Friend* down from 16 minutes to three-and-a-half and that didn't really work out. One radio presenter chose it as her Single Of The Week, but kept calling us Slo Moshing. Still, we got loads of mixing work through it, with people like Heavy D & The Boyz and Livin' Joy, so Dansa had a release out every two weeks or so, doing 1-2,000 copies, before we moved on. It was a brilliant time as Danny and I were right on the same page, musically. We really trusted each other.

In 1995, I got a call from Neil Macey at Network distribution who wanted a few tracks for his new label Ideal Trax. I asked him what kind of thing he wanted and he thought for a minute and said, 'Techno and house mixed together.' I interpreted this mix as best I could and recorded six tracks in total under the name Trackman. I hadn't thought of any song names and so they were labelled from one through to six. This EP came out as a double-pack on Ideal Trax as one of the very first things they did. Surgeon had a release on Ideal Trax too, which was a bit of a label from day one. That double-pack was re-released last year (2015) on a Berlin label called Infrastructure New York run by David Sumner (better known as Function) who has always played one of the tunes in his sets.

***

The gigs had stopped, but I was still DJing with Danny. I moved all the studio gear into one room back at the house and bought a bigger desk. I had been buying equipment for a while so I could make all the music I wanted. When I first started I didn't know how to make music at all and didn't know which drum machine or keyboards to use or how to produce music properly. I had a long waist-high shelf for keyboards and a rack with a lower shelf for drum machines. I moved all the equipment into the front room upstairs and insulated the whole thing with grey carpet up the walls and ceiling. Mike Bell the engineer helped out with the acoustics by spreading glue on the ceiling. It wasn't the ideal set-up in terms of a productive working day – with playgroups and kids' TV dominating – but my studio was a damn site roomier than the one back on Sandon Road.

Ken from Madagascar worked with me on a follow up to the Trackman tune after Neil Macey asked for some more material. Ken was really into techno and jungle and was always popping round. Most of the artists on Dansa were quite local and people would often phone up to see if I was about to work on various bits and bobs. When we went on a family holiday to Spain, we let Scott from Madagascar house-sit so he could look after all the gear and record some tunes.

Scott recorded loads of material while we were away and even went over some of our discs, which was a swine, but nothing was broken or damaged. We had a lot going on with the Dansa thing and were spending plenty of time in Stoke when we acquired the Bassroom Studios to do some Slo Moshun remixes. We had mixes out on MCA, 6x6, Transworld, Deep Distraxion and Club Buzz. There had been a big backlash on rave, but now was the time of the superclubs like Cream, Golden and Renaissance and things were looking up a bit. The problem was that Dan didn't want to be tied to one label – Network – and wanted to be able to record under his name for whoever he wished. We worked on a third Slo Moshun single together, continuing to steer ahead of the curve and spent money on getting a guy who worked with Soul II Soul to come in and help, but that track never came out.

There had been changes at Network with Neil Macey leaving and setting up Ideal Trax, plus Chris and I weren't about any more. Meanwhile, music had gone towards jungle and drum and bass. The jungle sound was completely different and I liked it. I had even started recording jungle mixes for Network, under the name OPD, but it wasn't where my future lay. I was always panting and wheezing, hence my nickname at Network, Old Pa Dopper (OPD).

Network never really put out a straight jungle single, but we put out a mix of Groove Corporation that was cut from the same cloth. I continued to work with Geoff Hibbert from Leicester. Geoff wanted a mix of his *Break of Dawn* from 1991 after Strike's *You Sure Do* ripped off his original. 'Let's mix it and put out a proper version.' But other than bits and pieces I was losing touch with the industry.

Network eventually paid Danny off to leave his contract and so that was the end of both Slo Moshun and Dansa. There had been a little battle between Danny and Network and I just went along with it all. Danny stamped his foot a bit and refused to play ball and I was the go-between really. There was no bad blood as such, but this didn't help my situation any.

Work might have been fading, but I managed to get myself on *Big Breakfast*. Peter Andre was doing the roving reporter bit and he had a mission to record an original track during the live show and get it played on radio by the end. They contacted Bassroom Studios which was opposite the local radio station in Stoke and so we were told to work on the track before it went straight over the road to get played on air. Peter Andre turned up at the studio and called me John, which was odd, if not unsurprising. He was a nice bloke actually, but clearly hadn't done any research. At one point, mid mix, he looked over and said, 'You want to keep this up, mate. You might get somewhere.'

Danny Taurus (Slo Moshun) *"I knew of him before I knew him. I didn't even know that these things he did were by the same people. I thought Nexus 21 were from Detroit because the music they did was so firmly techno and Network were licensing a lot of that. I was working in a record shop called Global Groove in Stoke, which is still running after 20 years and was hearing Mark's music all the time. I was aware of Altern 8 in the same way I was aware of Prodigy in the sense that this was rave-turned-pop. I wasn't that into the Altern 8 music as I was into a different sound.*

Lee Fredericks or 'MC Lethal' knew Mark and brought him into Global Groove one day. Lee walked in, and after him shuffled this shy guy staring at the floor with a big overcoat on, talking about music production. Lee asked if I had heard of this particular mixer and I was giving my opinion. 'Oh I've heard that's not very good.' That was my fairly unfounded opinion at the time. Ha ha. Then Mark piped up. 'Derrick May uses one of those.'

- *'I doubt it, but OK.'*
- *'Oh he does. I've been in Derrick May's studio.'* Lee then introduced him.
- *'This is Mark Archer from Altern 8 and Nexus 21.'*

I suddenly shrank into this tiny insignificant person in a record shop. We got on though.

Mark knew about equipment and I loved equipment. I had a home studio of analogue gear, synths, samplers and I loved the production process of music. I started buying synths and keyboards in my early teens; amassing all this gear. In Mark, I had finally met someone as obsessed with the actual technology as I was.

So we hit it off quite quickly. The manager of Global Groove, Pete Bromley, was a prominent DJ in Stoke and Mark asked him to do a remix for his next 12"; a good marketing move to ask the most popular DJ in Stoke to remix your stuff. Pete then got me involved. 'Mark has asked me to do a remix of one of his tracks. Do you want to come and help? You can be the intermediate between my ideas and Mark and the gear.'

'Cool.'

Pete and I went down to Stafford to Mark's terraced house. Upstairs in a tiny 6x4ft room was the most amazing gear. I was expecting a studio with a standalone, sound-proofed vocal booth, but I was quite naive at the time. Anyway, this room was a treasure trove of Akai samplers and an Atari Cubase, which I don't think even I was using then; by the time Atari became popular with musicians it was obsolete in the computing world.

So we remixed this tune for Pete and I got more involved than I should and Mark saw what I was doing and it led to other things. 'Have you got any other tunes? Any of your own stuff?'

I had started working on stuff that was more Jean Michel Jarre, Vangelis and Kitaro, doing covers and mixes. Then I started doing house and had three tracks I'd been working on.

So Mark signed my track and was instrumental in putting me on vinyl first. I was also credited on that Pete Bromley remix of the Golden Delicious track too, as Danny Weaver.

Danny Taurus was a character off EastEnders who was an ageing, failed rock star trying to steal Pauline Fowler from Arthur to take her away on tour. Someone in the record shop suggested Taurus as my recording name and as he was a karaoke singer, it seemed appropriate to me. So, under the name Danny Taurus, Mark put out my four-track Lies EP on Stafford South. That was my first foray into house. He gave me an advance of £1000 and that was the deposit on my first house.

Lies did OK, but I have never known any sales figures for anything I've put out. It did alright though and it firmly cemented our relationship for a few years after that. I credit Mark with so many things there. I'm really indebted to him. He won't take it though. My introduction to the whole music industry was through Mark: the star kid at Network. He had the ability to get you in and then you were made, just like the Mafia. Dang! That's amazing. So no longer were you paying up front for distribution, plus they did all the artwork.

Quickly after Lies came Bells of N.Y. We really wanted to do something together so we got an E-mu Proteus to do some sounds on Bells... and we played some riffs and added 909 drums. It needed a hook, though. Mark had been working on some hip hop stuff and we had these breaks at our disposal, so I suggested slowing it right down before going back to house. 'Could we do that? Is that a thing?' A Vicious Music track had already done it: a driving beat, then echoey and reverby before a hip hop break. It was the kernel of an idea, but quite inaccessible, so we decided to do that but with a proper hook. Mark did some scratching and turned the hip hop bit into a party vibe rather than a dark thing and that's how the 'House 2 House' name came about. House to hip hop then back to house.

Finishing it was a real trial and tribulation in itself. 'Yes this is so good!' And then the Atari crashed. The way the Atari crashed was it would just hang, so you could see what was on the screen. So with pen and paper I drew what I could see so we had something we could reconstruct the track from. I wish I still had that drawing, showing where bits came in and out. Because saving on a computer back then took a minute or two, with the disk drive chugging away, saving the data interrupted the flow of the work and so you didn't do it that often, you see. It was a fine balance between saving work and working quickly.

Bells wasn't exactly what it was; it was better! 'This is really big, with the potential to be massive.' We saw how other people had pulled little scams and marketed their records. Kylie Minogue had a remix with just a big 'K' on the label, so you didn't know who it was, which we thought was cool. Slo Moshun's Bells of N.Y. was by Ed 'Chunk' Rodriguez (Mark) and Anthony 'Monty' Montana (me); I didn't even know who Scarface was back then.

If you held a copy of Bells... you knew it wasn't an American import because of the shrink wrapping and the pressing. Any connoisseur would know, but people were more naïve back then and it worked really well.

DX Promotions, named after Mark's DX synth, mailed out copies to people like Graeme Park, Allister Whitehead and Danny Rampling. We had a fax machine at my house and we got the most amazing reaction reports back from these DJs. We were getting calls from all over the place to license this track. 'Is publishing available?' I was out of my depth. I didn't know anything about all this. But Neil was used to this idea of tomfoolery with music and worked the marketing angle very well and we got onto Renaissance and Cream albums. Someone once said to me: 'Isn't it weird when one of your songs is used on a commercial or something?' And I replied, 'What is weird is when it's used as background music on John Craven's Newsround. Or it's on in the café in EastEnders, totally out of context.'

Bells got to number one in DJ Mag and Mixmag Update. The reaction just blew us away. Then Neil announced, 'There is a very good possibility that we'll be on Top of the Pops. You get asked, you do it!'

- 'I don't want to do it. I will look like a dick.'

Then someone found out I wasn't with Equity, so I was fine. But we didn't get chosen anyway. There was this track Blow Your Whistle and that got on over Slo Moshun. We just had the vocal 'Pump it homeboy' which comes in twice and so that wasn't great for Top of the Pops back then. So I got a reprieve. Mark was fine with it, but I really didn't want to do Top of the Pops.

We soon descended into difficult second album territory. How do you follow that up? We got Ann Saunderson, Kevin Saunderson's wife, to write some lyrics and do lead vocals, along with Tracey Bilston and Andrew Peake, a couple of gospel singers who provided vocals and backing vocals. Help My Friend was our own Bohemian Rhapsody. It didn't do as well as we hoped it would, but when challenged, following Bells, we had gone back underground.

Dansa Records hooked in as many local Stoke and Stafford producers as we could. It was a really cool, collaborative community. We were also DJing as Slo Moshun all over the UK together.

Mark was in the loop with Network and had a contract, but I was thrown in at the deep end with Slo Moshun and they didn't know who I was. 'Come in and sign these contracts. This is your recording contract. Here's £5000 and you can continue to do stuff for us, under this name. Then you get more money. Here's a publishing contract.'

- 'What's publishing?'

It was like free money and I was none the wiser. 'Sign and get another five grand.' After a while I got more clued up with my rights and ownership."

***

Dave Barker rang me with the news. Network were to cease making music. All the wind left my sails. Shiiiiiiiiiiiiiiiiiiiiiiiiiiiiiiiiiiiiiiiiit!!! Not only were Network my employers, but they also provided the framework to my career and life. It was one of the moments when you know that the safety net has gone and all you can see below you is the ground, getting nearer and nearer. I felt sick. I hadn't seen this coming at all. So, Altern 8, Nexus 21, Slo Moshun, Dansa and now Network were all gone.

Network and 6x6 were to stop as active labels and so I was out of a deal, as it were. The money dropped off almost immediately and we went from being comfortable to having virtually nothing. I had used up a lot of the savings and there were no more Altern 8 gigs. Suddenly, the world was getting smaller and scarier. Life was genuinely frightening.

I had no real connections with any other labels at all and didn't know who might want my material. Once you lose your confidence everything seems fruitless. No one was asking me for anything. I had taken everything I had done to Network, but now the pipeline was blocked. Nothing was going out and nothing was coming in.

Network had lost a court case over its release of *Please Don't Go* by KWS and like Factory records had been a great label, if a rather poorly run business, spending loads on artwork and expenses. There was also a problem with Sony pulling out of a deal, which I believe was the final straw for Network.

Neil Rushton *"KWS had a number one-selling single with Please Don't Go and sold 399,000 copies. Then there was the most remarkable set of incidents. This tune was a number one for five weeks and a hit in America and could have set us up for life. But we lost the court case. We then did an album with a major, operating as a distributor and the company we set up with went out of business. But Network never went out of business; in fact, we are one of the only indie operations from that era that still retains ownership of the record masters and the song publishing rights. I suppose this is a legacy of us combining a maverick, almost punk-style vibe (which is why we were the perfect label/home for Altern 8) with a very sassy business-like attitude. We stopped operating when the new company we set up with Sony went out of business when Avex didn't pay us monies due. The Altern 8 and other early masters were not part of this, but essentially we had gotten too big and were distributing to more than 20 other labels and supporting them financially, which was crazy. We were also trying to make albums with artists who were singles acts. The KWS court case was a head fuck and a financial nightmare.*

In the last few months at Sony they would not give me the money to sign Daft Punk – who I saw at Manchester in 1996 – and I freaked because they reminded me so much of Nexus 21. Idiots. So I went back to finding obscure Northern Soul records."

Without a record company or working partner I was crippled by a lack of self-confidence. I had no one to give me feedback, support or direction. I didn't know if anyone would want the stuff I'd done. I could have been wrong. I felt I was really up against it. The year previously, I had my own label and Network plus extra work for Ideal Trax. There was Slo Moshun, Trackman, Xen Mantra and DJ Nex. But now... I had no output for the jungle tracks I'd recorded for instance and they just stayed on DAT, collecting dust. I was completely on my own and I wasn't getting feedback anymore. It was like being on Blue Chip again, but worse. No DJ reaction reports, no sales figures; nothing passed down to me. I was seriously losing my shit.

***

Liam was born two days after Emma's third birthday, July '96. I was to have a sound system fitted in the car on the Wednesday and the garage moved it to the Tuesday, which was lucky, as I wouldn't have had a car available for Liam's birth the following day.

I was spending even less time in the studio now I had two kids and no employer. I just didn't have the workload where I needed to be in the studio. The cost of childcare would have been too much as well and so I stayed home. I had virtually no time to do anything properly. I was used to getting an idea and turning the equipment on and starting work. Now I had half an hour to do something before Liam woke up. I was drowning. I had a son, though! I was beyond excited. I had always wanted 'one of each' and now Liam was born, the circle was complete. However, the struggle between work and family was getting harder with two children. If I tried to get any work done it was torture while they were up and about. When Liam was starting to crawl, he would often wander into my studio and start pulling wires out of samplers and whatnot and I had to block off the doorway with these big metal record boxes, which still allowed air to travel through into what was a very stuffy room. Liam could stand and balance himself against the boxes, but couldn't actually get in. Emma always wanted to stand on the studio chair by the decks with headphones on and it was only natural that the kids wanted to come in. The only time I could use the studio was when Karen was about to look after the kids, as I couldn't leave them downstairs. This continued to cause problems. 'Going in there again, are you?'

We had always worked up to having kids, the house and everything and so I couldn't complain and I wouldn't have changed a thing, because I saw my kids grow up. But work was dipping. My face was fading away from the scene as I attended playgroups and sat by the telly with a sleeping child in my arms.

Then just as things couldn't get any more difficult, Scott from Madagascar died in a car crash. I was devastated. It was the first time anyone I knew had died. The funeral had the guys from Stoke there, but I had largely stopped hanging around with them after things went sour with Danny. Only days before his death, Scott had talked about setting up a recording studio. It was horrible.

Around late '96/early '97, I bumped into Parksy again. Breakdancing was coming back into vogue and he had started going to Stoke to practise. We got chatting and agreed to go to breakdance convention Fresh '97 in Folkestone together, where I bumped into Kiddo, an original member of the B-Boys from Wolverhampton. Then weeks later, I saw Kiddo again in Funky World Records in Stafford. We got chatting and he told me he DJed quite a bit in Wolverhampton. He was a very confident geezer and offered me the chance to do some work myself. 'If you want to DJ at one of my nights, let me know.' I went over to Wolverhampton one evening and checked the clubs out (speed garage was popular back then). Kiddo DJed at the big Canal Club and The Light Bar, as well as lots of smaller bars and clubs. Kiddo seemed to be a person to keep in with, which was good, as I needed to make some money. FAST!

The Incredible Shrinking Man, Rich Tea Biscuits And Little Ballpoint Pens

My eyes came out on stalks when I saw a home video of me playing with the kids. I was pushing Emma around in a plastic car and I couldn't believe what I was seeing. I was totally shocked. I was a right fat bastard! 'That's it! I've got to slim down. That's just horrible!' I just hadn't realised how bad the situation was.

So I stupidly went on a Slimfast diet. Slimfast wasn't daft in itself; it was only when I cut out the actual meals that it got silly. Then I cut out the shakes! I got to the point where my diet was... wait for it: one Rich Tea for breakfast, one Rich Tea for lunch and, you guessed it, one Rich Tea for dinner. No wonder I was so hungry. But the weight just dropped off, which I guess is often the result of starvation. On the plus side, eating less food than a parrot was saving us money.

I had started DJing with Kiddo in Wolverhampton after Network closed and was starting to pull in £125 a week. I had gone from thousands each month to £125 a week. Whenever we needed something I used my savings until there was bugger all left. I had gone from big advances to biscuit crumbs. Literally.

DJ Kiddo *"Mark DJed with me, not for me. We were a little family of like-minded souls and Mark had a fantastic understanding of how to make great records. He felt a great idea and then did it. It could be just a feeling.*

I decided to give him a go DJing at a night I was doing in Wolverhampton called Life And Delirium. I wouldn't tell him what records to play, but I would steer him clear of some genres and 'No hit records!' The warm-up is the most important slot on a club night and the hardest. They provide the energy and feeling without sending people to sleep. They have to excite them with records they don't necessarily know. The main slot is easy: play good records. I shared my DJ knowledge with Mark and in turn I learned production from him. We worked well together.

We started making music in '97 and released Kiddo Kutz Volume 1, which featured Indigo Theme that went on to become a massive anthem in Wolverhampton."

Karen had worked at the local council since leaving school. She had a safe job there, which was lucky because I was in a right state. Karen's mother was in her element at this stage of course, as I had proved her parents right all along. They could rest assured that I had come back down to earth with a massive bump.

Karen and I would argue all the time. I was very grumpy and probably depressed. I was going out at the weekend DJing and then sat home with the kids watching cartoons and taking them to playgroups. My work/life balance was all over the place.

Kiddo was very positive about the future. 'We can do this and do that. By the time I'm 35 I'll be a millionaire.' When he DJed everyone was awe inspired and I got a real insight into what was expected. Kiddo taught me a lot about the warming-up process. If you were the warm-up guy for a big name they didn't want you playing monster tunes, as it would be next to impossible for the main guy to shine and they'd never book you again. People wanted you to accentuate the main attraction whilst getting people to dance. Kiddo was great at introducing me to the craft of DJing. Slo Moshun had a rather different view: 'If you don't want us to bring the place down, then don't book us – we don't play trance either.' This clearly wasn't the attitude I needed at this juncture.

Kiddo and I recorded some tracks together for an EP called *Kiddo Kutz*. I don't think he'd been in the studio before, but he was giving me some great ideas.

Early '98 Kiddo and I decided to go out to the Winter Music Conference in Miami, where everyone who makes music meets up with the labels. We wanted to get a deal for this track *My Lover* by Kama (Kiddo and Mark Archer) featuring Gee Haitch (Geoff Hibbert who wrote the tune) and needed a label. All the big fish would be out there looking for the next big tune for the summer and so I used the rest of my savings to fly out to Miami in a last-ditch attempt to try and get a deal, armed with cassettes, promos and T-shirts.

While we were out there I bought Karen an eternity ring. I convinced myself that this slump in work was just that: a blip. I knew I also had to work at my marriage too and the ring was my way of starting that process. Everything would come good again.

Nothing came of the Miami trip as our track had wholesale sampled a Chic record. We played it to the head of Atlantic, who owned Chic, so that didn't help. Ha ha. He asked us to call him, but it was a brush-off. The trip – and that track – came to nothing.

I did my usual routine in Miami of loitering around in the shadows. I bumped into Fast Eddie and Masters At Work, but didn't say anything. I met Armand Van Helden in the hotel lift and just stared at the doors. I went to a Masters At Work BBQ, which was an amazing experience, but the shyness thing reared its ugly head again. I just didn't have the bottle to speak to anyone, although I did get recognised. As we all had lanyards with our names on, this American dude sidled up and asked, 'Are you Mark Archer?'

-    'Depends on which Mark Archer.'

This fella recognised me, which was weird considering I'd worn a mask for three years. He had been to the gig on Jan 2nd 1993 in Detroit and had driven hundreds of miles to go to that show. He said that Altern 8 had changed his life. He was called Tommie Sunshine and he's a massive EDM DJ in the States right now. At this point Tommie was just starting out.

I came back from Miami and the arguments continued at home. The money wasn't coming in, the savings were gone and we had to scrap a family holiday we'd booked and lost the deposit. The trip to Miami was risky. If it had worked we could have been sorted, but failure rendered the journey an expensive folly. We were fucked.

DJ Kiddo *"We went to Miami Music Conference in '98 and had a great time. We set up a ghettoblaster by the pool with a Minidisc and speaker system and were playing all these house mixes. There were girls and DJs grooving with us. A well-known house DJ turned up and asked, 'Who the fuck are you?' I laughed.*

- *'Well, who the hell are YOU?!' and we continued to dance. I didn't give a sausage who he was.*

I remember the moment we suddenly realised we were eating pork scratchings in the lift of a kosher hotel. Pork Crunch they were, but still pork. Oops! We got up to so many crackers things in the five days we were there. They were tough times for Mark with work and marriage though. He was doing so many hours he didn't have time to make music any more. He's an upstanding human being is Mark. My dad, God rest his soul, said, 'Hold no friends. You don't find friends; friends find you.' I was 11 and said, 'Hold no friends? Don't be stupid! I have lots of friends.'

My dad was angry. 'Don't ever talk to me like that again!' Years later, I knew exactly what Dad meant."

***

I stuffed the car with all my records and drove to Birmingham. I wasn't DJing that night, I was selling my entire collection of hardcore. Not only was I not making music, but now I couldn't afford to listen to it. It was one of the hardest things I have ever done. These were the tunes that had nurtured my growth as a musician and here I was packing them into the car for a fast buck.

Even if each record was worth £1 per disc there was at least £1500 worth and many were worth way more than a quid a pop. Some of them were worth £30 each. I took them all the way to this Birmingham record shop and they offered me £300. It was ridiculous. A red-hot record collection for £300. I wish I'd told them to fuck off, but I didn't. I just stared at the counter and said, 'OK, then.' To top it all, I got a parking ticket. It was what you might call a 'turbo shit day'. Within days those records were selling for £15/£20 each.

Things were snowballing. We got a knock at the door one day and it was a bailiff. He'd been sent round to the house because he couldn't find Chris Peat. He'd been to a record shop where Chris was supposed to be working and had been given my address. The problem was an £8000 unpaid Altern 8 tax bill and as a member of the partnership, I was liable to pay if Chris couldn't. The bailiff said a guy in the record shop told him, 'There's no Chris Peat here, but I do know where Mark Archer lives.'

I was so scared that he was going to start taking my furniture that I agreed to pay the bill, as long as he gave me a day to sort it out. I promptly sold my car to pay it off. We part-exchanged the two cars for two crappy ones and Karen really wasn't happy. I couldn't blame her. Everything seemed to be going wrong. Chris had disappeared. Everyone kept saying he'd started up a computer shop in Stafford called Digital Dreams, (after a Nexus 21 track) but it wasn't his shop; he just worked there. Luckily it was at the other end of town to us as I didn't want anything to do with him.

By the summer of '98 Karen and I weren't even talking. On my birthday I was given a present before being left on my own. That was it. The hardest thing was that I had been brought up by parents who were a fine example of marriage. They had shared interests and went diving together and I had always wanted to be as happy as they were. I was also not the kind of guy who felt confident enough to go looking for anyone else and so the thought of leaving my wife and kids didn't sit right. But that's what I had to do. I had to leave.

It was the hardest decision of my life, but I couldn't stand the arguing any longer. I felt that I had let everyone down and that they would all be better off without me. Karen wanted some stability for her and the children and yet I had never really had a conventional career. That was fine when things were going well, but what could I do now?

I packed some clothes into a sports bag and left. The house and all the contents were for Karen and the kids. That home was where Emma and Liam were staying. I can't really describe the feeling of leaving your kids behind. It's beyond upsetting. I had the typical suburban upbringing where mum and dad stayed together and it killed me to walk away. Liam was only two and I hoped he knew no different. So I took my clothes and went to stay with my mate 'Spanish John' Birchill.

Every day I would come back and look after the kids – I just didn't live there any more. Then, as soon as Karen came home, we'd start arguing again and I would leave. Karen never really showed any kind of emotion at all and so I don't know how she felt about all this.

Apparently Karen had gone into the bathroom one day and screamed when she saw a spider. She pulled down the roller blinds and screeched, 'Marrkkk!!!' According to my friend Jon Saxon, who was using my garage/

studio as an office, this was the first time she'd really acknowledged that I'd left, as I was the one who always dealt with creepy crawlies.

Living in Spanish John's front room represented a learning curve. It was the first time I'd lived on my own, so to speak. I was now hanging out at the laundrette with a pile of 20ps. I was still DJing at the weekends for Kiddo and once the arguing with Karen stopped, I could have a tat in the home studio.

Spanish John was into the same music as me and he knew a mate of mine called Rob from the acid house days. We put some decks upstairs, which was quite nice and we had some great evenings playing tunes. It made a big change from being the househusband. I suddenly had some time to myself, but it came at a price: not seeing my kids as much.

John would be out at work during the day and so I'd go looking for a job in Stafford. I got a part-time thing at a pizza place called Gino's, working late at night. My job was preparing the dough. You'd get all the dough and lay out it in trays ready for the walk-in fridge. It was really hard work and I couldn't live on the wages, so it was lucky that I had the DJing with Kiddo.

Gino's had a very young manager there: Kath was only 18 (I was 29) and we soon started seeing each other, which didn't go down well with the owner. I'm not sure I should have been getting serious with anyone so soon after leaving home as I was in such a mess. But I was happy again, which was something.

I used to order pizzas quite a lot – well, all the time before the Rich Tea diet. In fact, it got the point where I would phone up the local pizzeria and this girl would giggle on the other end of the phone. 'Your usual?' My next-door neighbour came round for a pizza evening once and asked: 'Why do you order pizzas to be delivered? It's quicker to order and collect and then they're hot and quick.' So we went to collect this pizza and I saw this girl and thought, 'She's fit!' That was Kath. Then Spanish John and I went in there one Sunday night and Kath looked embarrassed. There was definitely a spark there. Once I got to know her, I started going in to help make the dough of an evening.

I had run out of time at John's – 'you need to find yourself somewhere' – and so it was back to Mum and Dad's in Gnosall. I was 30 years old and in exactly the same position as the 14-year-old me, only with less money and two kids. I would jump at any opportunity to get out of the house. Kath wanted to move out of her family home too and so we managed to save enough for a deposit on a little flat in Stone (just outside Stafford) for £13,000. The place was desolate when we got there, just before Christmas 1998. My whole life had been turned upside down since the previous winter, but I now felt as if I was on firmer ground. After all, I had somewhere to live and was DJing with Kiddo. I guess 'life' had taken over and music was struggling to get attention. Rennie Pilgrem from Rhythm Section contacted me, to get something new for his TCR label and I came up with *Nu Skool Breaks*, which was drum and bass with a house tempo, and he liked that. But that was possibly the only work I did that month.

Weekends were spent with the kids whilst playing out in Wolverhampton and money was scarce. I would spend the days walking around looking for a job in Stafford. I washed pots for a while at this French restaurant called Pierre Victoire and people would ask me what I'd done in the past. 'So why on earth are you doing this?' Well, I wasn't proud. I needed to pay my way.

I had lost all my records, but had kept hold of the equipment, although no one wanted anything from me, really. Plus, all my gear was in the Stafford house and so it was very difficult to make music. Then, from out of nowhere, former Network guy Neil Macey asked me to do some more Trackman work for Ideal Trax. Any interest when you're down on your luck is golden – if only to remind you of what, and who, you were. I was fast forgetting.

Neil had a spare room down in London and said he would pay for my trip down there by train. Neil had a plan. 'Move all your gear down to the offices of Ideal Trax and we will use it while you're home, and you can still use the studio each week to record.' It seemed like a reasonable idea to be honest, plus I got to spend some time in London. I wasn't in a position to say no to these things anyway. I was just desperate to get busy.

Looking back, it was the wrong time to try and make music. The scene was very disparate back then and I wasn't too sure as to what I, or other people, liked and wanted. I did some odd tracks, bits and bobs, but nothing came out. I had lost all my confidence and had zero inspiration. It's often when you need something to happen so much that it will not go your way. Music had always been my passion and my saviour, but it was slipping away from me. 'Why don't I give you an offer for the rest of your gear?' Neil Macey asked me one day. I couldn't think of many reasons to say no, and I had plenty of reasons to say yes. Kath had always said she didn't want kids, and it was something I was dead against at the time, but a year into the relationship she changed her mind. We now needed money to prepare for a baby.

Neil agreed to pay me £4,000 for £20,000 worth of gear. Ping! The 202, 727, 909, 808 and 303 were gone. Everything I had ever worked for, and worked on, had gone. I recalled the afternoons spent with Emma and Liam, tatting away on the keyboards and the tunes I'd made on that gear. All gone. I didn't even have any decks at the new flat.

Neil Macey *"I left Network in 1990, but went back again in 1993. By 1995 I was out on my own again with a new venture called Ideal. Basically I was allowing musicians to deal directly with me, no signing away of rights, on a release-by-release basis. It was to give freedom to the artists and unlike traditional P&D deals (press and distribution) we would deal with artists as well as labels. Give us the artwork and we organised, manufactured, sold, distributed and promoted it.*

Ideal was also a label too (Ideal Trax) and if Mark wasn't the number one choice to record for us, then he was in the top three. Musically, things had moved back to pure house and techno and Mark came back to us with the Trackman EP catalogue number: IDT1. Labels back then communicated what the listener was to expect and if you deviated from that you alienated the core audience. However, if you stuck to the brief, you could accurately predict what they would sell, given the number of people around the world who wanted this type of music. Mark had gone back to Detroit, as it were, and was spot on with this Trackman release, which he did with Ken Clarke. Don't Stop is just an incredible techno masterpiece. A storming, monster of a record which sold fairly well. Trackman's Don't Stop is one of the records I'm most proud of releasing.

I felt bad about buying Mark's equipment in '99, but he said he was desperate for cash and I paid the asking price. But it felt like I was capitalising on his misfortune somehow. I paid for him to come down to London and record, and fed him and put him up, but he was so distracted and uninspired. Network going bust had left him feeling lost. It was the wrong time to make music, looking back, but we tried to get something together, although it proved fruitless. Mark was in a bad place, personally, and had lost the thread. I couldn't help feeling that I was putting a nail into the coffin of his career."

You know things are bad when you can't afford the petrol to get to the job centre. I walked 12 miles every day from Stone to Stafford only to

Chris, me and Joey Beltram backstage at the
Limelight, New York, 1991

Mansion House, Dublin, 1992

Blue Chip studio, 1992

Stafford Newsletter photoshoot, near
Pennycroft Flats, Stafford, 1991

Mask photo for E-Vapor-8 promotional
campaign, 1992

The change of suits and new masks.
They didn't last long

Mixmag front cover, 1992

Energy at the Eclipse, Coventry where we
appeared on Hitman & Her, 1992

E-Vapor-8 video shoot, Cannock, 1992

Crez and me, post gig, 1992

Backstage at Phobia, 1992

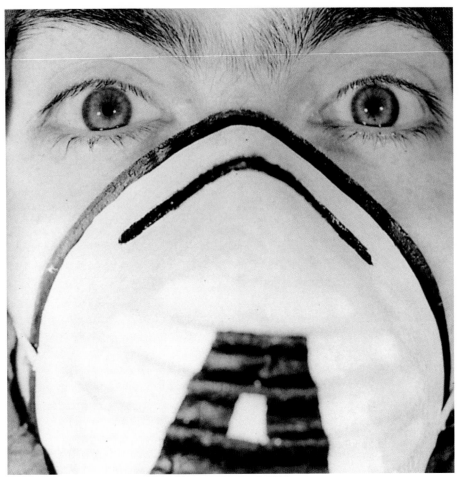
Album photo shoot, 1992

LA's 18 Hour Hardcore Fest flyer, 1992

New merchandise with the 88 Revival logo, 1992

Altern 8 and the mighty Carl Cox

Me and Chris at the Quasar album launch at Stafford Ten-pin, 1992

Opening HMV in Hanley, 1992. Take That were our warm-up act

Altern 8 in Red Ruth with Sara Cooper, 1992

Judgement Day, Stafford, 1992 with a 'genuine' witch doctor

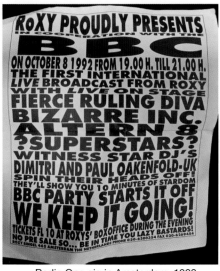

Radio One gig in Amsterdam, 1992

In the very cramped Sandon Road home studio

Ticket for the Greece gig, 1993

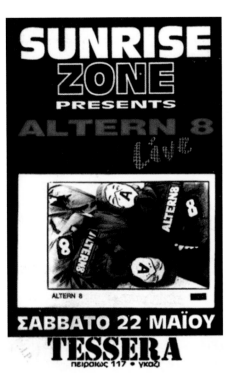

Sunrise Zone, Greece, 1993

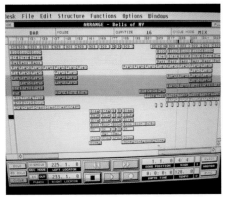

Danny's hand-drawn Dansa logo after we
recorded Bells of N.Y.

Bells of N.Y. Cubase arrangement screen

Front cover of Echoes, 1994, at the height of
my love affair with Wimpy

Emma and Liam in 1996

Emma in my newly refurbished home studio, 1996

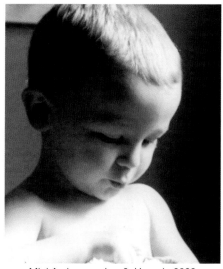

Mini Archer number 3. Harry in 2002

First ever Bangface gig with the Stormtrooper cut-outs we robbed (Sorry James), 2005

Bangface's Revenge of the Synth

Altern 8 fans at the Bangface tent, Glade, 2006

be totally disheartened by the lack of jobs. I had no discernible skills to offer anyone. 'What can you do?'

- 'Make music.'
- 'Anything else?'
- 'Not really.'
- 'Well, there are not a lot of opportunities for that.'

My confidence was shattered into a million tiny fragments. I was so tired and just not thinking straight. Things had gone to shit, so damn fast. It wasn't that long ago that Slo Moshun were getting rave reviews and yet now I had to motivate myself to get out the front door. The split with Chris and the tax bill had been a major blow to my marriage as well as my wallet and Network had fallen away too. I was a 30-year-old divorcé with two small kids and what seemed to be no hope of recovery. The world was moving on and I was going backwards, plus we were trying for another child.

Kath wanted kids and although I had been upfront about not wanting to go down that road again, she'd had a massive change of heart. All of a sudden it was the only thing we talked about. We had a massive difference of opinion about this, plus there was this big age gap. Kath wanted to control me although I was 12 years older and there was no way I was prepared to let her. Life just seemed to get confusing without me realising what was going on. Why did Kath suddenly want kids when she was still a teenager? I left at one point and was about to give up on Kath.

I shouldn't have gone back, but I did and as a result she gained a bargaining position and it wasn't long before the baby was suddenly an urgent matter. 'Who am I to stop someone getting what they want out of life?' I had already sold all my equipment in anticipation of family life.

A chink of light, money-wise, came from a most unusual source. Kath had wanted to leave Gino's for a while and she was getting quite excited by a typing test she'd arranged for a job at an Argos call centre by junction 13 of the M6. Kath passed the test and got an interview and by the time she got home, bingo! She had a job on the telephone order line. Kath enjoyed the job at Argos and suggested I went for one too. At that point, the thought of any routine coupled with a sense of stability was tempting. I just wanted to stop feeling so down. The typing test was basically a spelling quiz. You had to type fast from a leaflet and make sure that what you typed was spelled correctly. I did the test and passed. A job offer came soon after. From Altern 8 to Argos. You know what? I was chuffed.

So, I had a job on the order line and when people phoned Argos to place an order for a bed or a hairdryer or whatever, I would take the details, check if the item was in stock and note any detail about the delivery. If the item was not in stock, I would rearrange delivery. If nothing else, this job represented a start. Something to move on from.

I did my training and really felt like a part of the team. Kath was in a different department, but we could still see each other at lunch. It felt so cool having a new bunch of friends who took me at face value. So I worked during the week and would get the kids at weekends when I was still DJing with Kiddo in the evenings.

The DJing was my last remaining link to music, really. It was a source of income and it helped my confidence no end. I worked really hard playing all the little venues as Kiddo looked after the bigger ones. I was starting from the bottom again there too, but I was learning a lot.

In 1999, Miss Moneypenny's from Birmingham decided to buy the Canal Club and so I went from warming up the little bars for Kiddo to some main slots, when he moved to Moneypenny's in Birmingham. I would sometimes get both an early and a late gig. Often big guests would play and I would close the evening. Then another bombshell hit. Moneypenny's wanted to bring in all their own DJs over to Wolverhampton. Shiiiiiiiiiiiiiiiiiiiiiiiiiiiiiiiiiiiiiiiiiiiiiiiiiiiit! All that warm-up work had led straight into a brick wall. It was getting to the point where I truly wondered if it was all worthwhile. I did everything I could to look eager and never turned work down, but music just seemed too much of a struggle.

Moneypenny's bought the Canal Club, installed their own DJs and went glam. Everyone wanted to be seen in there: trannies, models and dancers on the bar. It was very different to the rave thing.

The job at Argos genuinely helped me though and gave me security and stability, but music was still my passion. I just felt a bit lost although I counted my blessings that I had done the things I had. I played Brazil with Moby, appeared on *Top of the Pops* and had hit number three in the charts. At least I had those memories, even if things were looking bleak.

Mum rang me one evening, not long after the DJing went south, with a telephone number. They had a message on their landline from someone who wanted to get into contact with me. The way my luck was going it was probably a bailiff or something, but I decided to ring it anyway.

I don't know how they'd got my parents' number but this guy certainly wanted something I had. I was at Argos when I got the booking for the Altern 8 PA. 'I don't know if you're aware, but we split up in 1993,'

I explained. 'I have also fallen out with my partner Chris.' This fella didn't seem bothered. 'As long as you wear the suits, I don't care who it is.'

I hadn't seen this coming at all, but I was overwhelmed with excitement. The gig aside, just being linked to the past and what we had achieved gave me a boost. The band was getting back together. Even if it was for just one night.

So I got Parksy, Dan and Butler together for the triumphant return of Altern 8. As I had coughed up for this £8000 tax bill I saw this as a way of clawing some of that money back. It wasn't to piss Chris off; it was about me trying to fill the hole that the tax bill had left in my bank account. A tax bill that contributed greatly to my divorce when things were going downhill fast. Danny Weaver (Taurus) from Slo Moshun agreed to play the keyboards, which was great, as Chris and I were still not speaking. Even the thought of seeing Chris made me jittery.

I hadn't seen Danny or any of the Stoke lot for a couple of years. Scott (Madagascar) had died in the car accident and the last time I saw the Stoke crew was at his tribute night, which coincided with the eventual launch of his record label (RIP) a year or so after his death. Kath and I went up together, but we didn't stay long as it wasn't her kind of thing and she didn't know anyone there. I met up with Danny and Lethal Lee and the others who had not seen me since I was 16 stone; I was down to nine by then. They were shocked at the difference in me.

I thought the PA would be a one-off as revival circuits – we were part of the old-skool '88-'92 scene – would often go in fits and starts. A one-off was better than nothing, though. I had no equipment of course, other than a Yamaha DX100 keyboard and an Akai sampler. Danny had a broken old keyboard and we had an X stand each. I dusted off the suits and masks and looked forward to getting back to those karate-chops on the keys.

When we went abroad in '93, we couldn't take the As and 8s and so we needed something we could take with us. In another stroke of DIY genius, I got a one-inch plumber's pipe and made a giant A by placing sections at 45-degree angles. I then attached canvas, which I painted black with fluorescent paint on top. It was lightweight and you could lift it with one finger. You could also roll them up into a guttering screw-top. I still had those.

Crez couldn't make it, but he was in a good place as a director at Kindertons, an accident management company. I had kept in touch with Parksy though, and he was bang up for it. I had known Rob Bairstow from the acid house days at Frenzy and he popped round Spanish John's now and again when I was there. He had danced with Bizarre Inc and agreed to share the stage with Parksy. Butler was cool for MCing.

We hadn't done a live PA for six years, but it felt like yesterday. It was an amazing night. Everyone was on point and it felt almost spiritual when I placed that mask back on. I fitted some new elastic to the masks and got a new chemical suit for Danny. The Marcus Garvey Centre in Nottingham, went right off. It was just like the old days; we'd played that venue a few times back in the day. It was January 1st 1999 and it was the best possible way to start a new year.

It was like being in a trance on stage; all these memories came flooding back. It was so joyous. Even my body knew that this was what I should be doing. The crowd lapped it up.

We did the gig and as we were getting all the gear offstage I stumbled on these concrete steps. I was carrying an X stand, keyboard and the big A when I slipped. I put my elbow out to stop me and there was a pebble right where the bone landed. Aaaarrggghhh! I banged my ribs, which hurt like fuck and my elbow went numb. I went to the dressing room and said, 'My arm hurts a bit.' I rolled my sleeve up and there was a perfect circle of a hole punched into my elbow. The fall on to the pebble had plunged it straight into my skin. I thought, 'Oh well, at least it's not bleeding.' As soon as I thought that, blood started pouring down my arm. I held my arm up and covered it with green paper towels when this geezer came in. 'What a wicked gig! 808 State – you were wicked!' he boomed, and as my arm was in the air, he hi-fived it. 'Aaarrggh!' He didn't seem to cotton on to my predicament and kept hi-fiving me, over and over. So I turned my arm round and showed him the damage.
- 'So sorry mate, so sorry.'
- 'And we're not 808 State.'
- 'So sorry mate, sorry.'

I ended up driving back from Nottingham with my arm held straight. It had gone completely stiff and I could hardly move it. I kept it lolled over the steering wheel and it looked like I was trying to touch the windscreen. I went straight to A&E in Stafford and waited there for an hour to get seen by someone and eventually they put a plaster on it. That was it! I could have done that! Over the following weeks the hole in my elbow turned into a massive scar that resembled what can only be described as a pert nipple.

CH. 27

Fridges, Gigs And A Bad Case Of Karma

Kath was majorly happy when she got pregnant and promptly left Argos. But as soon as Harry was born, the honeymoon was well and truly over. The stress levels hit the roof. Life was a constant stream of arguments, rows and sleepless nights. I loved Harry to bits of course, as I did Emma and Liam, but life was a mess. Kath took control almost immediately as she finally had what she wanted. I think my close friends and family must have thought I'd really lost the plot at this point. Looking back, I was just trying to steady a ship that had already hit a few icebergs. I just wanted an easy life – something I never quite achieved.

The relationship soured very quickly. I had developed a temper I found hard to contain. You can always blame people for things, but it's up to you to change it and I guess I hadn't been tough enough in a way. Kath was messing me about. You're in a flat, a little flat, with no money and you're changing the baby and looking out of the window where there's a 'for sale' sign outside your house. 'Some idiots have put a for sale sign outside our house.'

- 'That's meant to be there. We're selling.'
- 'What!!!? When were you going to tell me that?'

Looking back, it was a very difficult time. I was in love with Kath and had Harry who was now six months old and during that whole time I was always trying to win her back. Then she hit me with a hammer blow. 'You don't make me happy. You never have. We shouldn't be together.' It was totally crushing. Could my life get any more miserable? It wasn't long before I was booted out again. Next stop: Mum and Dad's.

Dad was cool with me following music and doing my own thing, but he would get grumpy over my personal life. I now had two sets of kids with different mums and I wasn't living with either of them. I got in one night very moody and Dad was a little drunk. He'd had a skinful, actually. 'I have a little advice for you, son... lay off the pussy!' Although he'd put it in rather crude terms, I knew exactly what Dad meant; my life was being ruled by my need to be with someone. I guess it helped my self-esteem to have a girlfriend. My marriage had earned me little affection and so I craved it. I didn't like being on my own.

***

Maybe John McCready knew something I didn't when he kept banging on about washing machines and laundrette raves in those early press releases for Network because here I was at Argos, selling Hotpoints and Zanussis. When the ordering department got moved from Stafford to a call centre in Widnes, I was called in to help with Argos's foray into white goods. Selling fridges and tumble dryers was a new direction for the company and when Argos did something, they had to be the best. So if they did toys, they had to outsell Toys R Us. I was chuffed when they asked me to help steer this new direction.

The Altern 8 gig had been a one-off and although fun, it didn't feel like anything more than that. My DJing had all but gone and so now I could concentrate on my day job. It wasn't what I wanted to do, but it was what I had to do. Argos moved six agents to this new white goods department and I was one of them. I'm not sure what would have happened if I'd not been chosen but, much to the dismay of my team leaders, I was. I don't think my line managers wanted me to progress. I didn't make a conscious decision to go up the ladder, but there you have it. I was on my way up! I was a 'team second'. I was always keen, happy and chatty at Argos and would always be on hand to help anyone out. I think it was important for me to be around other people.

It was quite weird because this girl I'd been chatting to at Argos got the idea that we were going out together. I had done nothing to encourage this and was more than a little worried that word would get back to Kath, as I still hoped we'd get back together. We went for a team meal one night and I bumped into an old flame (I dated her for about month while Kath and I were separated) and this girl from Argos got the proper hump and even told her dad, who threatened to beat me up, because she was so upset. It was so odd. What was happening? It was my fault, according to the managers who had an emergency meeting about me. I was oblivious to all this. Suddenly my career at Argos had hit some turbulence.

***

Even apart, the troubles with Kath continued as I tried to see Harry as much as I could. I found out one afternoon that Kath was going out that evening with the girls and was leaving Harry with her dad. Now I was his father, but she decided not to ask me. I was already missing out on seeing Emma and Liam grow up and now this. I phoned Kath and there was lots of arguing and slamming of phones before she handed over to her dad. 'You've got my son and she's going out on the piss and I can't see him. I'm working dead hard here and yet I can't see my son!' Kath's dad then got my blood boiling. 'There's a train on the line!' The phone went dead. I went to Kath's parents after work to get Harry and they threatened to call the police. I was so pissed off. I stormed out and sat in the car for a bit. Driving back to Mum's I went past the Top Of The World and parked up. There was a massive queue outside. There was a time when life was carefree and I was waiting to get into that club for a night out. Now I was a middle-aged man with all sorts of problems. There was a tap at the window. It was the police. Because I had my hood up, I looked quite shady and so they got me out of the car in front of all these clubbers who were jeering. Life was shit, but as the police patted me down, I promised myself that I would win Kath and Harry back. I drove back to my parents, but the door was locked and so I slept in my car.

Gigs were slowly coming in while I was at Argos. I had no one sorting bookings for me and if people didn't have your phone number, you missed out. I probably lost loads of gigs as this was the early days of the internet and I had no presence online. Butler and I did the odd PA together and it was always old-skool. A bit like a typecast actor, people always wanted 'that character' no matter what you'd done since. I had done Slo Moshun, Nexus 21, Trackman and Xen Mantra, but everyone wanted the mask.

We did a New Year's gig in 2000 while I had split from Kath and I bumped into a lad who used to live near me. I was always walking past his house while he was washing his car and he would often play Altern 8. Phil had moved house to Doxey (a mile or two outside Stafford) and told me that next-door was up for sale. I told my brother Paul, who was living in the married quarters at the RAF base, knowing he wanted to get on the property ladder. 'I will get it and you can rent it from me,' said Paul. Yes! Now I could finally leave Mum and Dad's to live on my own, in a fully functional babe lair.

Living in Doxey allowed me to get my head together. I needed time to work out what was going on and to get my head around the past as well as the future. I decided to be as positive as I could and offered to give Kath lifts if she ever needed one. Eventually, Kath thawed and we became friends again, and in early 2001, we got back together. It was boom or bust and we had a big sit down and talked about not repeating the errors of the past and moving on. To show how committed we were we decided to get hitched.

'I want a car,' Kath announced one day. She hadn't even passed her test and yet she wanted a car. So, we started saving for a Mini and a wedding.

So my typical day was up at 7am with Harry, then 2pm to 10pm at Argos and then home by 10.30pm. Weekends were spent DJing too as I saved money for the wedding (and the car). I would always see Emma and Liam on a Sunday at Mum and Dad's.

So we bought Kath a Mini and a short while later she passed her test. I was often on the order line when the phone would go. 'I've broken down at the traffic lights... the car has stalled... loads of cars are beeping at me.' I had these calls every day. 'There's nothing I can do about it, Kath. I'm at work!'

-   'But they're beeping!'
-   'Don't worry about anyone else. They won't kill you. Just calm down and get through this.'

Every day was the same. It drove me mad.

We got married at the Isaac Walton Cottage in Shallowford (Walton was the real-life J.R. Hartley from the famous *Yellow Pages* TV adverts). The cottage had really low ceilings and was a cracking venue. The wedding was brilliant even though Kath's mum and dad weren't particularly arsed with getting on with me. It was a great day, though, and the future suddenly seemed bright. The three of us were reunited and now we had a house in Doxey.

Things were progressing nicely at Argos too and I did well as part of the white goods team. Management wanted me to become a team leader. My team leader didn't like this idea at all, but I went through the interview process and was surprised as anyone when the call centre manager promoted me.

I now had a team of young lads (17, 18) who would go out to lunch and get stoned. They were the kind of kids who knew more about computers than the IT department. These fellas knew all the security cheats and could wipe machines clean and remove the disc drives. My team were playing games on sites they weren't even meant to visit and this made me quite proud in a way. They could have been a great asset to Argos, but they were lost in the machine, as it were.

We had a competition between different sales teams and my team were expected to come last, so it was a surprise to everyone – including me – when they came out on top. One guy accused us of 'fiddling it'. I have no idea how we won, but we did. Woah! Go Team Archer!

The office buildings were either side of a huge warehouse and Argos had a bus that would take staff around this enormous business park. This bus driver spent all day driving in a circle around Argos. We called the vehicle the Venga Bus. That bus was important, though, because if you missed it, you had to walk and that could ruin your stats for the day.

Kath wrote the Mini off not long after we got it when a guy pulled out in front of her. He was in the wrong, but there were no lines on this weird junction and so he had the law on his side. Kath was very vague at times. I would come home and ask if anyone had called and she'd always say no, then I would find out days later that all sorts of people had spoken to her. I had to interrogate Kath to get any semblance of a conversation out of her. I was madly in love with her and I wanted to be a proper dad, – I felt I had failed Emma and Liam – but it was hard work. Still, I was trying to make a go of our marriage, as much as I could.

Then the white goods department moved to Widnes as well. I was then moved into the training department and was tasked with getting new recruits up to spin. You had to put in a little performance in this new role and so you had to be quite confident and outgoing and I had no mask to help me this time.

I am bad at picking up on signals and for a while I was chatty with this woman at Argos, who I later found out had a thing for me. Anyway, this girl contacted the BBC people to get me on *Never Mind The Buzzcocks* in that identity parade thing they do; you have to spot the washed-up musician among the ringers. The show thought it was a great idea and I was booked.

I told the show's researchers how to get the exact same suits, but they said they'd already sorted them, as well as the masks, although they looked nothing like mine. One of them had a light green rubber zip-up suit with wellies. Anyone who'd seen a pic of Altern 8 would have known. They then gave us silly names and we were told to just stare at a point in the studio and not to react. I was Masturb8 and there was Black & Decker Workm8 and Who 8 All The Pies. Phil Jupitus picked me and said I looked like I was high on ether or something although the strongest thing I'd ever taken was that cigarette with Poddy. They then played a bit of *Activ 8*.

You can see how people lose sight of their dreams. Life just takes over. Argos, childcare, marriage and weekends with Emma and Liam – how could music get a look-in? 2003 had been quiet on the DJing front – I did a few nights with Butler – although things did pick up a little in 2004.

We went out to Ibiza when Butler and I got a gig DJing, after I mixed a CD for Danny Donnelly's Suburban Base; he was putting out some pure garage and R&B CDs and the Euphoria series of trance and old skool. Danny was out in Ibiza at the time and so we planned to meet him out there. Kath and Harry were able to come too and so I was really looking forward to having some fun in the sun.

I did a mix of old skool for Danny's CD and got it spot on and my confidence was well and truly boosted. Studio mixing is odd compared to live mixing, in that you can do it perfectly when you're playing out, but as soon as you take the pause button off in the studio, the recording fucks the mix up straight away. Ask any DJ. But I was eager to carry on with the work for Danny.

These *Euphoria* albums were great for getting new gigs as they were advertised on TV. Suddenly I was going to Ibiza with Butler to play old-skool at The Judgement Day Trance Party on the back of it. This trip to Ibiza was different, though, in that Kath was with us.

Kath could be quite difficult on nights out. New Year's Eve at the Q Club in Birmingham, for example. Mark and I decided to take our partners and he and Lisa drove down to give us a lift. It was New Year's Eve and we were booked quite early on and were already running late.

Just as we were getting ready to leave Kath popped down the stairs and asked how she looked. Bearing in mind we were late, and waiting for her, I told her she looked fine and that we had to go. At that point she threw a strop. 'I want more than *fine*!' She came back down again in pyjamas. 'Look, I don't want to be late. I can't be late, it's New Year's Eve! It's a good gig.' We had to leave without her. 'I hope you meet someone else and fuck her!' she texted.

In Ibiza, Mark and Lisa looked after Harry one evening so Kath and I could go out on our own. But Kath didn't feel like it. I was getting tired of all this. The next night she went out with Lisa and came back at 6am and slept all day, meaning that I missed my meeting with Danny Donnelly as I had to look after Harry. That was the point where I gave up. I still loved her to bits, but I gave up trying to get through to her. She just did what she wanted, when she wanted and didn't see how this was affecting our marriage.

I deeply regret what happened next and how I went about it because karma came around and bit me fair and square on the arse.

***

I was working at Argos with a girl called Pippa and she was arguably the fittest woman in the whole call centre. She didn't think she was, but every bloke did. My mate Stuart Higgins would rib me about it all the time. He was as surprised as me that I won the leader board that time as he would go home every night and swot up, yet I was totally winging it. Stuey kept going on about Pippa because she was spending so much time with me, talking.

I would get in early to start at 2pm, and every day Pippa came in and sat down with me. She was sending all these signals, but I couldn't read them. Stuey started calling me a 'stupid gommer' because I couldn't see that she was into me. I just thought she was being polite. Pippa was on her last warning for being late to work and yet she was actually getting in early, to talk to me.

I went to the pub after work one Friday and we ended up at my mate Rob's afterwards. Pippa was there that night and it became a regular thing. It was clear, even to me by now, that Pippa liked me and so it began.

I deeply regret seeing Pippa behind Kath's back and when she correctly suspected something, I lied. I could have come clean and sorted it, but I was still in love with Kath. Of course things came to a

head eventually and Kath even phoned my mum, who I really didn't want involved. She put it straight: 'It's me or Pippa!'
-   'I will stay with you if you can make me happy…'
-   'I'm not going to change.'
-   'That's answered that, then.' Kath moved out.

Kath waited until I was at work one day and took nearly everything from the house. Marriage number two was over for good now and the future was, yet again, far from certain.

Not long after we split, Kath dropped Harry off on a Sunday morning and I had to say it: 'Bloody hell, your boobs look big!'
-   'It's the bra.'
-   'Are you sure?'

It turned out that Kath was pregnant. Pregnant! I wasn't the father, however. It turned out that she had been seeing an ex, on and off, during our breaks, but this guy was married and wouldn't leave his wife and so a baby was not what he wanted. I still loved Kath, even if we were over. I could tell that she was upset and worried and tried to help her out as best I could. I had to make sure she was OK, as I really did love her, even though we were finished.

This bloke went on holiday to escape the situation with Kath back home and while he was away, Kath lost the baby. I took her home from the hospital to keep an eye on her, as she had just lost a child with someone who wasn't interested. I didn't know it at the time, but I was getting to the point where I couldn't stand any more stress. I was getting very anxious and at times was unable to sleep as I was so depressed and jumpy. Dad had suffered a funny turn around this time when he went out into the garden and had a fit. He went completely blank and started sweating and didn't say anything for a bit. When he came to, he was dizzy and didn't know where he was. He had forgotten loads of stuff. Mum waited quite a while before she said anything as she didn't want to bother me.

Dad didn't have Alzheimer's, but a form of epilepsy, and this stopped him driving straight away; he couldn't be having fits in the car. This and Kath had my nerves all over the place.

I went to work the day after the hospital trip with Kath and started my computer up. I could see Pippa at the end of the row of desks, as hundreds of emails popped up on my screen. I looked at the monitor and nothing made sense. It didn't mean anything at all. I just scrolled up and down and up and down before pushing the keyboard away. I was done.

CH. 28

I'm Drowning

I wasn't sure where I was, what I was doing, or who I was. Everything seemed to be slipping through my fingers and falling to the floor. There was too much to worry about. I had no idea how I could get over this. I had forgotten how to smile. I was drowning...

A female colleague asked me if I was OK and it was the worst thing she could have said. I pleaded with her, 'Please don't ask me that. I'm alright. Please!' Then I snapped. Something went. Tears ran down my face and I ran downstairs crying uncontrollably. I gripped onto the handrail in the stairwell to stop myself falling. A colleague followed me down and called a cab. I was shaking like a leaf and unable to think straight.

My second marriage was over. My dad was ill. My new relationship was causing problems at work. My wife had just lost a baby after seeing someone else and my career in music had faded into a distant memory. It was all too much. Argos sent me home.

The doctor said I was suffering from clinical depression. I was dreading going back to work and so he put me on antidepressants. However, those pills were really messing with me and I felt suicidal. 'Everyone would be better off if I wasn't here.'

One of the side effects of these particular antidepressants was linked to suicidal thoughts. What?! I thought they were meant to cheer you up. 'Don't make any big decisions,' the doctor advised and that really helped. I saw a counsellor too. 'You have to realise this isn't you; it's something happening *to* you,' she said. But life was just going to shit and I couldn't stop it. I don't know where the days went. I was in such a state. I was on the outside looking in, scared stiff of what my life had become. I just couldn't do it anymore.

My therapist said a lot of my problems went back to school and the bullying and these heightened feelings of sensitivity were a result. She seemed to be on my side and that meant a lot. We went through everything that had happened to me and that felt good. I felt justified about feeling this shit and this was important. Sometimes you just have to stop torturing yourself. I was only on antidepressants for a few weeks, but it was just masking the situation. It wouldn't go away until I dealt with it. You're not supposed to simply stop taking these pills, but that's what I did.

I couldn't even consider dealing with the public at Argos in the frame of mind I was in. I was all over the place. My sleeping patterns had changed completely and I was an emotional wreck. I would cry all day, every day, for weeks. It was an outpouring of emotion I just couldn't stop. I just couldn't hold it together. I would come down the stairs in the morning, have breakfast and then just curl up on the sofa, sobbing. I had been set unrealistic targets at work and was much more stressed than I let on and so that pressure had been building up for a while. The situation with Pippa was bad too, and colleagues saw me as a love rat because I was married. I had started to hate being there; there were a few people on antidepressants at Argos. Then splitting up with Kath and not being with Emma, Liam and now Harry was just too much. I had three kids and wasn't with any of them. The job, coupled with Kath's miscarriage, really pushed me over the edge.

Just hearing the Argos office in the background when Pippa rang from work would send me off into a spiral. I couldn't breathe. When the sick pay ended I knew I had to quit. There was no way I could return. It was hopeless. I was drowning.

After a while, I realised that money was now an issue again. I needed some. Quick! Just going to the Job Centre was so depressing. I would want to burst out crying within minutes of entering that office. I had no relevant experience. No managerial training. If Pippa was with me I'd panic and bolt for the door. I felt bad for putting her through it all. She was so young. She didn't need all this.

I went home after another joyless trip to the Job Centre and locked myself in the bathroom. No one could bother me in there. No one could tell me it was alright because it wasn't. There was a disposable razor on the side and I picked it up and looked at it. I thought about snapping it in half to get the blade out. 'This could solve everything. I am not going to feel like shit any more if I just move this across my wrists.' I really felt that crappy. 'I am just useless. I have failed at life.' Pippa banged on the door and I woke up as if in a trance. I wasn't holding the razor against my wrist; I was just in a daze, staring at it. I unlocked the door and she walked in looking really scared. She got me to put the razor down.

I wasn't out of it all the time, but it was draining, coming as it did in fits and starts. But once I started crying I just couldn't stop. I didn't even know why I was doing it and no one knew what to say. A girl from the order line team came to the house to see me one morning and I couldn't handle that at all. She realised how delicate I was and there wasn't much she could do or say. But I really appreciated what she did. I could be quite nasty too as I felt so pressured when people were paying me attention. It was really difficult for Pippa.

I was offered another DJ gig in Ibiza that July and as screwed as I was, I took it. I just wanted to escape and so I took Pippa with me. That trip couldn't have come at a better time. It was a complete break from what was going on at home. The sun was out and I had a smile on my face, although there was still a lot going on under the surface. It was like music was pulling me out of that flat and all the trouble that seemed to follow me around like a black cloud.

We went to a house night at Eden where Howard from Take That was DJing. Pippa loved Take That and had a great time. We listened to a lot of R&B together and Kath had liked the same sort of music too. It was nice to have the sun on your back and I could proudly show off my new tattoos. As soon as I met Kath, she got a tattoo after her dad told her not to. She got a butterfly just above her panty line. I was desperate to have one too, but Karen never approved. She really frowned on such things. But I got a tribal band around my arm as soon as I met Kath and I thought it was ace. But once you have one, the whole thing starts up. Tattoos are very addictive. Like Pringles, once you pop, you just can't stop.

We had a great time in Ibiza and although my problems hadn't disappeared, I had at least forgotten about them for a bit. I just needed to break the routine that the depression had created.

Pippa helped me a lot and I was mad keen on her. Back home we started clubbing together every Saturday in Stoke at a night run by Lethal Lee. Danny (Taurus) was often DJing there too as was a young lad called Vasco. Having Pippa on my arm was a real boost to my self-esteem, which had hit rock bottom. 'You and Pippa look inseparable,' Danny once commented. People said there was an aura around us. I admit, I fall in love far too quickly and Pippa was no exception. I tell girls I love them within weeks/days/hours. I am a soft git.

One particular night just before Christmas 2004 a few people came up to me and said that Pippa had been talking to a certain lad. I just brushed it off. 'He's her age, it's OK,' I said. She was 19. I was 35.

Of course, she ended up getting off with someone at this club and it was like the whole karma thing had come back to bite me again. I have to admit I was in bad shape psychologically and Pippa was far too young to get involved with all that. That said, she was still round my house all the time, as she had pretty much moved in, which was a big deal for her mum and dad, who were obviously protective of her. The only problem was that she wanted to live with me *and* see other people. I might be soft, but I wasn't that pathetic and told her she needed to go back to her parents. Early 2005, we split.

I had lied to Kath and saw how miserable that made her and now it was happening to me. I made a vow – now I was on my own again – never to tell another lie. A lie becomes another lie and trouble is always near, and so I vowed to be honest and take any consequence that might result. Instantly I felt a weight had been lifted.

I was still in a state and prone to serious bouts of depression. I had lots of concerns, along with crippling financial worries as well as two sets of children by different parents. No matter how fragile I was, I had to get a job.

I saw a cleaning job in the paper one morning and got it. It was hardly any money at all, but I felt as though I was doing something positive. DJ work was so sporadic you couldn't live off it and so I ended up taking the job as a cleaner in order to ease the pressure. I would get up early and go to work in offices and shops, cleaning the floors and emptying bins. It seemed as if the physical nature of the job, coupled with the lack of interaction with others, suited me for a while. You'd get a list of places to go, or just one. I was home by lunchtime. If there was a big contract you might go with other cleaners. JCB had a place outside Stoke, which was its main HQ with a helipad and stuff, and we would often go and clean the social club. I would sometimes spend an hour at one place, an hour at another and then you were done. Once I was home I felt as though I'd done something.

Pippa had started seeing someone else and that was weird. There was a period where I felt crappy again and it was a lot to take in, but I tried to remain friends with her. This new bloke wanted to take her to Ibiza and to all the clubs I took her to, which was odd. Apparently, this new fella was even copying what I was wearing and hanging out at the same bars and venues.

I did a lot of soul-searching around this time and was learning a lot about myself. I was also lonely and would start texting Kath as I walked around Stafford drunk. I had never really been a drinker, but I think alcohol simply filled the gap. I'd wake up the next day and realise what I'd done. Texting whilst drunk was *always* a bad move.

MSN, Bottles Of Port And Ebay Rage

McDonalds don't want me. Kwik Save don't want me. Jesus Christ! I've been turned down by McDonalds!

My brain was clear of worry when I was cleaning, but it was a far cry from playing a Manhattan nightclub with Moby. Cleaning wasn't going to stress me out and I couldn't have anyone expecting anything more of me at this point. I would get up, go clean a few places, get home later for lunch and be a miserable arsehole for the rest of the day. It paid a pittance and I couldn't even afford to pay my brother £150 a month for rent, but the DJing was slowly picking up and I was getting gigs in different places, but this in turn raised a flag to Chris.

Chris would phone me up to threaten court action. 'You're using Altern 8 to get gigs and that's me and you. You can't use the name. I am making a folder of all the gigs you've been doing and I'm taking it to the police.' The situation was so desperately shit. Chris would often phone promoters to get the gigs cancelled. Some of the promoters weren't that old and just didn't want the hassle and the threat of legal action. 'You can't put Altern 8 on the poster!' Chris would warn them. I think these promoters often passed my mobile number to Chris and then he would be on the phone constantly. I don't know how many times I changed my number.

If Chris rang me, I'd put the phone down. Then he'd ring again. I'd leave the phone ringing for ages. Why would I answer, when I knew what was coming? 'You're not Altern 8!!!'

- 'But I was a member of Altern 8!' It just went on and on.

Neither of us owned Altern 8 and the music was the property of Network which had named and bankrolled the band. We agreed to split the profits from the music before we dissolved the partnership, even though I had done most of the work, but that was it. I had even paid Chris's half of the tax bill. In my eyes, we were done. But for Chris, it was an ongoing battle.

I started getting a little bit of work from a new web community called Myspace, which seemed to be working well for new bands. Myspace was also useful to older hands who wanted to reconnect with their audience. Most of the work I got was DJing, but offers of PAs were trickling in. It was weird cleaning the office of an insurance company on a Friday morning only to find yourself flying to Ibiza later that evening to play a club. But that's what life was like back then. Schizophrenic.

When your passion is your job it makes up your entire identity. It's not so easy to move on from it, either. Music might not have been paying my mortgage or giving me confidence, but it was more than that. It was a part of me. Fortunes peaked and troughed, but music never disappeared altogether. It would tease you with a few bits and pieces before withdrawing for a while, leaving you confused and hungry. When the chance to perform came along it energised my entire body and mind, and for those precious moments I felt I could conquer the world, just like those people on the dance floor. I guess that is the whole point of what we do. But hours later I'd be worrying myself half to death over a credit card bill.

***

I went out to Ibiza again and did a gig at Deja Vu and told work I'd be back on the Friday, but the cab failed to materialise to take me back to the airport. The taxi driver said he'd knocked, but he hadn't. He eventually came and got me to the airport, but I missed the flight and was rescheduled for the next day. Then I spent another four hours waiting for a cab back into town. To cheer myself up I went to Space and had another night there. But because I hadn't shown up for the cleaning job, they were quite arsey. So I resigned. The bank had lost their quite considerable patience too and were closing in on me. I was only getting £180 a month from cleaning and so the bank stopped my overdraft, took away my cheque book and card and gave me a special withdrawal book. I had to discuss finances with a member of staff before they signed anything. It was a real slap on the wrist.

As much as I wanted to keep music alive, I kept climbing the ladder only for another rung to snap. 'At some point I'm going to have to sack this off.' But then I'd get a call for another gig and my eyebrow would arch. Feast or famine when I really needed a regular income.

I ended up getting offered a job at a clothes shop in Stafford called Mode, owned by a good mate of mine called Matt Zalepa. Mode was very fashionable at the time with lots of flight jackets and caps. This job at Mode came at a good time because I finally felt I'd left the middle-aged lump I'd become with Karen behind and now, with tattoos and a slimmed-down frame, I didn't feel completely over the hill. I'd had my fair share of disappointments with work over the years and was actually turned down by Kwik Save and McDonalds, which did nothing to boost my self-esteem. I mean, I got rejected by McDonalds and if there was one person who *knew* burgers it was me! However, when someone gave me a chance I always did my best and that's exactly what I did at Mode.

So I was working in the clothes shop during the week and DJing at weekends and this calmed my nerves a bit. My brother wanted to sell the house in Doxy and he kindly offered me first dibs on buying it. So I mortgaged myself right up to the hilt, thanks to the job at Mode, which had suddenly brought credit back into view. I had lost quite a lot of weight and sometimes got paid in clothes, which was good, so my fashion game was through the roof.

I was so hurt by previous relationships I started getting quite fussy with dates, but I still really wanted a girlfriend. When you're young you know what you like, but you haven't learned yet what you *don't* like, because it hasn't happened. But by now I knew very clearly what I didn't like. If that makes sense. I was on my own quite a lot after working at the shop and although I was lonely, it was much better than being trapped in a negative relationship. I would go home, turn the computer on to MSN or I'd go on eBay. I had a thing about port at the time; I only ever bought the cheap stuff. My dad loved port and I started to get a bit squiffy on the stuff, which in turn would lead to trouble online. I had got quite into eBay and was always looking for toys and stuff for Harry, but shopping online and getting tanked on port didn't mix too well.

Say there was a Disney/Pixar movie out and people were selling those free Happy Meal toys from McDonalds; well I'd be on there, baiting them. 'That's a free toy! Why are you selling a free toy, you tight arse?' I'm not proud of this, but I'd look at an auction and if they'd misnamed a character from the film, I'd send them a shitty message. This was after a few glasses of port. 'Don't you know anything? That's not the crab's name! You're so stupid.' Then I would go to bed and forget about it. The next morning I'd load up my emails. Bong! Bong! Bong! *What gives you the right to say this?* And I'd look at my 'sent post' and think, 'Oh shit!'

I hadn't turned to drink exactly, but it deadened things for a bit and I stopped worrying so much when I was a few glasses in. I was briefly seeing this girl Libby and one night my brother Paul and I had drained three bottles of wine when the phone rang. Now the answerphone kicked in after 31 rings or whatever, but it kept ringing and so I picked it up at the point it started recording, as I was getting fed up with it. When I got up the next morning I saw the red message light flashing. 'Ooh I've got a message!' I pressed 'play' and it was Libby ringing me from the previous night, and there I was, on tape. I was just so slaughtered. Libby, 'Hello Mark...'

- 'Aaarggh basart, aarrgghh.'
- 'Are you OK?'
- 'Aaaarrgghhh, blaadddy blaaahh, aarggh!' Not a legible word at all.

I couldn't remember a thing about it either. As you can tell I'm not great with drink.

Unbeknown to me, Butler had started accepting and taking solo bookings as Altern 8. Butler was never a member of the band and I found out what he was up to when he played an old-skool gig in Liverpool. I explained to him that this was something I had built up and that he couldn't just accept money as Altern 8. Mark was also taking smaller fees, which was damaging my ability to command higher prices. He saw my point of view and could see how damaging it was to the band name and agreed to pack it in. This was the last thing I needed with Chris sniffing around.

I was on my own for the first time and it really gave me time to think about things. I was still sensitive from the depression thing and needed to reach out to people, but was scared. I joined a web forum based on the old-skool community, which featured file-sharing and the chance to chat to people. I wondered if this could work for me in the way that CB had when I was lonely. I was nervous as hell, but took the plunge anyway. It's quite stressful when you join an established community as a newbie; everyone already knew each other and I was often ignored. Some of the people on there were pretty abrasive, to be honest. Then, one regular user started on me over nothing and I just turned the computer off. I didn't even log off. Just turned off the power and walked away, utterly devastated. 'Never again!'

A friend of mine told me not to be so sensitive and to get back online. I wasn't convinced, but eventually I agreed to chat to a few people on this '88-'94 old-skool forum. I signed in as Mr Nex – the name Jon MacDonald gave me – and took a bolder approach and started chatting to loads of people. I think a few of the guys suspected I might be a musician and started PM-ing me, asking me questions about myself. Eventually they sussed and I told them I'd been in a band. Things got much easier after that, although I'd get the odd loon telling me how much better Prodigy were. Maybe it was payback for the eBay abuse?

I got to know loads of people online that were based up in Liverpool and, after a while, we all agreed to hook up at a gig I was doing there. We were to swap some records at the venue too. They were a lovely lot and we had a real laugh at their flat, but I soon realised after I'd arrived that I'd forgotten my records. In the end I had to go through their vinyl in order to do the show, which was a pain anyway, as mixing old skool is notoriously hard. I had a bit of a sweat on, trying to establish a set list that would flow properly, but got there in the end.

I was seeing/not seeing this girl in Liverpool for a while, but that got quite nasty too. I really had the carpet pulled from under me on that one and we haven't spoken since. But although I'm saying all this, I was getting stronger. I still don't know what was going on there, but it seemed that the guy with the mask was a lot more interesting to this woman than the one without.

Around the time I split with Kath, I had 'Mr Nex' tattooed on my back in an act of teenage rebellion. Now, a year and a half later, the Liverpool crew knew me as 'Nexy' and that tattoo seemed to symbolise a new era as I put the past firmly behind me.

I started hanging out in Liverpool most weekends. I was just DJing really and was doing precious little production. DJing costs a lot more than you'd think and you need wheels. When my car started playing up, I had to really scrutinise the fees set against all the expenses. DJing can cost you money sometimes.

I put together some more Trackman work for Neil Macey and bagged some mixing work too. I also did a remix of an old-skool tune for Danny Donnelly (*Sons Of Da Loop Da Loop (Altern 8 Revival Mix)*, but my output was minimal. Danny Taurus and I mixed Gwen Stefani's *What You Waiting For* and the Martin Solveig house tune *Rocking Music* in an acapella style, but within an hour of being up on Juno we received a 'cease and desist' letter from AM:PM although we'd sold every copy. Oops.

Danny Taurus (Slo Moshun) *"I was working in a studio in Crewe with the Dario G guys and we asked Mark to do a remix. After that we decided to do some more stuff together in the spare room studio at his parents' house in 2005 under the name Waxton's. Waxton's was a colloquial insult. If something was Poobar Waxton's, it wasn't very good. It also had zero results on the internet, so we could get the domain name. Ha ha.*

Mark and I worked really well together. It was a very fluid relationship. One goes forward and does their bit then the other; no falling out or disagreements. I worked better with Mark than anyone else. I can be quite dominant, but then so is Mark and he has such a heritage. I can defer a lot to him."

I would meet up with the guys from the forum a lot and it really helped me emerge from my depression, but my confidence, workwise, had taken a battering. Sometimes you just can't get that feeling back and things don't seem to flow as they should, even when you get the work. I knew it could lift at any moment and so I just had to keep plugging away.

I had done some techno tracks in the style of Nexus 21 back in 1995 and they had stayed on DAT when Network stopped. In the madness that ensued after Network ceased making music, these tracks were largely forgotten. I started playing these tunes to people on the forum and they loved them. 'You need to get these out!'

I sent a tune to one of the Black Dog guys in Sheffield who was running a label called Dust Science. He really liked it and eventually pressed a limited-edition run on a sub-label called DS3. They put out the EP *Songs For Einna*, which came out under my own name (the first ever release to do that) as handmade, individually numbered vinyl copies (no digital) of what was the label's first release. This EP eventually came out the following year (2007). It was the guys in Liverpool who made that happen. I bought a copy of my own record and sent it to Transmat in Detroit. I got an email back from James Stevenson at Transmat who looked after us in Detroit in 1993 and he said he played it in the car whilst taking Derrick May to the airport one day. He put the record on and said nothing about it. 'What was that music?' asked Derrick. 'That reminds me of Detroit techno. How it used to be.' The bloke who influenced me to make techno; the man who came up with that *Wiggin* bassline said that!? Wow! Now that was mind-blowing. I bumped into May in Liverpool in 2006 and was astonished when he suggested I write a book. Who the hell would read that?

A Bang In The Face, I Love Acid And LA LA Land

Like two pharaohs, The Men In Masks floated across the sea of heads on an enormous bed. Thousands of people screamed as the music shot down from the heavens through a man in the sky. The masked men looked all around, surveying the scene, jaws dropped. 'It's the moment they've all been waiting for!' The bed travelled upon the arms of the worshippers to every corner of their vast kingdom, as The Men In Masks nodded their heads and pointed people out. 'It's the moment they've all been waiting for!' The Men In Masks finally took to the stage. Arms behind their backs, heads bowed, they waited for the signal. When it came, delirium filled the air. 'It's the moment they've all been waiting for!'

One day, out of the blue, I got contacted by an agency that had got Butler and I a few gigs. It was a booking for a night called Bangface, which was meant to be a mental experience and so I was very curious. I have to say that I wasn't in the greatest frame of mind at this point. I had lost loads of weight again and was still a little depressed, but maybe a bang in the chops was what I needed.

The thing you sometimes forget with music, is how what you did two decades or more ago communicates to the young of today. As a lot of the original ravers started buying Dido and Coldplay, so there was an entire generation emerging that were totally up for getting sorted. Bangface was not just nostalgia, it was new to those who were mere twinkles of an eye in 1988 (if that!).

The Bangface gig was totally different to anything else we'd ever done. The music that had been hardcore had moved on to gabba and splintered into breakcore and our old-skool stuff was pretty laid back compared to this. The crowd was really mental, with people jumping about like monkeys and it was completely different to many of the old-skool gigs. Bangface had a monumental effect on me. The night was called Revenge of the Synth – based on the *Star Wars* prequel – and behind the decks were two life-sized cardboard cut-out Stormtroopers. Being *Star Wars* fans, we swiped those Stormtroopers on the way out. Bangface made me feel young again and I loved the vibe. It was so therapeutic and Bangface loved the old skool. It was such an open-minded approach to music, with breakcore, wonky techno and gabba. We thought we might not be an exact fit for them, but we couldn't be more wrong as the agency – Mickey Finn's Urban Takeover – booked us for the following year. 'Bangface want you to play Glade Festival.'

Glade was the first festival I had ever attended. I never considered myself a Glasto type – not my kind of thing, but this really changed my mind. I went to Glade, at the Wasing Estate in Berkshire, with a bunch of the old-skool forum crew and did an Altern 8 set with the suit and mask. Butler and I also MCed and DJed. I would play three records and Mark would play three. The audience was incredible and quite tired by the time we came on and totally in the mood for some old skool. It absolutely went *off*. I have goosebumps recalling it. There were lads down the front in suits and masks climbing up the barriers.

I ended on *Strings of Life* and the place went bananas. Absolutely crackers! It was the first time we noticed the Bangface inflatables. Every hour or so they would release another load of blow-ups: skeletons, saxophones and bananas. Bangface was great fun and the closest to back-in-the-day rave I have ever seen. The whole tent was rammed and going bonkers. There was crowd-surfing and moshing. The crowd was full of promoters from smaller clubs there and so we received an influx of gigs after that. We even got a call from Japan to do Sonar Sound in Tokyo. We played Japan in 2006, which was sorted by Urban Takeover. We were looked after by a guy called Nik Sliwerski who did all the translation as he showed us the sights of Tokyo. What an amazing experience.

Then we were off to Brazil again and, because we hadn't topped up our inoculations, we had to go through all that pain. I was probably working at Argos when the top-up jabs could have been done and I must have thought I'd never see Brazil again. But music seemed to be coming back into view now. It had taken a while but, just as you can feel when things are turning bad, I think you can also tell when things are getting better.

We got a lot of grief if we didn't wear the suits, even if they hadn't asked for them. We got caught out without our suits in Japan and they insisted we sort it. So we found some white boiler suits in a Tokyo hardware store and sprayed the Japanese flag on the back. We got some masks from the same shop and sprayed them black. I was drying them under a hand dryer in the toilets when a member of the Yellow Magic Orchestra came in. Woah!

It was like Beatlemania in Japan. I played *Strings of Life* at the beginning and we stood at the front of the stage with arms folded. When a certain bit of the song kicked in, we turned round and the crowd saw the flags and went mental. There were girls at the front screaming and shaking their heads.

We had to cobble some suits together for this gig in Brazil too and eventually found two green football tracksuits with hoods and 'Brazil' across the front. The promoters had decided to recreate the *E-vapor-8* video where we woke up in bed. It sounded weird, but we went along with it. The venue was a massive warehouse with big girders holding the ceiling up. There was one rig of lights pointing up and a massive amount of scaffolding. The DJ booth was really high.

The promoter had created a giant inflatable bed for us with two poles either side. We stretched out on the bed and, like two pharaohs, were carried out into the enormous crowd. Everyone had their phones out and the DJ was scratching two copies of *E-vapor-8*. '*This is the moment they've all been waiting for... this is the moment they've all been waiting for...*' We were taken from one side of this warehouse to the other on this bouncy bed and the crowd went nuts and sang every word to every song, louder than the sound system. There must have been more than 5,000 people there that night in Sao Paulo. I've been back to Brazil another four times since. They're not great payers, but the experience is always fantastic.

The next few years followed the same wayward trajectory. Massive highs and humongous lows.

Butler and I were offered a mini-tour of Australia in 2009 playing a host of dates on a 10-day run. It was a great experience and we did London to Bangkok, Sydney to Perth, Melbourne to Sydney and then Brisbane before finishing back in Sydney. We did 40,000 miles in 10 days, which represented a lot of travelling. They were wicked gigs and I loved Australia although it was somewhere I'd never really wanted to go;

I was positive I'd get bitten by a black widow spider. This cockatoo flew past our window one morning and landed on a roof and I couldn't believe it. 'That's a real cockatoo!' That was such a rewarding and tiring trip.

***

I treated myself to an Audi TT: the dream car I'd always wanted, to cheer myself up after I wrote off my Passat on the way back from Liverpool (after a Hazy Daze booking). When I pulled into my road in Doxey, the girl driving in front of me, simply stopped. I went to go round her as she hadn't indicated, but she hadn't seen me and just went straight into my side and wrote my car off. I wasn't hurt but, because I was going round her, it was my fault. If anyone had seen it, they'd have thought that I was in the right, but on paper, I was stiffed. The insurance company wouldn't play ball either.

This Audi was my last-ditch attempt to try and get a girlfriend. I was in my forties and five years single and I wanted this car to help me snag someone. It was ridiculous really. Ha ha. But I was willing to try anything. This car got me into a lot of debt, though. I was wrapped up in a mortgage with a few loans on top and I'd increased my borrowing to get Christmas presents for the kids. I had to make sure the children had a good Christmas.

Through spending a lot of time on my own I had finally got to know who I was and why I behaved the way I did. I realised just how sensitive I was and how I had this massive desire to be with someone. I hated being single, but slowly got used to it. I had my own routine now and felt as if I was becoming a better prospect for someone as a result.

Being on my own reignited my interest in birdwatching, something Dad got me interested in as a kid. Dad got me some binoculars when I first showed an interest. I'd always studied ornithology books and watched birds wherever I went. If there were birds nearby I'd stop and watch. There were marshes near the house in Doxey and I'd go and observe all the geese there. They used to fly over the house at night, honking away and it always brought a smile to my face. When I look back to that time on my own, I always think of those geese.

***

It was hard managing my finances; not only was work erratic, but sometimes you didn't always get the money you were promised. Often a promoter would get you booked and yet act as if they were doing you a massive favour. Then, if the venue wasn't full, they would dock your money. It was so hard planning your life when nothing was guaranteed. I have been stiffed many times. Some people claim that they haven't got the money on the night – when a thousand people or more are paying in cash – and so promise to pay you the following day online. Then you get home to find that they've unfriended you on Facebook and won't answer the phone. You might have had a bill that needed paying and yet these people refused to honour their word.

Not only are things tight for many DJs and musicians – unless you're David Guetta – but everyone thinks you're rolling in it. I was cleaning carpets and working in a clothes shop – and still racking up debt – despite playing out in front of thousands of people at the weekend. But if it wasn't for Bangface and I Love Acid, I might not be here today.

I contacted I Love Acid on Facebook back in 2007/8, just because of its name really. Josh Doherty from I Love Acid replied almost immediately saying that they would love to have me DJ one night. I'm not good at blowing my own trumpet – and it's very rare that I message people I don't know – but it worked. Josh was upfront regarding the money – they didn't pay a massive fee – but he said he'd love to see me at one of their nights. I Love Acid was being held at a tiny club called Ginglik in Shepherds Bush – it was an underground Victorian toilet. It was a very small club, but a wicked crowd.

Josh Doherty (Posthuman, I Love Acid, Balkan Vinyl) *"I first met Mark in 1998 or 1999 while I was doing a SKAM Records night at the Music Box in Manchester and he was the headliner. It was my first gig as Posthuman and had just signed to SKAM, so it was all very new to us, yet Mark was an old hand who had seen it all. He did Altern 8 and Nexus 21 sets while we were in the other room playing electronica. Graham Massey was in the room dancing to our tunes all night, so we were pretty pleased with that. I then met Mark backstage with the Gescom guys. The underground scene still had a lot of love for Altern 8 and Mark was a seriously underrated producer.*

Our paths crossed again in 2007/8, when I was running a club night called I Love Acid (still running) and booked Mark after chatting on Facebook. I got him to do a DJ set on the acidy side of rave and he was very good. Mark was immediately friendly and easy to deal with and he ended up playing again and again. We soon became friends. Mark became a resident at I Love Acid during those days at the Ginglik."

I played Bangface a couple of times in 2009 and did the Bangface Weekender in Southport, but I was still getting grief off Chris: 'You can't use the Altern 8 name!' Often I would insist on Altern 8 being placed in brackets on posters, but many promoters just ignored me and printed the posters the way they wanted. Then Chris would ring up and start banging on again. Some people would drop me unless they could use the name large on the flyers. It was a difficult situation. The way I saw it was that I was in Altern 8 and simply carrying on the name. Network had given me permission to use the music and that was that. I was constantly having to try and adapt my live work to avoid Chris. I had played a load of Altern 8 tunes one night – without the costume – and just scratched over the top with a dancer and MC on stage. But people wanted the mask.

To play nights such as Bangface with music that was now 20 years old was a dream come true. Up there and in the zone, all the money worries just ebbed away. I knew then why I was doing what I was doing. I was connected to something higher and more uplifting.

As you have seen, life has had its fair share of ups and downs and when the economy collapsed in 2008, the first thing to die off was men's fashion. Mode closed not long after. It seemed as if blokes would make do with their old jeans when money was tight, whereas girls would shop at Primark. The shop suffered massively. I was stood in there some days and not a single person would enter the shop. Suddenly I was out of a job again.

Not knowing what to do next I started to make music again. No one had really heard anything from me since 2000 although the *DS93* vinyl was released in 2007 to some very positive reviews. Josh from I Love Acid asked me to do a track for a new label he was starting up called Balkan Vinyl. I had no equipment of course so I went through some old DATs, one of which had the Trackman work on there that Ideal Trax hadn't picked up. We had recorded four tracks; and Ideal picked up three so I had this extra tune. I was 41 at this point and so placed the number next to the 21 from Nexus and called the track *2141*, which was put out alongside Luke Vibert and B12. God, it felt good to be putting out music again, even if the world was constantly crumbling beneath my feet.

***

Altern 8 were booked to play LA again in December 2008 and it was not the most glamorous jaunt. We flew to Chicago and we were to connect to a flight onto LA when Parksy – who looked like he had stolen some gear from Justin Timberlake's wardrobe – was pulled over by security, who were obviously suspicious of his fancy trilby and bandana. We had no visas and really didn't want to be pulled and so I was getting jumpy when they started interrogating Parksy. 'What are you doing over here?'

- 'Dancing.'
- 'What are you getting?' Parksy told them what he was earning.
- 'Who are you with?' Parksy pointed to Butler.

They were pulled into interrogation rooms and Butler managed to diffuse things, but we ended up missing the connection. We then heard that the snow was so bad outside the airport that flights were being cancelled all over the place. We were at the airport for nine hours. We managed to get on to a plane, only to be told to get off again an hour later as the weather was so bad. We spent the night in a hotel, flew to LA the next day, arriving at midnight to do a gig at 1am. 'We're sending a cab for you now,' said the promoter. We were shattered.

We did the gig, got paid in cash and put the bag – with all the money inside – into a secure room at the hotel. When we went to leave I couldn't find the money anywhere. We'd been cleaned out. Parksy had also put a load of wine on my credit card for the room, which was annoying. Just as things couldn't get any more frustrating, Chris phoned me at the airport and threatened me. The whole fiasco had cost me time and money, then Monday morning it was back to looking for work. Chris seemed to have a habit of calling me when I was at a particularly low ebb. Sometimes things got so stupid you just had to laugh. I'd flown to LA, played a gig, lost the money and been shouted at as a result. Ha ha!

I was sitting in the airport on the way home from LA when I noticed a couple talking in the departure lounge. I'd been single for five years or more and just watching this couple made me feel so alone. I had vowed not to get myself in too deep again, and was now quite fussy; any little alarm bells and it was over. However, in that moment I really wished I had a girlfriend. It would have just finished everything off. Music seemed to be returning to me, albeit in fits and starts, and now I felt that the time was right. I just wanted to share these stories with someone.

CH. 31

Dance Island Romance, Frozen Prawns And Billy Bunter

A gig in Cambridge saved my life. July 2009, we were playing Dance Island and the constant bickering with Chris was really getting to me. I hate to say it, but I just couldn't be arsed with this gig. Work was sometimes difficult. For one, Parksy was cancelling at the last minute before shows. We had a gig in Manchester at Music Box and everyone had known about it for ages when Parksy pulled out again, leaving me no time to find a replacement. He said he was on holiday. Then we got to play Bestival and Crez couldn't do it, but he told me straight off. So I really wanted to make sure that Parksy could do it and yet come the week of the gig, he announced that he wasn't available. I decided to draw a line under it and booked some dancers to come in and take their places. Bestival was great fun, but one downside was that they didn't pay you on the day. I didn't know this and so I went to the production office to get the money for the dancers and was told that it wasn't happening, which was awkward. It was great fun though and we did the Afterburner stage, where I was high up in a booth while Butler had to MC on a ladder that led up to the DJ box.

Back to 2009. I was very lonely and in a foul mood at this particular Dance Island gig in Cambridge. 'You'll never find a girlfriend while you're looking,' friends would say, 'but if you really want one you mustn't *stop* looking...' What?!

I saw these two girls walking around backstage at Cambridge just as I was about to go on and wondered who they thought they were, as they seemed to be walking round like they owned the place. I went out, plugged in the filter pedal – I could trigger samples from a CD deck and mess about with them thanks to the filter – while Parksy, Crez and Butler did their thing. I was looking around the venue when I caught the gaze of this girl I'd seen walking round before. 'She's nice,' I thought. 'What can I say to her?' By the time the gig had ended she was gone. What I didn't realise was that she had been to see us at Gatecrasher in 2008 when we had the suits on. That night Mark wasn't MCing and local MC, NRG took the mic. I couldn't hear this MC – I'm totally unaware of what's going on when I'm playing – but according to fans, he was awful.

I got home from Cambridge and was looking at the Altern 8 fan page on Facebook when this girl from the Cambridge gig appeared, making comments. We had a brief chat and she said thanks for Saturday night and mentioned the Gatecrasher gig and MC NRG who rabbited all over the set. She had apparently thought that I was the sound man until she went through the pictures I'd posted. Ha ha. She then sent me a friend request.

I went on her Facebook wall a few hours later and was gutted when I saw a profile pic of her and another fella. So I hid her. I didn't want to know. But according to a friend of mine on Facebook it wasn't her boyfriend in the picture. This reignited my interest no end and that's how I met Nikki.

We started seeing each other and I was absolutely buzzing. We just clicked. She was 17 years younger than me, but I was no spring chicken any more. The relationship just gave me a real lift in so many ways.

***

Chris was still pissed off with me using the Altern 8 name and so when someone offered me a merchandise deal I contacted him to see if we could let bygones be bygones. 'All we have to do is yay or nay designs and they do the rest. We get a cut for doing nothing.' Chris seemed pretty amicable, although maybe we were running before we could walk. He asked for an email with the proposal, which I sent him and I felt optimistic. It felt good to talk.

Chris was good to his word and got straight back to me; via a solicitor's letter telling me to stop using the Altern 8 name. Great. It was all happening again. Everyone was like 'Don't worry, he's not got a leg to stand on,' but I felt so depressed. I just couldn't make any headway with it. I had obviously lost the income from the clothes shop as well and so this latest spat with Chris really got me down. It came at the exact wrong time. What did I have to do to earn a living and pay the bills?

I got a few bookings here and there and a mate from Portsmouth called Ben booked me a few times for his nights down south – and that won't be forgotten – but I was getting desperate. I had a £600-a-month mortgage and had overstretched myself getting it. I could only just manage the mortgage at first and when it went interest-only, it was upped to £670 a month and it was killing me. The gigs weren't enough to keep the house on, never mind all the other bills on top of that. I just wanted somewhere to take the kids and ideally I wanted to keep it on and leave it to them when I popped my clogs; that was the big plan. But I was finding the fight to stay afloat so tiring. Every day was a battle.

So it got to point where I had to give up the house and move in with Nikki. I contacted the bank, having gone into arrears on a few occasions, and agreed to drop the keys off. That was that. Liam and Nikki helped me move out and filled the van. I left loads of stuff there because I couldn't have the van for any longer. Gone. I'd bought four houses since leaving home and all of a sudden I was back to square one.

Although Chris wasn't happy with me using the name I carried on using what I considered to be 50% mine. Network were fine with me using Altern 8 as they came up with it. That mistake in the naming of that first EP had made things very easy simple, as neither Chris nor I had come up with the name. Network had named us Altern 8 and they had no problem with me playing the tunes. No one was going to hear this music any more if it was buried. Slipmatt, Ratpack and Shades Of Rhythm were still keeping the scene alive, and I felt that it was my right to use my heritage as I saw fit.

Since the recession I had to stop working with Mark on the smaller gigs and went alone as the fees plummeted. I had tried to repackage Mark and myself as 'MarkII', but there was no real interest.

I first bumped into Billy 'Daniel' Bunter at a Raindance do at SE1 in 2004. Billy 'Daniel' Bunter was a ball of infectious energy and he showed a real interest in what I was doing. He had been playing Nexus

21 when he was resident DJ at east London's legendary Labrynth in 1989. I told him I had these unreleased jungle tracks from '94/'95 and Dan loved them and was always playing them on Kool FM. 'Why haven't you done anything with these?' he asked. I told him they were done through Network and I had no way of releasing them. Dan seemed very interested.

I didn't know just how far back Dan went. Dan had more passion for acid house and the warehouse scene than anyone I knew and was obsessed with restoring the heritage of rave. Dan got me on to his Kool London show as a guest and blew my trumpet in ways I have never been able to. I was so embarrassed. 'But I'm just Mark from Stafford.' I played him some unreleased stuff, which later came out on his Music Mondays label.

Dan loved what I'd been doing and wanted me and Jerome Hill to do an acid CD called *One Night In '88*. It was a great concept and they had some wicked tunes on there, plus they wanted some brand new remixes. It was a brilliantly received CD.

Billy "Daniel" Bunter (DJ, musician, label boss, publisher) *"Nexus 21 sums up my love for early British house and Detroit techno because my first ever sets in the heart of east London were filled with their music. When I first saw their name in 1989 on the Blue Chip label, I was instantly fascinated. (Still) Life Keeps Movin' was typically Detroit, but you could tell it was from Britain. My earliest memories of bunking school and going to record shops are of Nexus 21. A year later, in my first sets at Labrynth/2000AD, I featured lots of Nexus 21 and they hold such a special place in my heart. There was also a sense of mystery about this pioneering British act. They were sublime. Nexus 21 really worked well in London, as they had a London-centric sound. Infiltrate 202, which still had the smooth edges of techno and what progressed into hardcore, worked in London too, but Altern 8 were soon frowned upon by the London DJs and it didn't quite work as well. Then they were massive and the whole Vicks face mask thing was going on and that wasn't really a London vibe either.*

At the time I had no idea that the same people were doing these tunes. That's what fascinated me about Mark's history. I found out about it all so far down the line.

Mark was Midlands and I was London and we never really connected. I met Mark at Raindance and even then the connection never really happened. Then when I met Mark and spoke to him properly, I found out what he'd been up to. I was fascinated. I booked Mark for my Kool London show and he brought all this unreleased Nexus 21, DJ Nex and Altern 8 stuff. I interviewed him and it was such a great story. I then decided to put out the DJ Nex tracks, which were drum and bass-esque. Mark stands tall in acid house and Detroit, bleeps and bass, rave, hardcore and house, but never drum and bass. Yet he had these proto-drum and bass gems and I loved them. These tunes were 20 years old and totally smashed it.

I love all the new acid house house coming through right now and had an idea for an album called One Night In 88 after hearing all the acid house Mark was making and so I got him and his mate Jerome Hill hooked up on this album. It was amazing.

In short, Mark is UK dance music's biggest secret. His story is so fresh. I didn't know he was doing stuff back in '87, adding breakbeats and acid before Nexus 21. Mark Archer's place in the history of British dance music is as potent as A Guy Called Gerald, but his name was never as well known. I made it my mission to get Mark Archer out there. I want the world to know that Mark Archer is as important as A Guy Called Gerald and Prodigy and that was the buzz behind putting out this book."

Nikki really stood by me when I needed it most – just as Dad had – and urged me to carry on with the music. I was never work-shy and would do anything I could to survive. I'm not a proud man in that respect. I was brought up to keep my feet on the ground, even if my mind was elsewhere.

To supplement my DJing I took a job packing frozen food at a local factory. I'd be up at 5am emptying bags of frozen prawns into boxes to try and put some money into the pot. I also did some building work for Wayne Bayle from Redditch after meeting him at a gig. He could see I was struggling when the agency wasn't getting me any gigs and he offered me some building work; I'm no builder, but I did my best. That really helped me out too.

Nikki supported me through all this and I can never pay her back sufficiently. Nikki gave me the chance to keep the dream of making and playing music alive when many partners might have grown tired of this obsession that often makes no financial sense whatsoever. Nikki hadn't even benefited from the good old days at Network with the holidays, cars and house. When you hear the music of your favourite bands or go to see them live, spare a thought for people like Nikki, because without them, there would often be nothing to see or hear. So for a few years, it was pack some prawns, play some tunes before back to packing fish. It's funny to think that The KLF burned a million pounds back in 1994 and yet here I was slinging bags of frozen cod on to forklifts. But we survived and it's fair to say that night in Cambridge, back in 2009, saved my life.

Butler, Jeff Mills and Me, Japan Sonar Sound, 2006

Sonar Sound, Tokyo

White suits at Sonar Sound, 2006

Me, DJ Andy and Butler in Brazil, 2006

Solo photo shoot around 2006

Secret gig for Tiga album launch, 2006

Life festival (DJing in a barn), Ireland, 2007

Me and Frank Fieber in Bath 2009 -
doing the 'secret' hand signal

One of my career savers, James Bangface
and me in 2007

Impromptu fill-in set at Bangface Weekender,
2010

The Mark Archer Logo courtesy of Robert
'Bobzilla' Page

Eamon (Liquid) and me at Bangface
Weekender, 2012, doing a Liquid-8 live DJ set

Me and Tommie Sunshine at EDC, Las Vegas, 2013

Nikki crowd surfing in a dinghy (Bangface tent at
Glastonbury, 2013)

Altern 8 graffiti up in Gateshead by the Ghetto
Method Collective

A very excited Nikki in Times Square, New York, 2013

Me and musical hero Tyree Cooper, Amsterdam, 2014

The Arcadia stage, Glastonbury 2015. 40,000 people! Damn!

The wife (Glastonbury, 2015)

Being interviewed alongside Bunter for his book 'The Love Dove Generation'

An almost life-long dream came true, Christmas, 2015. It's me!

My amazing kids: Harry, Liam and Emma

Finally marrying my soul mate, Southport, 2016

The onstage wedding, Bangface Weekender, 2016

CH. 32

"Altern 8 Saved My Life!"

Tommie Sunshine
(DJ, producer, musician)

"Growing up in Chicago is crucial to all of this. I lived in the south-west suburbs, 40 minutes from Chicago, in a very white, upper-middle-class neighbourhood. I was 'sleeping out' for concert tickets for INXS or something and, because it gets very cold in Illinois, my parents would leave me a car to sleep in, parked outside the record store. I was flipping channels on the radio when I discovered WBMX, which would break up broadcasts into hour-long segments. You would have classic house with Salso and West End, followed by an hour of imports featuring Alexander Robotnick, Telex, Kraftwerk and Italo disco; all the European stuff. It all sounded good to me, but there was nothing better than when they said they were launching into an hour of acid house. It was the first time I'd heard the 303 other than on Shannon's Let The Music Play, but didn't know it made that sound until I heard Chicago acid. That was life-changing for me in 1986-'87. I spent the next five years trying to piece together what that music was to become.

Chicago had some house parties and you could see Ron Hardy at the Muzic Box, or go to Medusa's where Armando and Lil' Louis would play and in Chicago you had the very beginnings of the scene, but it was small. It was odd in that the only way we were informed as to what was going on in Chicago was through reading the British press. I would drive into the city and go to Reckless Records and buy The Face and I.D., NME and Melody Maker. These magazines were our lifeline as to what was going on in Chicago and England. The only way you could find out what was going on in Chicago was by looking in those magazines. No one in Chicago was writing articles about Fast Eddie, Adonis and Mike Dunn. House music had taken England by storm and in turn had shone a light on Illinois.

I graduated high school in '89 and house music was falling apart at the seams, drifting into hip house, which got weird. The bigger guys were signing major deals: Larry Heard signed with MCA, Lil' Louis signed with Columbia, but although major labels, the tunes were hardly house. That was the beginning of that transition period and for an Anglophile like myself there was nowhere more interesting than the UK and the Manchester scene. The connective tissue between acid house and the rave scene for me was Happy Mondays, The Stone Roses, The Charlatans, The Orb and The KLF. If a record got a good review in NME, we would go to Reckless and get it. All of my early experiments with drugs were sound-tracked by KLF's Chill Out and The Orb's Adventures Beyond The Ultraworld. Right around that time was the beginning of the American rave scene, which hit the coasts before Chicago. Los Angeles was the first really and I'm not sure why, other than the fact there were lots of expats there. LA and San Francisco were the entry points of rave here. Then Frankie Bones went and played Energy in the UK (1989), came back to LA and was like 'Gosh, this is what it's like in Britain.' This led to Frankie's Storm Raves in New York.

1991 was when the first rave parties started to creep into the Midwest. It wasn't until '92 that it picked up steam. The first time that there was a real rave in Chicago, and not in a nightclub, it was so illegal, underground. These guys had broken into a junior high school on the West Side of Chicago and set up a sound system in the basement. If the cops had showed up, we were all going to jail, what with all the drugs going around. It was spring '92 and someone had brought in a DJ called The Music Maker who played the most irrational, darkest, scariest music of my life. I was on acid for the first time. He played O Fortuna (Apotheosis) and I thought the world was ending. They turned all the lights off, so only lights from the 1200s and mixers were on, although the DJ was wearing a coal miner's hat. We then started a train or conga and the entire party was doing it. O Fortuna came on and I'm sure he played it twice because it went on for fucking ages. I thought we were being swallowed up into the depths of hell. From now on I had to go to where these parties were. I didn't care how far away they were; I was a raver for life. Look at a map of the States. Look at the radius of our 'dance bubble'. From Chicago our journeys stretched to Madison and Milwaukee, Wisconsin. Ann Arbor and Detroit, Michigan. Columbus, Cincinnati and Cleveland, Ohio. Indianapolis, Indiana. Lexington, Kentucky and St Louis, Missouri. Kansas City, Kansas, Iowa City, Iowa and Minneapolis, Minnesota. Wherever the best party was. I spent hours on the telephone to people from these cities. 'Who have you got? Who's playing this weekend?' 'Kioke playing Cleveland, Richie Hawtin is doing Detroit, but Frankie Bones is playing St Louis. Fuck it – let's go and see Frankie Bones.' Eight hours away in St Louis and we would take drugs all night long and then I would get behind the wheel of my car and drive past all these cornfields, peaking on acid, the most irresponsible person on earth. I never got pulled, never had an accident, which isn't bad considering that for 60% of the time, I was driving back on acid or ecstasy.

I was buying a lot of music from Gramophone, which was the DJ record store in Chicago. This would have been around the time of Eon, T99, Altern 8 and Jam & Spoon and the early blueprints of what was coming together as 'rave' music. We were not part of a big thing here. I was one of 10 people in the USA who knew who Altern 8 were.

I really loved the mythology of Altern 8. Every part of it worked for me. The masks, the suits, that shitty B-side recorded from the car park of Shelley's, all fed into this crazy narrative in my head of this music, which was clearly a pastiche of Chicago and Detroit that had been put together in a way that hadn't been done before. I would drive into Chicago to go to all the raves and made a tape called the 'Going To The Party Tape' and 40-50% of that was Altern 8. Activ 8, Armageddon and Frequency were my soundtrack to going out to the shows. This all came together at this beautiful party on Jan 2nd 1993 when Kevin Saunderson brought them to play Detroit. That was the craziest thing.

Detroit isn't necessarily close to Chicago; it's about a four-and-a-half-hour drive. In the Midwest snow, those drives can get pretty hairy. I was driving with my friends in the car and sometimes when our ears needed a break from the Altern 8, we listened to Reflections by The Supremes. We were creeping along the highway when my car started to spin 360 degrees in two feet of snow. No plough had been down that stretch. We were only doing 30mph anyway and so it was going to take us six hours to get there, but no one was going to get between me and seeing Altern 8 in Detroit. I was not deterred by what was in front of me, but then the car started spinning in circles. It went around *once, it went around again and then, when it finally stopped, I was facing the opposite direction to where I needed to be, in the middle of the highway. Suddenly there was this truck coming towards us and the lights were getting bigger and bigger and it was driving right at us and we had two feet of snow packed under our car. This truck swerved out of the way with about a second to spare. When we looked out of the side window it missed my mirror by about an inch. It was mental. The truck passed, we got the car started and a friend suggested we stay at a hotel. 'No way!'*

We drove through the snow, got to Detroit, parked the car and got into the party. Two minutes after our arrival, we heard: 'Ladies and gentlemen, Altern 8!' We went ballistic. To us, it was like seeing The Beatles, we were the most excited people in that room. We went berserk. We knew all about the songs, samples and mythology. It was incredible to be at one of their shows and such a highlight for me. Of all the people making music at that time, they were the only ones with whom I felt a real affinity. I don't have any stories like this about Eon or Baby Ford. I loved those records, but I don't have stories like this connected to these other people.

Time has passed and music has evolved into many other genres, but I always found myself going back to that album. Full On: Mask Hysteria was the benchmark.

Altern 8 saved my life. That's what it really boils down to. When I was that kid in the Midwest living in brutal suburbia, Altern 8's music represented endless possibilities. There was so much depth in the chaos of those records that after hearing them, anything seemed possible. It was so inspiring to me; after all, who has the balls to sample Derrick May? That was remarkable, so crazy to sample Derrick May. I genuinely appreciated how punk they were. The idea of just fucking off and never letting anyone see your face. Sampling Kraftwerk with reckless abandon. There was a lot to be inspired by.

Suburbia, to anyone with an ounce of intelligence or a shred of artistic yearning, is the death of life. I couldn't wait to get the fuck out of there. I didn't belong where I grew up, and that music represented a way out...

It was only the mid-nineties when I decided to have a UK hardcore revival in my head. I had moved from Chicago to Atlanta where I ran Satellite Records. I was first DJing there, playing acid house and older rave records that were so un-chic at the time. 'Too soon!?' The scene hadn't even ended and yet here I was trying to bring it back.

Many people bitched and moaned about EDM, but why take it away from these kids? These kids are having a moment of discovery. This is the very first time for them. This is their point of discovery. Think about what you were listening to when you first discovered electronic music and I bet it wasn't sophisticated. I'm not sure I can really rationalise Sesame's Treet to anyone or A Trip To Trumpton. It makes no sense, but you don't have to have a sophisticated palate when you come into this and nor should you. Whether it's David Guetta or Skrillex, that's OK. I wear all of that proudly, like a badge. EDM breathed life back into the dance scene and the music that means so much to me.

Everything I have ever done as been informed by acid house and early UK rave music and the attitude permeated everything I have ever made. So yeah, Altern 8 pretty much saved my life."

CH. 33

The Church Of Altern 8, A New York ST-8 Of Mind And A Bloody Big Spider

It took a while, but Americans finally *got* the electronic dance music they'd created all those years ago. Many in Europe and indeed the States, looked down on EDM as some kind of soulless, commercial, backwards step, but for many of us, this enormous movement provided opportunities when the landscape had been looking quite bleak. Suddenly musicians like Tommie Sunshine were trying to book the original ravers to appear at these massive events in the US. For many youngsters it was the first time they'd been to a rave and old-skool dance sounded just as good in 2010 as it did in '88. I was more than happy to pop over the Heron Pond to keep the spirit alive.

Scotto *"I put together the NASA 20th party in 2012 and Mark came back for that. Mark joined N-Joi, Joey Beltram (all NASA originals) and 808 State. I spent £10,000 on flights and it lit a fire under Mark and prompted him to get Altern 8 back. To make a go of it again. He played a blinding set."*

EDM energised the UK scene even if some wouldn't admit it. We needed a bit of help, to be honest, as we all took such a hit when people started file-sharing and giving away music for free. EDM paid massive amounts of respect to its forefathers and many original ravers started returning to the scene, along with a new, young crowd, hungry for dance music. You could feel the energy coming over from the States.

In 2013, I was made aware of a campaign by a guy in Brighton to get Altern 8 back into the charts as the Christmas number one, to rival *X-Factor*, much like Rage Against The Machine had. Nikki showed me this Facebook page one morning and there were 600 people in the group at the time.

It was really flattering that someone liked our stuff so much that they had started a campaign. I was proper gobsmacked, actually. It was such a really nice thing to do. But there was no real planning behind it at all. I offered my help and spoke to Josh at Balkan Vinyl, suggesting he get on board. Neil Rushton at Network was interested, too. The rules had changed with charting: you needed a legitimate amount of sales on iTunes and Altern 8 wasn't on there at the time. So we put that right first.

The track we chose was *Activ 8* and we had the *Vicks Vapour Mix* and *Hardcore Holocaust* from '91 and got those remastered. We also got talking to iTunes. Neil said we could do with more remixes and so from late October, we worked like hell to get all this work done prior to Christmas.

I called in a huge heap of favours. Mark Breeze sorted out a mix (RocketPimp did a dubstep version), DJ Phantasy did a drum and bass version and Shadow Dancer gave it an acid house treatment. I put together a Xen Mantra house version, Lucius Project did a deep house mix and Tommie Sunshine moved it into EDM. The campaign had a YouTube channel and was on SoundCloud and Neil Rushton got fully behind it all.

Yet again, radio wasn't supporting it, just as they failed to pick up on us the first time around, Mark Goodier aside. Radio 1 did a 'Race for Christmas Number One' slot with all the contenders and mentioned AC/DC and Orbital, but when it came to us, this girl audibly sneered about this 'bunch of old ravers'. Yet one show on Radio 1 made it Single of the Week and suddenly our 600 fans on Facebook had swelled to 27,000! It was genuinely flattering.

This 22-year-old tune received no help from radio and yet we still got to number 33, which was higher than some of the tips Radio 1 *had* supported. So it was by no means a disappointment. Loz Russell was the man behind the campaign and I can't thank him enough.

We got a load of crap from some foreigners, though. I'm not sure where they were from, but they seemed to think we were evangelists as they could see the word Christ in Christmas on the web page. 'You're promoting anti-homosexuality.' They even posted a picture of me and Josh with devil horns and flames behind us, chains around our necks, saying we were homophobes. We reported it to Facebook, who couldn't see anything wrong with it. We said to these people, 'It's a Christmas number one, we're not homophobes.'

- 'No, no, no! You don't tell me what I am telling you...' they replied.

Josh Doherty *"In 2010, I started Balkan Vinyl and I really wanted to release some work with Mark and so he would often come down to London to work with me. Mark is an ideas person rather than a technical producer, which is my forte, and so it worked really well.*

Mark and I went over some of the Altern 8 tracks he wrote on his own, like Armageddon and Frequency, and released remixes of them on Balkan as coloured vinyl. We had remixes by DJ Markie, Ceephax and loads more. Many people were totally unaware that Mark was in Altern 8, so we wanted to build up the name Mark Archer to get him some work. We did Frequency from the original samples and recorded it in a studio (not a bedroom) and even did it in stereo! As a cover version it also meant no arguments with Chris. We even did an AGT V A8 show at the Ginglik with all the tracks mashed up.

The Armageddon Rave Survival Pack we put together was a limited edition of 100 with each set containing three records, remixes, face mask, white gloves and a pot of Vicks. It was a great nod to the old-skool. I then helped Mark with the Christmas Number One Facebook campaign, which was interesting, to say the least.

We called up so many favours for remix work as part of the Christmas scam. 'You have five days to do it, and we have no money!' we said to these DJs. Ha ha. It was real seat-of-your-pants stuff and the Facebook page was going mad. It was the most stressful thing I have ever done. The campaign was a magnet for lunatics and SPAM. There were a few people who thought Altern 8 was a cult, which they claimed was perpetuating oppression.

The problem with these campaigns is actually getting people to buy the record. It got to number 33 in the charts on hardly any sales.

Shows how few records you need to sell to have a chart hit today. We had 15,000 sales, across ten remixes, so that was 1500 of each. Some people bought all 10 from Amazon and iTunes and some people bought 50, so less than a thousand people got involved from 50,000 who said they would. That said, another 3,000 and we would have made the Top 10. After all that work we got a cheque for £300!"

Network were brilliant with the Facebook campaign and they always have been. They allowed me free rein in the use of the name and the track and even encouraged me to do new material. Network ploughed so much money into videos, trips to Detroit and such like, but they never charged us. They gambled on us being a success. Everything, from a DAT tape to a cab fare, the label paid for it all in the short and long term.

We musicians don't make the money in the way we used to any more. Live music is where you get the money, but to get the large fees you need something marketable. A record might not make money, but a hit will see your gig fees treble. I met Eamon Downes from Liquid at a Bangface gig back in 2011 and that sparked two singles from a new project we called Liquid 8. Eamon was great at boosting my confidence again and we've remained good friends since. I call him the Liberace Of Rave.

When the agency closed, Nikki took over my bookings and that took a lot of stress off my shoulders. Having someone else fighting your corner is so much easier. I don't like 'talking money' and I really don't like selling myself. I should have had a 'Nikki', a long while back.

Not only did Nikki re-energise my career and put a roof over my head but her mum even got my teeth replaced. I have always had problems with my front teeth, especially the right one, and ended up getting a plate after years of it falling out all the time and me literally gluing it back in (the dentist wasn't happy). I was being sick one time and managed to flush my plate down the toilet. I was so skint I couldn't get a new one, but Nikki's mum paid the £400 for my new teeth. Rock and roll!

I started doing live PAs with Josh from I Love Acid/Balkan Vinyl and they went amazingly well. There were no DAT machines this time and it felt more like a Nexus 21 gig where you actually had to do stuff. You fuck up, it fucks up, so I was still nervously biting my nails and everything.

We got Jerome Hill to play at one gig we organised. Jerome is one of the most versatile DJs around, who can play any style from hip hop, electro, old-skool to techno. Luke Vibert played, too. Our new dancer Rory, Rich (Benson) and Crez got some real energy from the crowd, who were singing along to all the words. Every time it dropped to a stab pattern or bassline, they didn't stand there filming on their phones. They were bang into it from the get-go. The gigs motivated Josh to put some new Altern 8 music out and so we worked together on new tracks and a reissue of the album. Josh helped me put together a *Rave Armageddon Survival Pack*, which we funded through Kickstarter. You pledge so much for one 12", two 12"s and so on. The box set was all wrapped up in tape with bio hazard stickers, Vicks, white gloves, glasses and three 12"s – all on Balkan Vinyl. We went properly overboard and it made no money, but it looked really good and we got loads of remixes as a result. Josh's attention to detail was amazing.

Josh Doherty *"It was quite surreal when I started performing as part of Altern 8. It was for the Bangface Weekender. We had Crez, Benson, the girls and breakdancers. We didn't get as much time to prep the set, and hadn't done a rehearsal, but it was amazing, brilliant fun – if a little terrifying. I then learned why Altern 8 used the Vicks. You sweat like a bastard in those suits, even though the charcoal lining had been removed. I put my mask on at a Dublin gig and nearly vomited. It really stank and so the Vicks was a lifesaver.*

We then played Bloc weekend together – I ran a stage there – and Mark brought the suits. I got drunk and went back to the chalet and put the suit on. So while Mark DJed I decided to get up on stage and dance. I kept bumping into him and knocking the equipment and he was getting really annoyed. My suit was flapping up and showing off my belly. I was very drunk.

Just recently we remastered Full On: Mask Hysteria on vinyl. The original was on a single record and was an awful pressing and not properly mastered, so I got the DATS and CD rips to put across three pieces of vinyl. The more tracks on a record, the quieter it gets, so these new pieces can be played out now as they're properly mastered. There are 888 copies and we remixed a couple of tracks and added a few new ones."

Tim Garbutt (Utah Saints) *"I still bump into Mark about twice a year and we keep going forward. Utah Saints have done one or two old-skool nights, but we try and stay current as well. I don't want to be totally old skool, so we like to mix old and new. I have always respected Mark and he knows his stuff. I totally get what he did with Altern 8. I remember when Mixmag pronounced the 'death of rave' with a Liam Howlett cover claiming him responsible for the scene's demise in 1993/'94. There was a lot of rubbish about, but it's cool again now.*

After 25 years Mark is still doing it. He knows his shit. Mark is totally underground and I wouldn't want to go on a Mastermind special up against him. He knows more about music than 98% of the record industry. I see him as a spokesperson for that whole generation. Go through the history of house and his name is always there."

***

In 2015, I closed the Arcadia stage at Glastonbury in front of 30-40,000 people. I had played the same stage at Boom Town the year before when I opened proceedings on the Sunday night and there were about seven people waiting as I set up. 'What time are you on, mate?' It was that intimate. By the time I finished there was a good crowd around that stage, which was shaped like a giant robotic spider.

Closing at Glastonbury was very different. Groove Armada and Too Many DJs were on before me and I was shitting it. Lose this crowd and you can watch them leave, so there was a real pressure to keep them there. There was an area around the back of the stage where artists sat to get ready and so I had no idea what was going on out there. Rory and Crez were dancing and I was DJing. Ben from Arcadia came over and said, 'Before you go out, have a look at this.' I took a few steps up to stage level and there were people as far as you could see. There were people beneath the spider stage too. Everywhere you looked there was a sea of heads. Christ on a bike! After a heavy weekend partying, people really went for a bit of a piano-y house and that set was the best of my entire career.

Crez "Glastonbury was amazing. We played there in 2015 with Rory and Josh. It was a really good show. It feels more invigorated now, somehow. I remember seeing lots and lots of heads in the dark. The Chemical Brothers had just finished one of the main stages and we were in the next field. Anyone with any sense came over to us, to carry on."

We got Rory dancing for us after seeing him commenting on a lot of our posts on Facebook. Rory was an Altern 8 fan and he posted a clip of himself at a gig dressed as a giant banana. Anyway, in this clip the banana goes bonkers. After chatting online for a bit Rory dropped his YouTube link. Rory had appeared in the Moby video for *BodyRock* and loads of other stuff. Rory played a dancer in this video that had Moby hanging round the back of some shops in a council estate car park. Then Rory, stood by a ghettoblaster, asked Moby to press 'play', before dancing like a madman, doing the 'running man' and more. It was an amazing video, especially when this large fan blew all this stuff at Rory. Rory had done a lot of cool jobs, he played an Austin Powers-type in a Cadbury's Creme Egg ad and had done quite a bit of acting. He was perfect for Altern 8, as interest in us started to rise.

Mark Mortimer *"Mark was the guy who directed Altern 8 and I had a real affinity with him. It was such a great time; sheer stupidity and beautifully chaotic. There was so much laughter. There's no better tribute than that because Mark had a lot to do with it. Altern 8 were the rave generation's Monkees, but with the bastard DNA of punk rock running through their veins. No one took themselves too seriously. We were like the Merry Pranksters in 1967 and the first Summer of Love.*

Slo Moshun was a whole different vibe. Mark is very musical, very clever and Bells of N.Y. was a brilliantly produced thing. Mark is one of the most important musicians of that era. Very underrated."

Me, Josh, Rory and Crez – who had come out of retirement – are now joined by the original MC Richard Benson from Astrix And Space. We've done some wicked sets at Bangface and suchlike. Having had music taken away from me for so many years it was so heartwarming to be back doing what I felt I was born to do. I had by no means given up on music at any point and although I had sold all my records and equipment and taken to mopping floors and selling washing machines, it was always there. No matter what life had thrown at me, I couldn't give it up. Playing live with my friends is the best feeling in the world.

Richard Benson *"Then Facebook arrived and the old social network got us back together. We hooked up at some old-skool gig in Sheffield and it felt just like old times, all water under the bridge as it were. Altern 8 were enjoying a bit of a rebirth at the time. I booked him as a DJ in Nottingham for a night I was running and then again as Altern 8. Mark then asked me to MC for him at Bangface and I thought, 'Why the fuck not?'*

Bangface went down really well and we do quite a few gigs together now. I'm 44, so pogoing around on stage with a mic in hand is bloody hard work, but it's a real laugh. Mark's music is still standing the test of time and continues to tear the roof off everywhere we play.

We had a mad time, a really mad time, back in the nineties. I just wish I could remember more of it."

Bangface has a real place in my heart for rekindling my love of music, as well as getting me back out playing. The first time I took Nikki to Bangface was back in 2009, and she couldn't believe that people were crowd surfing in a rubber dinghy. The crowd was mad at these nutty events. Then I proposed to Nikki at Bangface Weekender, Camber Sands…

Ian Bland (Dream Frequency) *"I turned 50 last year and my missus asked if I wanted a party and I was like 'Oh no, I don't want all that malarkey.' But then I reconsidered. I can either hide under the covers and pretend it's not happening or I can have a laugh. So we had a rave at this club in Burnley. The person I wanted to DJ was Mark Archer, in the suit. He wore it as well. There he was DJing and dropping all these proper Blackburn rave tunes and Altern 8 when some woman walked up to Mark and asked if he had any R&B. We were all sat back laughing as this 60-year-old tried talking to this man in a mask and chemical warfare suit as to whether he had any Rhianna. It was class. A top guy is Mark."*

***

I am Mark from Stafford and I always have been. I owe so much to my fans, the people who bought the records and tickets. I am nothing without you, which is why I will always take time to talk to people at gigs and online. It doesn't cost much to be kind. You gave me all these wonderful experiences and without you I would have been truly lost. Now, old-skool ravers are turning up to gigs with their kids and it's always a joy. I have had several young fans turn to me and say, 'My mum thinks you're amazing!' It's a really heartwarming thing to hear.

Lee 'MC Lethal' Fredericks *"Mark was making records in '87 and predates a lot of people from that scene; he just needed someone to market him. Very few people have been going as long as Mark. He's a very genuine guy. He's not a chest-beater, although he might do it jokingly, like a throwaway comment. He's not one to say how great he is and that can be the difference between Mark and someone more successful, yet slightly less talented. His musical knowledge and dedication is amazing. He's not musically trained to Grade 7 piano, like a lot of these in the house music scene today, it's more about feeling than musicianship and Mark is the real deal. To me, Mark Archer is the godfather of UK techno. And I can only see things getting better for him."*

Music has taken me on all kinds of trips and I have met so many kind and talented people along the way. If you had told the 13-year-old me that all this was around the corner, I'm not sure he would have believed it, but it just goes to show that anything can happen. Anything.

Daz Partington (808 State) *"We're sometimes on the same bill and if I'm on before him or the other way round, there's a real respect in the handover. Some DJs just play all the big hits and jump off, but we understand each other and know how to hand-over properly.*

Nexus and Altern 8 are English, from our shores, and they totally smashed it and that's a major thing. It was good for us Brits to prove that we could take on that mantle of house and really understand it and not just duplicate it, but put a stamp on it. I have a strings and electro version of Infiltrate 202, which I play when I DJ. I play that all the time. It's a good electro mix and nice to pull out at the events. People love it.

Mark is genuine. A raver. A punter. Yes, a producer also, but there's no distance between him and the crowd and that keeps him honest and fun to be with. If I'm doing a gig and he's there, it takes the gig up a couple of notches. I look forward to seeing him, because he's going to make me dance. Mark makes me dance. He's always in my top 5 DJs and never left it. I'm grinning like a Cheshire cat when he does his stuff. He's earned his badge."

Mark Goodier *"For a while I did a bunch of TV voiceovers for a guy called Nick Moran who produced dance compilations and there was a whole range of hardcore albums. On every album you'll find an Altern 8* track. I heard one not that long ago, and you know what, it might be an oldie, but it still stands up!"

I still wonder what would have happened if Karen hadn't bought that box set of house records back in 1989. It's mad, isn't it? That box set started Nexus 21. Sadly, in 2015, Dad passed away. Dad, just like that box set, was a major inspiration to me and was there from the start. Dad brought me up on music and he and Mum always put me up during the several low points of my life. I was playing Temple of Boom for Dan Bunter the day after Dad died and I was in a real state, but I won't let anyone down unless my arms are broken. The man who stepped in and pulled me into this world, as that umbilical cord wrapped around my neck, had gone, but the fact I am involved in music at all is down to Mum and Dad, who supported me all the way. Mum's brilliant and very resilient. She was very ill when Dad was in hospital but, true to the Archer family spirit, she wouldn't let on. It's lovely to know that Mum is happy for me. I know she has worried about me in the past and for good reason. Dad knew I was happy before he died and that's special. I also have the best older brother in the world and the greatest kids. And *wife…*

Danny Taurus *"I'm in LA now and relaunching Dansa Records and I am super proud that Mark's still doing the Altern 8 thing. He put so much hard work into it. He flies 12 hours, spends one night in a hotel, plays 45 minutes in a club then does 12 hours home. Such hard work. But he loves all that. He is keeping the name alive. He's had his fair share of troubles yet he's one of the most positive and upbeat people I have ever known.*

During the lean years he told me he had a job. 'What do you mean, you have a job?'

-   'Needs must. I have to pay the bills.' I was gobsmacked.

Mark is a hard worker and has given a leg-up to more people than he would care to admit. A lot of people owe an awful lot to Mark."

Neil Rushton *"One of my standout memories was going to America with Altern 8 to play the Limelight on a Friday night. Mark, Chris, Crez, Parksy and Butler all doing their stuff till the early hours of the morning. Joey Beltram did a crazy remix of Activ 8. I was in New York and really jetlagged as our band boomed out of one of the best sound systems in the world. I didn't know where I was.*

I loved shooting the video at Shelley's too. I played the part of an outraged man who wanted the shoot shut down. I was desperate to get the police involved, to generate some hype for it. I always got on with Mark as he was always really into what was going on with the music. Mark was ultra-aware of all that and fanatical about the whole rave scene. I'm from a soul background and yet I really got into the electronic stuff and had loads of ideas of where we could take it. Mark was totally happy to go along with all the pranks and scams.

Mark is not the typical pop star. When it came to the rigmarole of promoting and releasing music he was fine with it all and totally understood it. They were the odd couple really, Mark and Chris. Mark was bang into the music and Chris wasn't so much, but odd combinations can work sometimes and for a while Mark and Chris were on fire."

John McCready *"Altern 8 were grubby, daft, kamikaze; a junior KLF. It was a beautiful moment in that it was unpolluted by common sense and career-building. Altern 8 were a pop band in rave clothing and part of a long chain of British suburban lunacy stretching from Screaming Lord Sutch and Wee Willie Harris etc. They were momentary and they knew it, but burned brightly for a minute back there.*

Mark is socially a gentleman. I can understand why he is still working in the sense that people like being around him. Musically, he is a bit of a silent genius really, having been making records for so long and being able to turn his hand to anything required. But he is serious about dance music and techno; it's just that he has no ego and isn't po-faced about it. So he takes the Altern 8 thing with a necessary pinch of salt and welcomes memories of the fun people had to the music he made back then."

***

Nikki had always wanted to go to New York and when I got invited to play the NASA 20th anniversary with Joey Beltram, N-Joi and 808 State in 2012, I vowed to take her the following year. We queued at silly o'clock in the morning to get to the top of the Empire State Building. Once we got to the top, she burst into tears. It was a perfect moment in time when everything came together. I've had my ups and downs, but there are a lot of people who have had it tougher than I. So here we were, on top of the world, looking forward. Together. A lot had happened since that first trip to Detroit and yet here I was 20-odd years later with a girl I loved, still doing what I was born to do in this land that created so much crazy music. Thank you so much for joining me on this journey and allowing me to remove this mask for a bit. Remember that no matter how hard life gets, never give up on your dreams.

Mark from Stafford

Michelle Kidd (social services/fitness instructor) *"I first saw Altern 8 on 20th Feb 1992 at the tender age of 14. I had been into hardcore/ house since I was introduced to it late 1990 by older friends who went to Shelley's and Introspective in Stoke. By the summer of 1991 I was hooked on the music, the culture and everything it stood for. Being from Longton, I was lucky to be surrounded by such a flourishing dance scene. I used to go to under-18 nights around Stoke, but my favourite was at the Leisure Bowl in Longton on a Monday as that was where I got to hear all the underground tunes I still love to this day, such as Infiltrate 202. That bassline had me hooked! I remember saving my pocket money to buy Infiltrate in the summer of 1991 from Replay Records. I also got the remixed Vertigo EP (orange) and later bought the silver version. Later on that year came the massive Activ 8, which has one of my all-time faves on the B-side: Re-Indulge. I bought a copy of the Rage magazine which featured an interview with the band as they were dropping Christmas puddings on Stafford. They were fast becoming my heroes!*

My cousin rang me one evening to say that someone had been giving flyers out at his school for an under-16s night at Shelley's featuring Daz Willot and few other local DJs, as well as Altern 8. It was what I'd been waiting for. I remember going down with loads of my friends, some of whom were well over 16, but they all wanted to see Altern 8. It was held on a Thursday night and was only £2 to get in. I got what I thought was 'dressed up', with my blue 'PG Trips' top and red Nike bottoms and Adidas Gazelles.

Shelley's was really busy with teens at the bar ordering juice and ice pops, and loads more on the dance floor dancing to Tech G. For a club full of kids – who had taken nothing but a shedload of sugary drinks – the atmosphere was ace.

I remember Altern 8 coming on stage and I was just in awe! They wore their trademark yellow dust masks and chemical warfare suits, followed by two dancers and an MC. I'm sure they started with Activ 8. I was totally transfixed on Crez, who threw me a Mr Freeze ice pop! That was also the first time I'd heard Frequency.

The whole PA was amazing and although I already had a connection with the music, it seemed to make more sense hearing it in a club, with the smoke machines and lasers. Just being around others who were into the same music was ace! I still see a lot of them now when I go out clubbing. Everyone in there was dancing, making loads of noise and just loving it.

That was the only time I got to see them in the nineties. I continued to be a massive fan, though, and bought every single 12" and became a member of the fan club and had a 'Watch yer bass bins!' top! To this day I am still a proud owner of an '88 acid revival' badge sent to me by the Altern 8 Fan Club.

I got to see them again in March 2016 at the Shelley's Reunion and the whole night was so emotional with loads of DJs and MCs. However, it was seeing Altern 8 on stage again that made my night. My 14-year-old self re-appeared for a moment and I was overwhelmed with excitement! Even though 24 years had passed, the feelings I get when hearing the music still remain. Thank you so much for the music and the memories!"

Tommie Sunshine (DJ, producer, musician) *"Altern 8 made everything that happened here (US) with EDM much more tolerable and palatable to me because I knew we were having that moment for the first time. Yes, you could go to an underground rave with a thousand people but never 20-30,000! Dancing to electronic music in America was a small-scale thing until 2010. I first met Mark in Miami in 1998. There was a finite number of people who made music at that time, so if someone new turned up they were curious. 'My name is Mark Archer,' he said. I gasped. I couldn't believe it.*

'Altern 8?!' I gushed. Mark looked at me like I was crazy. 'How would you get that from my name?' I told Mark that he was talking to someone who basically modelled their lives on Altern 8. So we met briefly then and lost touch. Then SoundCloud came around and I reached out to Mark and told him my stories.

I started to befriend Pasquale Rotella, who runs Insomniac EDC at Las Vegas, which is massive. So I posted up some old-skool Altern 8 from Top of the Pops, so young people here could hear them for the first time because they're not going to hear them in a club on a Saturday night and Pasquale got in touch. 'Oh my God I fucken love Altern 8!' and we got talking. The basis of our friendship is based around Altern 8. I have played four Electric Daisy Carnivals and it's all down to Altern 8. I asked Pasquale if he wanted me to put him in touch with them (Altern 8). 'Get out of here!' So I put them on an email chain together and that was the year Mark played EDC.

Mark closed out the final night with the Sunrise set at the Electric Daisy Carnival, 2015 and it was such an amazing moment. He was playing such incredible music and hearing these tunes at sunrise was too much. All the records were from that era. There were 120,000 people raving to Mark in Las Vegas. My wife stood by the stage in her wedding veil, as we'd got married that day. We were dancing to Mark on our wedding day. It doesn't get much better than that."

OUTRO...

15th April 2016, Southport.

Hymn 303
Give me joy in my heart, keep me raving
Give me joy in my heart I pray
Give me joy in my heart keep me raving
Keep me raving till the break of day...

I mentioned to James 'Lord St Acid' Gurney that we wanted to do the wedding at Bangface. Give James an idea and he'll just run with it.

We went up to Bangface at Southport Pontins real early on the Friday and dropped our stuff off at the chalet. There were plenty of people milling about and guests turning up to come to the wedding. Nikki hired this girl from Southport for hair and make-up and she had no idea what was going on with all these ravers wandering about. It was a brilliant atmosphere.

My best mate Shaun Crist was wearing a suit owned by a friend of ours called Barry, who had sadly passed away the year before. Nikki burst out crying when she found out. Barry was one of the funniest people I have ever met. Even the hairdresser was crying at that news. I had Dad with me too. I thought about wearing one of his National Service badges on my inside pocket, but my brother Paul had something much more personal. My dad wanted to be cremated and so the ashes were cast around the cottage in Gnosall, but because of all the rain and snow that year, there was still this pile of ash at the old place that stubbornly refused to shift. So, inside this little vial, tucked away in my pocket, was Dad.

I sometimes whistle when I am in supermarkets now. Dad used to do that. You often couldn't see him, but you could hear him on the other side of the aisle, whistling away. Dad would do this whistle when you entered the house as well. Now, I find myself doing that exact same whistle, as if it keeps a connection between us or something. I never thought I would, but boy do I miss his whistling now.

We went to Southport Town Hall Registry Office for what was an amazing ceremony. I had been married twice before and Nikki once, so we knew what to expect. You could tell just how happy everybody was when Nikki's best friend started a Mexican wave. It was astounding and once we were married we went on to Bangface.

The main room was packed by the time we got there. There was a big archway all lit up and to the side was a big gunk tank and a seat for ordaining witnesses into the ceremony. The ceremony itself was all scripted and Josh had even mixed the Wedding March with *Amen* breaks to bonkers Bangface music. Nikki came on and two witnesses ordained and performed the ceremony. There was even a choir to help the crowd sing along to Hymn 303 (to the tune of *Sing Hosanna*) 'Give me joy in my heart, keep me raving...' The whole crowd sang along to this hymn as pictures of Altern 8 flashed up on the screen.

James then started the Bangface wedding. The 3,000 ravers went mental following the vows and then these big industrial-sized confetti cannons blasted as lasers zigzagged around. Nikki and I stood on stage – just us two – in bright yellow masks (me in full Altern 8 suit). Nikki's mask said: 'Mrs A'. The first dance was to *E-vapor-8* and we slow-danced in the middle of the stage all the way through, accompanied by a full Altern 8 PA. Josh was there on stage in the boiler suit with Benson MCing and Rory and Crez dancing. Everyone went nuts. I then carried on with the PA, which went down brilliantly. A wedding, a rave and an Altern 8 PA – what more could you want from a weekend?

8 Tracks That Changed My Life

1. The Night Writers – *Let The Music (Use You)*
2. Armando – *Land Of Confusion*
3. Mayday – *Wiggin*
4. Baby Ford – *Fordtrax*
5. Afrika Bambaataa And The Soul Sonic Force – *Planet Rock*
6. Malcolm McLaren And The World's Famous Supreme Team – *Buffalo Gals*
7. Grandmaster Flash – *The Adventures Of Grandmaster Flash On The Wheels Of Steel*
8. Unique 3 – *The Theme*

The Man Behind
The Mask

In the 28 years that I've been making music and DJing, one thing has been constant and always there - you guys, without you there would be none of this and for that I am truly grateful.

Thank you.

: AARON "AZZA" HAJZYK

: AARON DAVIS

: ACID88

: ADAM "LANKY STANI" LANCASTER

: ADAM BURTON

: ADAM DUKES

: ADAM MUSSETT

: ADAM OLD SKOOL SHAVE

: ADGIE LEXI BLAKE DAVIES

: AJAY CHAND

: AKIHIRO TAKANO

: ALAN MACPHERSON

: ALAN MCDONALD

: ALAN WALCHESTER

: ALEX BURNS

: ALEX DOWNES

: ALEX NEIL

: ALEX WRIGHT

: ALEXANDRE BANSE

: ALEXMCLEAN (G)

: ANDREAS GARBE

: ANDREW ATCHESON

: ANDREW DONOGHUE

: ANDREW FISHER

: ANDREW FORDYCE

: ANDREW UTTING

: ANDY

: ANDY FINNEY

: ANDY HOOPER

: ANDY KEZ FINNEY

: ANDY MCMANUS

: ANDY MENNIE

: ANDY RUDGE

: ANDY SIMPSON AKA DJ TOILETTE

: ANDY SMITH :-)

: ANDY SWANN

: ANDY T (HEREFORD)

: ANDY TURNER

: ANDY WYLIE

: ANIL SHARDA

: ANT READ RUGBY ALTERN8 CREW

: ANTHONY RAFFERTY

: ANTONY DALY 586 RECORDS

: ARTUR KLIMECKI

: ASHLEY DANIEL STOTT

: BARRY FINNEY

: BARRY GRAYSHON

: BARRY HOLLAND

: BARRY LAWFORD
: BEAN-HEAD
: BEAU RICKERBY
: BEN DEADSILENCE
: BEN DEXTER
: BEN KOU
: BEN 'SKIMMY' STOTT
: BEN TODD
: BENNY HELL
: BEX
: BIG AL
: BILLY MURRAY
: BLUEBEATPETE
: BONS
: BRADLEY LADE
: BREGT VANDEREYKEN
: BRENDAN
: BRETT J BUTLER
: BRIAN "PLUGDIN" LAWSON
: BRIAN (BOB) O'BOYLE
: BRIAN HORTON
: BRIAN LAURIE
: BRIAN PARR
: BRIAN RENDELL
: BRIAN SMITH
: CALLUM 'DJ SPYRAL' JOHNSTON
: CARL PALMER
: CARLOS ACIARES MÃ¡RQUEZ
  (DJ CACIARES - CHILE)
: CATH MACKENZIE
: CATHERINE BERE
: CHARLIE FANTAZIA
: CHEREEN WALSH
: CHRIS
: CHRIS COOPER
: CHRIS CURTIS
: CHRIS J HENDRY
: CHRIS MARSHIONIST MARSH
: CHRIS MCNICOLL
: CHRIS PROLE (PROLE MUSIC)
: CHRIS YORK
: CHRISSIE B
: CHRISSO
: CHRISTOPH BUERKI
: CHRISTOS CHRISTOU
: CLARE CANNON

: CLARE CIELECKI
: CLIFFY BURROWS
: CLIVE BISHOP
: CLIVE HARRIS
: COLIN "RATTY" RATCLIFFE
: CONRADIO :)
: COREY ASHTON
: DAISUKE MIYAMOTO
: DALE CROWTHER
: DAMIAN DAVIES
: DAN "ABBOTS" SIMPSON
: DAN "DABJ" LURINSKY
: DAN BEECH (DJ DAN)
: DAN BRUFFELL
: DAN FRAIDSO MCGLYNN
: DAN HANSON
: DAN HICKS (DJ LEVI)
: DAN SLEE
: DANIEL JAMES WALSH
: DANIEL WHITING
: DANIELLE SHERRINGTON
: DANNY SMITH
: DARREN DAVIES
: DARREN E COWLEY
: DARREN MILLBURN
: DARREN PIZZY
: DARRYL LEE - MINDWAVE RECORDINGS
: DARYL FITZGERALD
: DAVE BENNETT
: DAVE DOBSON
: DAVE GRAY
: DAVE KILLINGBACK
: DAVE TANCOCK
: DAVE WILCOX
: DAVID
: DAVID "EXPRESSION" KERSLAKE
: DAVID "MAZE" VAN BRENK
: DAVID CONWAY - "UK DAVE"
: DAVID GRIERSON
: DAVID HERSEY
: DAVID J BROWN
: DAVID ZIPPY ARMSTRONG
: DEAN
: DEAN BLUNT
: DEAN CUTHBERT
: DEBBY HALLAM

: DEBS E
: DEEPZ
: DEREK MATTHEWS
: DEVA ONE
: DJ BAZ HAY
: DJ GREEN
: DJ HAIRYMONSTER
: DJ KSD-MARK "PASTY" ASTLEY
: DJ MARZO
: DJ NOAH
: DJ PERKY
: DJ PLATTS
: DJ SMITT-E
: DJ STEVE ABRAHAM
: DJ TC BROWN
: DJ TRADEMARK
: DJ TREV TREVOR A BROADBANK
: DOM WELGE
: DOMINIC PERRY
: DONALD SISSON
: DYLAN DJ DYJOMAT TROYER
: ED "DJ ED-STRON" BROWN
: EDDIE GALAVAN
: EDWARD HIPKISS
: EGG BOTTOM DOOR MANNY'S
  KETTERING
: ELAINE KENNEDY
: ELE BEATTIE & HENRY MORRIS
: ELLIOT "SHADES" SMITH
: EMMA STEDMAN
: EZY RYDER (ASH)
: FABULOUS FRANC/SONIA@JUNO
: FIONA CALLAM
: FLEUR
: FLORIAN MEYER
: FRANÃ§OIS KITCHING
: FRANK FIEBER
: FRANK HENDERSON
: FRASER BUDGE
: 'FRESSSSHHH' ED LOMAS
: GARETH DARBY
: GARRY SHRIMPTON
: GARY CROCKFORD
: GARY MCKENNA (GARY THE PHONE)
: GARY ROMAN MAKOWSKI
: GARY WALKER

: GAVIN GLYNDWR JAMES
: GAVIN LOCK
: GAVIN MICHAEL BURNS
: GAWAINE JONES
: GAYLORD MICROBAT
: GAZ BARKER
: GEERT SERMON
: GEORGE CRAWFORD FROM GUELPH,
  CANADA, AND AN ORIGINAL TORONTO
  JUNGLIST & OLD SKOOL RAVER
: GEZ "LFO" VARLEY
: GIB DUFFY
: GILES HINKIN
: GLYN ALLAWAY
: GRAEME DUB-L-G GENT
: GRAEME JONES
: GRAHAM PODMORE
: GREENBINS
: GRIP JEAL
: GRUM TAYLOR
: GUVNOR B
: GUY J H TAYLOR
: HAYES STUART
: HEATH DAVIS
: HELEN GOODWIN
: HELEN QUINN
: HUGH MULHALL
: IAIN DAVID WOODS
: IAMSCOTT3
: IAN BOYD WALKER
: IAN QUIGLEY
: IAN VOID
: IAN WAINWRIGHT-JONES
: INGO LÃ¶MKER
: INVOCATOR666
: JAKE LEVINE
: JAMES (CYNISTA) LOCK
: JAMES ASHFORD
: JAMES BRITTON (AKA JB)
: JAMES GREGSON
: JAMES SMITH
: JAMES THOMPSON AKA TEK
: JAMES VINTER
: JAMES WILSON
: JAMIE HEADSPEATH
: JAMIE LEVIT8 THE REPROB8 HOLMES

: JAMIE RUSSELL
: JAMIESON WESLEY
: JAN (CORECRACKER)
: JAN-PAUL ANTEMES
: JAROD PRESTON
: JASON CRABBY
: JASON CRAWLEY
: JASON 'JR' RIDER
: JASON TROWLES
: JASON WALDEN
: JAY ELLIS
: JAY WILDE
: JEFF SHRIMPTON
: JEN IN NC - 1972- _ _ _ _ - GERIATRIC RAVER (CIRCA 1990)
: JENNIE HARRISON
: JEREMY SENA
: JEREMY WHETTELL
: JETHRO REDMORE
: JEVFB BECKMAN
: JIM MCCORMACK
: JIM SIMONS
: JIMMY 'MACKINNERS' MACKINLAY
: JODY WOOD EXETER
: JOE BEATTIE
: JOE COSTIGAN (AKA LUMPH4MMER)
: JOHN ARROWSMITH
: JOHN CAPEL
: JOHN CONLON
: JOHN KINSELLA
: JOHN MCGAW
: JON MASCIANA
: JON 'TEEBS' SAYELL
: JON TURI
: JONATHAN (DJ JON-E) NOBLE
: JONNY HENFREY
: JOOLS FOY
: JORDAN EWAN RAMSAY
: JORGE "THE8" PRIETO
: JULIE ASQUITH
: JUSTIN COLLINS
: JUSTIN HAWKINS
: JUSTIN ICKE
: JUSTYN W G FELTHAM
: KARL LOBLEY
: KATT CHAPMAN

: KEITH "CUFFY" ANDERSON
: KEITH FOWLER - STAND FREE
: KEITH HOLIDAY
: KEITH S PLEASANT
: KENNY ROBB
: KENNY W THOMPSON
: KEVAROO
: KEVIN SOUTHERBY
: KEVIN VAUGHAN
: KING JIM
: KIRK 'ALTERN8' ARCHER
: LAN CREW
: LAURA DAYGLO
: LEE "SILKY" HOUGHTON
: LEE (REPLAY) BANKS
: LEE BARRETT Âᵒ
: LEE BOREHAM
: LEE CAP MAIDSTONE
: LEE DEE E
: LEE MCCOY
: LEIGH OLD SCHOOL EDWARDS
: LEON PACKALEW
: LIONEL SMITH
: LITTLE RED
: LIZ LUMBY
: LIZA BERRY
: LIZZ HOLDSWORTH-WHITE (LEEDS CREW)
: LUKE HANDSFREE
: LUKE MATTHIAS STAMMERS
: LYNDSEY SWIFT
: MACK
: MALCOLM SHARP
: MANDY WINTER
: MARC A SMITH
: MARC 'ARGYLECYMRU' WOODWARD
: MARCUS FOX
: MARIUS SANDE
: MARK
: MARK
: MARK & HELEN BAMFORD
: MARK ABYSS WRIGHT
: MARK ADAMSON
: MARK ASTON AKA SHOOMS AKA LORD SHOOMINGTON OF SHOOMS MANOR AKA THAT INAPPROPRIATE CUNT WITH THE MASSIVE COCK

: MARK BAKER
: MARK D
: MARK 'DOOG' DOUGLAS
: MARK GALLAGHER
: MARK GRIMACE
: MARK INNES
: MARK LEWIS
: MARK LUSCOMBE (LUZ)
: MARK MARSHALL
: MARK SPINDIZZEE TAYLOR
: MARK TURNER - DJ MARK T
: MARK VICKERS
: MARK WARING
: MARK 'ZAMMO' NICHOLLS
: MARKC
: MARKUS "THE KOMER" HERKOMMER
: MARKY RUSSELL
: MARTIDOG303 MCCUE
: MARTIN HARRIS
: MARTIN HAYHURST
: MARTIN JAMES
: MARTIN MURRAY
: MARTIN MURTAGH
: MARTIN NORTON AKA NAUGHTY
: MARTYN LEVITT
: MARY LOUISE DONOGHUE
: MATHEW EDGE
: MATT ACIDIC-THE RAVE YARD
: MATT BENN
: MATT BROWN
: MATT BUDD
: MATT COPLEY
: MATT HIGGINSON
: MATT 'MEDIC-8' STEPHEN
: MATT PARKES
: MATT ROBSON
: MATTHEW ' SNIPS ' PARSONS
: MATTHEW BLACKWELL
: MATTHEW CAWLEY
: MATTHEW MILNER
: MATTWARD808
: MATTY SHAW
: MAURIZIO VITIELLO (SMILE IT MUSIC)
: MAXIM D CARP
: MICHAEL BETETA - AKA ACID88
: MICHAEL BFG DEAN

: MICHAEL CANTY
: MICHAEL DOUGLAS
: MICHAEL FORSHAW
: MICHAEL SMITH
: MICHAEL WORTON
: MICKEY CROFT
: MICKY 'ROCK IN YER HAMMOCKS'
CONN
: MIKAEL KLASSON
: MIKE A
: MIKE ANDERSON
: MIKE FLEET
: MIKE SPEED
: MILENKO HOUSLEY
: MITCH THRAVES
: MORGAN MOG
: MORGAN OSL GIBBONS
: MOZZA PAUL
: MR GRIMEZ POET WARRIOR
: MRS P
: MY BROTHER'S KEEPER
: NATASHA
: NATHAN DESS
: NEIL DJ TED RATCLIFFE
: NEIL ELKINS
: NEIL HICKLING
: NEIL KWIF BRO PLEASANT
: NEIL MCMEECHAN
: NEIL MOTTRAM
: NEIL PARKES
: NEIL PURVIS
: NEILIO THE BOXROOM RAVER
: NIC "ST1X" WHATMORE
: NIC SERPELL-RAND
: NICHOLAS DAVIES
: NICK CASWELL
: NICK NEWBOLD
: NICK WILKINS
: NICK WOODCRAFT
: NICKY (DJ NO) WILLIAMS
: NICO
: NIK WILLIAMS
: NOKESY
: OLI DODD
: OLI DREAMTRAK
: OLIVER RAFFERTY

The Man Behind The Mask

: OLLY REVEST
: OWEN 'BUMP' DAVIES
: OZZIE
: PABLO VERDE + MAREE MOOEE
: PATRICK HORNE - THANK YOU FOR THE MUSIC!
: PAUL "THE RIFLEMAN" WILLIAMS
: PAUL A SPRINGER (ILF)
: PAUL 'BRUCIE' HUGHES
: PAUL BURKE
: PAUL DOUGLAS
: PAUL EVERATT
: PAUL F M COLLINGS
: PAUL IMRIE
: PAUL J WEBB
: PAUL LOCKER
: PAUL MESSENGER
: PAUL MORRIS
: PAUL O'DONNELL AKA DJ REVOLUTION
: PAUL OSMOND
: PAUL ROONEY
: PAUL SANDERSON
: PAUL SENIOR (SENWAR)
: PAUL, JENNY, CONNOR & JORDAN BRUMBY
: PAULEJAY
: PCR CREW
: PER LINDKVIST
: PETDUO - ANA & DAVID
: PETE CLARKE
: PETE DI-MURRO
: PETER APSEY
: PETER HARRINGTON
: PETER IRVINE
: PETER JAMES MORRIS
: PETER SCOTT
: PHIL "BLUNT" GILL
: PHIL HARLL
: PHIL HORNER
: PHIL 'JUDDERZ' ADAMSON
: PHIL YOUNGMAN
: PHILIP 'PHILOOSH' MERRILL-WEAVER
: REN KAINTH
: RHUMBLE
: RICH BROWN-KENNA (RBK)
: RICH 'ENERGY FLASH' HARVEY
: RICH YATES FROM SWAD
: RICHARD ÄŠTYEMCÄBOARD
: RICHARD GREEN
: RICHIE 'EARLGREY' ELLIOTT
: RICHIE LEE
: RICK HORSFIELD
: RICK TOZER
: RICKY GEE
: RICO 'RICHT' THOMPSON
: RITCHIE PRIOR
: ROB CHAPMAN
: ROB LEARNER
: ROB WALSH, RAVER
: ROB WASE
: ROBBIE "BOBBY DAZZLER" F
: ROBBIE DUNSMORE
: ROBERT BLOOR
: ROBERT RENNIE
: ROBIN GRAY
: ROCKIN'N'SHOCKIN
: RODNEY ANTHONY PAUL TAYLOR
: ROGER CHURCHFIELD
: ROGER COOK
: ROSS BOWERMAN
: ROZ SUTORIS
: RUDE STU BEAUCHAMP
: RUFFAGE HYPER-KAYNE DUDLEY
: RUSS BILLINGTON
: RYAN BLAIR
: SAKARI KARIPURO
: SALVU SEQUENCHILL MUSCAT
: SAM "DJ GOATRIDER" PETTETT
: SANAE KIMURA
: SANDER ZEGVELD
: SANDY DUFF
: SANDY HUNER
: SCOTT GEDDES
: SCOTT HALLAM
: SCOTT JOHNSTON
: SCOTT OG HENNY LOC RICHFORD
: SCOTT WILSON
: SCOTTIE MCCLYMONT - AKA THE MORNING GLORY LTD - 'GET RAVIN' IN THE HOUSE!'
: SCRAWNY
: SEAN DAKIN AKA WEZBASH, ORIGINAL

310

RAVER, GALLERY AND JOY CREW!
RESPECT ALL THE GALLERY CREW!
: SEAN GERMAINE
: SEBASTIAN HOFF
: SEBASTIAN LÄ¶TTERLE
: SHAMAN
: SHANE KEHOE "NEVER FORGET YOUR FIRST RAVE"
: SHAUN WESTON
: SHAZZASPANNERED & DAVE SKYWALKER
: SHERIDAN J EARLE ESQ
: SIMON ASHLEY OPTIMUS PRIME LAKE
: SIMON BAULK
: SIMON CONNELL
: SIMON DIBBLE
: SIMON DRISCOLL
: SIMON HORNER
: SIMON LIVINGSTONE
: SIMON SIMKIN
: SIMON VAN DER BURG
: SIMON ZEUS LAVER
: SKRIBS
: SMITHY 76
: SPARKY ED
: SPENCER ROBINSON
: STEPHEN "DOUBLEDROP" LAUNCHBURY
: STEPHEN "STARKY""CLARKE
: STEPHEN BORLAND
: STEPHEN HUNT
: STEPHEN PEOPLES
: STEPHEN TYMAN
: STEPHEN YORK
: STEVE ""FUNKYFRESH"" PETCH
: STEVE BELLAMY
: STEVE 'BELLBOY' BELL
: STEVE BIRDTASTIC BROWN
: STEVE KELLY
: STEVE KETTLE
: STEVE 'STEIL' O'NEIL
: STEVE WICKS
: STEVEN BOOTH
: STEVEN SANDIFORTH VICKYLEWIS
: STEVIE 'DJ BOY' NICHOLL
: STEVIE E

.: STU
: STU - C
: STUART "TOKEN ASIAN FRIEND" GOMES
: STUART BARROWCLIFF
: STUART PARKINS
: STU-E @ FORCE FM
: TAKAHIRO INOKUCHI
: TANZ
: TAZ "MAJOR BIZZLE" BENSON-WEST (PROTOKOL)
: TERRY HAYNES
: THE DJ FOZ
: THE DOUBLE K
: THE FRID
: THEO LUIS
: THOMAS O'SULLIVAN
: TIM (MELODIZE) DALCHAU
: TIM BENNETT
: TIM BETTERTON
: TIM PROCTOR
: TO ALEX LOVE FROM JAMES! XX
: TOG HOWARD
: TOKYOACIDCRU
: TOM WOOLLEY
: TOMMY G WILLIAMSON
: TONI KURKIMÄ¤KI
: TONY & JASON OSMOND
: TONY BRITTEN
: TRACY PAUTSCH
: TRAUMA LIVE
: TRAVIS GENTLEMAN BASTARD KAMEN
: TREVOR WILKES
: TRISTAN JUMUNJY
: VAS SELVARATNAM
: VERNON GAY
: VLR
: WAYNE TOMLINSON
: WAYNE 'TRIPLEXL' CHAPMAN
: WAYNE TULLY
: WEDGY
: WOLSKIE HYLANDER
: ZENITHSOUL (KELBFTN)